Black Women, Identity,
and Cultural Theory

Black Women, Identity, and Cultural Theory

(Un)Becoming the Subject

KEVIN EVEROD QUASHIE

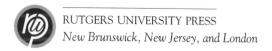

RUTGERS UNIVERSITY PRESS
New Brunswick, New Jersey, and London

Library of Congress Cataloging-in-Publication Data

Quashie, Kevin Everod.
  Black women, identity, and cultural theory : (un)becoming the subject / Kevin
Everod Quashie.
       p. cm.
  Includes bibliographical references and index.
  ISBN 0–8135–3366–X (hardcover : alk. paper) — ISBN 0–8135–3367–8 (pbk. :
alk. paper)
  1. American literature—African American authors—History and criticism—
Theory, etc. 2. American literature—Women authors—History and criticism—
Theory, etc. 3. African American women—Intellectual life. 4. African American
women in literature. 5. Identity (Psychology) in literature. 6. Women, Black—
Intellectual life. 7. African American photographers. 8. Group identity in literature.
9. African American aesthetics. 10. Women, Black, in literature. 11. Women
photographers. I. Title.
  PS153.N5.Q37 2004
  810.9'9287'08996073—dc21
                                                                    2003007035

British Cataloging-in-Publication data for this book is available from the British
Library

The publication program of Rutgers University Press is supported by the Board of
Governors of Rutgers, The State University of New Jersey.

Manufactured in the United States of America

for Esther Pemberton, Monique J. Savage, and Donn A. Boulanger, Jr.,
who are creativity's best friend and love's best measure

Contents

Acknowledgments   *ix*

Introduction: What Becomes . . .   *1*

Chapter 1   The Other Dancer as Self: Notes on
Girlfriend Selfhood   *15*

Chapter 2   Self(full)ness and the Politics of Community   *42*

Chapter 3   Liminality and Selfhood: Toward Being Enough   *78*

Chapter 4   An Indisputable Memory of Blackness   *98*

Chapter 5   The Practice of a Memory Body   *111*

Chapter 6   Toward a Language Aesthetic   *129*

Chapter 7   My Own, Language   *148*

Conclusion . . . What Is Undone   *173*

Notes   *179*
Works Cited   *207*
Index   *221*

Acknowledgments

Insufficient gratitude to my parents, Calais and Mary, who got me here; my sisters, Cindy (for "getting" this and me), Fay (for saving me all those times and for "the dance of joy"), and Janelle (for being, always, my favorite, for being my heart at home; and for her husband, Francis); to my nephews, Paul, Anthony, and Sereau, whom someday I hope to be worthy of; to my aunt Mercedes for kind words; to colleagues at Smith, especially Brenda Allen, Ann A. Ferguson, Paula Giddings, and Vicky Spelman—all of whom have been supportive intellectually and otherwise; as well as Andrea Hairston, Yvonne Daniel, Adrianne Andrews, Darcy Buerkle, Marilyn Schuster, Kum-Kum Bhavnani, and Terrilyn Cooley (whose editorial help was invaluable); and the Provost's Office for financial support; to Eugenia Delamotte (still the best close reader of my work), Myriam Chancy (whose classes and encouragement were formative, constitutive), and Susan McCabe (for guidance in how to read theory), who supported me through graduate school and an early early version of this book; to my peers in Tempe who mattered: Lenore Brady, Claudia Nogueira, Irena Praitis, Ruth Butler, Vanessa Holford Diana, Don Wilson, Ruth Kocher, Rashid Robinson, Richard Yanez, Jeanne Clark, Regina Spillers; to my editor, Leslie Mitchner, who is capable grace, as is her staff; to Elizabeth Gratch for a keen eye, elegant prose, and that heart; to Dennis Miehls and his patience; and to the anonymous reader whose feedback shifted aright my vision, over and again.

I have been loved well through much of this, including by Esteban Monsterrate, Felipe Gonzales, Roland Zamora, Steven Fullwood, CJ Oliver, Matthew Bokach, Michael Stancliff, Don Wilson, Shawn McGuffey, Gerold Ebner, Tetsuya Fukuda, David Roeder, Lance McCready, Hilton Kelly, Eric Carriera, and Eric Boring. And Eric Waggoner.

And these (former) students have been especially helpful: Cypriane Williams, Binta Jeffers, Lindsey Dawson, Helen Hwang, Yashira Pepin, Sara

Feldman, Georgiana Goodman, Mecca Sullivan, and especially especially Michelle Medina, who often approached flawlessness intellectually, emotionally, spiritually, and is now a friend in all ways. Jessica Horn's quiet questions propel me still; Allison (Alley) Hector's skill with the cover as well as her gracious ear as I missed and recovered my grandmother, was saving. Those sisters of the yam at Adrian College from over ten years ago, especially Karena Benford and Lizzie King, and those awe-full women in the Friday poetry group at Smith throughout 2000 were instructive—we one another's yearning.

And for these three women—Lenore Brady, Claudia Nogueira, and Monique Savage, who are blessings manifest and who are my heart's coauthors . . . I can say no more. Now.

Black Women, Identity,
and Cultural Theory

Introduction

What Becomes . . .

To be loved, to be held, to remember: these basic human impulses, sprawling and imprecise, are each metaphors of selfhood; they mark a subject and articulate her function but also imagine and suggest an other who is engaged in the act of be-ing. As they gesture to selfhood as a tension between at least two subjects, these elegant humanities are allegories of poststructuralism and its fascination with the project of subjectivity. To be loved, to be held, to remember.

The gifts of poststructuralism, which I am loosely imagining here as the umbrella for more specified discursive bodies (postmodernism, psychoanalysis, deconstructionism, and postcolonialism, for example), are many and far-reaching, especially the disruption of the subject and the suggestion of a multiplicity that is frustrating and fruitful. But rarely has it been considered that Black women are encountering, reflecting on, challenging, poststructuralism's architecture. This then is my book's motivation: not to explore as if the question is on the table but to assert that Black women's cultural production in the last thirty years *has* influenced and been influenced by the debates and discourses that characterize contemporary cultural theory, especially the notion of identity. Their poststructure is the idea of the girlfriend, an oscillating identificatory process between self and other, a Black feminist idiom of subjecthood. This idiom, the girlfriend, is where the self becomes and is undone, the site where the politics of self, nation, and difference are evaluated through cultural landscapes and ethical sensibilities relevant to Black women, where the necessary anti-identity politics coalesce.[1] In the book at large I am arguing that girlfriend subjectivity is a critical icon through which

Black women artists reconsider and reframe self and then memory and language—these canonical conceits of cultural theory. This is my study of how Black women's cultural idioms shape and engage contemporary critical theory.

To ENGAGE THE construction of identity necessarily means encountering essentialism. Articulations of Black subjectivity have often struggled with essentialism as a principle of Western thought. At once the idea that there is something essential—defining, necessary, representative, and totalitarian—about Blackness as a marker of racial identity is attractive and repulsive, an easy justification for nationalism and predetermined buttress for claims to cultural integrity as well as a ready-made validation of doctrines of racial separation, doctrines that are often (always?) hierarchical. Still, essentialism is an evocative concept precisely because it highlights that identity is a politic, a venture or argument, that has a direct relationship to power and resources, social and otherwise, and that is relational and collective; that identity always invites and implicates a plural body (a group, a community, a nation) and is unfaithful to individuality. As such, the consideration of identity is often (always?) contested, always of interest to more than just a self.

And even the terms of that last sentence are, by poststructuralist standards, inadequate: the idea of the "self" is troubled and unstable; the word *identity* has been surrendered for the more sophisticated *subjectivity*; the notion of the individual acknowledged as a modern(ist) fantasy. But I use them anyway because they are so familiar to our discourses and because they are evocative: they point attention to something more, which is also what I think *essentialism* as a term of cultural debate does.

Let me use, though he is not a Black woman, W. E. B. Du Bois to begin not only because doing so unsettles the idea of essentialism—though I am not quite ready to throw the term away—but especially because his place in cultural studies is so grand. I am not interested in his famous articulation of "double consciousness" so much as I am with that fascinating first paragraph of the opening chapter of *The Souls of Black Folk:*

> Between me and the other world there is ever an unasked question: unasked by some through feelings of delicacy; by others through the difficulty of rightly framing it. All nevertheless, flutter around it. They approach me in a half-hesitant sort of way, eye me curiously or compassionately, and then, instead of saying directly, How does it feel to be a problem? they say, I know an excellent colored man in my town; or, I fought at Mechanicsville; or, Do not these Southern outrages make your blood boil? At these I smile, or am interested, or reduce the boiling to a simmer, as the occasion may require. To the

real question, How does it feel to be a problem? I answer seldom a word. (37)

Du Bois's expression here is of a Black subject that is delayed, suspended, a thing rendered as a metaphor of itself at least three times over, a tepid corpus because it does not, nor is it needed to, appear. His paragraph is populated with anxiety, with terms of hesitation and sl(e)ight: unasked, delicacy, flutter, half-hesitant, curiously, smile, reducing, as well as the use of the subjunctive may require. The subject in question never manifests on the scene and is never in the interaction, which happens anyway; no subject, for that matter, manifests. Instead, there are these awkward statements of deflection that gesture toward the profound, awkward but still unarticulated (and therefore unreal, to disagree with Du Bois) question—how does it feel to be a problem?—a question that is itself a deferral, for it never speaks the words it really means, words that would surely be terms of affinity made by the speaking subject to and about the nonspeaking (and Black) one. Maybe the real articulation would be: I love you or its synonym, I hate you. Or I am afraid of you. Or you are me, or are not me, depending on the vagaries of the day. Whatever the case, the question that Du Bois rightly says remains unasked is only at best a trick, a delay of the real question and a withholding of two subjects from the stage of consciousness. The *it* of Du Bois's "how does it feel to be a problem" is precise because it means everything and nothing at all; the question is, as Marita Bonner might term it, "an empty imitation of an empty invitation."[2]

The metaphorical shimmer in Du Bois's series of deferrals is an exact articulation of the conundrum of essentialism: the subject is fluid and even fails to appear, though the outlines and meaning of its corpus are well known, even definitive. These two qualities neatly partnered—fluidity, even absence, coupled with precision; or even better: that such deferral (and its synonym, *deference*) is a characteristic Black experience, an essentialism, the irony being that the expression is so unstable (so unarticulated) that it is almost the exact opposite of itself.

There is a raging debate about race and gender essentialism as it relates to Black women that my reading of Du Bois's paragraph is intended to evoke. That debate is an old one; it can be heard in Sojourner Truth's destabilizing of the category "woman" through her discussion of class, labor identity, and religion (but not really race, for it is already there and also is not a profound category in many expressions of antebellum consciousness; the term *slave*, which at this point subsumes race, is more enunciatory), even as she points precisely to her body as the site of proof (see Painter 164–169). The debate is also evident in Anna Julia Cooper's struggle to articulate specific aspects of

Blackwomanness. In her 1891–1892 essay "Woman versus the Indian" Cooper positions the Black woman as (categorically) essential to the success of post-Reconstruction U.S. society: in an argument about the place of manners and courtesy as indicators of the nation's health, Cooper writes, "as the chemist prefers distilled H_2O in testing solutions to avoid complications and unwarranted reactions, so the Black Woman holds that her femininity linked with the impossibility of popular affinity or unexpected attraction through position and influence in her case *makes her a touchstone of American courtesy exceptionally pure and singularly free* from extraneous modifiers" (93–94; emph. added). Cooper's use of the language of science is not so startling in context of a time concerned with biology, technology, and race; yet it is her positioning the Black woman, the "when and where I enter" Black woman, as the *touchstone* of American courtesy that interests me, because it suggests that Blackwoman is a category of *extreme* social relevance and power—essential more in its relevance than as biologized essence.[3] This her entry into the essentialism debates.

But, if I am going to engage poststructuralism broadly, it is appropriate, even essential to consider those expressions of Black female subjectivity in the early 1970s, about the time that poststructuralism itself exploded on the U.S. academic stage. In this context a signal expression would have to be the Combahee River Collective's "A Black Feminist Statement," a manifesto that is determined to speak for and about Black women in a complicated way. To this end the statement offers this lovely sentence that is an underacknowledged complication: "As Black women we find any type of biological determinism a particularly dangerous and reactionary basis upon which to build a politic" (17). It is curious, and for sure intentional, that the sentence begins with the categorical *as Black women,* a gesture that marks certain bodies within a race and gender discourse while disavowing "biological determinism." This ambivalence represents the anxiety of essentialism as well as an attempt to make it useful: not merely strategic essentialism, as Spivak has suggested, but a more sustained commitment to a category of identity, a marking of self as part of a larger group that has some inexpressible affinities.

Maybe the best way to understand the construction of essentialism in the Collective's statement is to consider the idea of difference as essential: that it is not only the marking of a Black and female subject as different/difference that is the essential principle or characteristic—the defining swath that makes the group a "collective"—but also the commitment to difference ideologically that permeates whatever boundariedness the definition of the collective self takes. This commitment is evident in the statement's expression of intersectionality, the sense that Black women are and experience many subjectivities; there is, then, not only one hegemonic Blackfemaleness, but, at the risk of irreconcil-ability, there is a recognition of many Blackfemalenesses, each gaining integ-rity from the vagary of themselves, each becoming more and more unnameable as itself—the disintegration of the politic, which is itself the politic. This privi-leging of difference and intersectionality is clearly poststructuralist, a gesture that at once appears and fades.

The other key document of Black female subjecthood from this thirty-year arc would have to be Barbara Smith's essay "Toward a Black Feminist Criticism" (Smith is also a primary author of the Collective's statement). Here Smith makes a bold claim for a body of Black women's literary theory, and, although she was neither the first nor the only to make such a claim, it was her effort that paralleled and motivated the rise of writing by and about Black women in the late 1960s and early 1970s.[4] Smith's essay was widely criticized for its perceived essentialism, however, its suggestion, as Deborah McDowell notes in *The Changing Same*, that there is a specific and particular Black women's *language*. McDowell's criticism notwithstanding, I think that Smith's essay warrants another reading and a more generous appreciation, especially because I read hers to resist the capitalization of Black femaleness by express-ing its definitiveness in a loosely conceptualized lesbian identity. She disrupts the idea of an oppositional and narrowly defined Black femaleness that is in complete service to intersections of whiteness and maleness—and, instead, offers an expression of Black female relationality, a kind of self-centeredness that is a necessary political gesture and that suggests, if Evelyn Hammonds's argument is right, a subjectivity that Black women hardly know.[5] Something under-engaged or maybe even new. In this way Smith's articulation of Black femaleness is committed to difference, a commitment that undoes its stabil-ity but also is its integrity. Her centering of Black women's identity in their relationships with one another destabilizes essentialism because it rejects the oppositional binary that fuels the inarticulate, absent, and evocative Black sub-ject and because it localizes the experience of selfhood, puts selfhood back in a subject-to-subject context, as a thing accountable to the (im)precise articu-lation of one subject in an unpredictable dance with another. Smith's engage-ment of familiar categories of social identity is not only anathema to poststructuralism's disarray; in fact, hers implies its own disarray and abandon.[6]

And whatever Smith's errors of overstatement, whatever presumptuous integ-rity she ascribes to the dalliance between one Black female subject and another, her statement's usefulness is not mutilated. Nor is the larger case I am making: that Black women's cultural expressions are encountering and grappling with post-structuralist terms and, in doing so, are articulating their own poststructure, their own guiding principles of the subject's becoming and undoing.

I am attempting to argue for a useful essentialism, a complicated thing that unbecomes as it unfurls: something that will be articulate of the recurring tension between the need for a sense of "true selfhood" in and against the impossibilities of such an achievement. It is not possible to give up the categories of selfhood, socially constitutive and imbedded as they are, but it is also not fruitful merely to genuflect in their wake. Not a selfhood as a site of nation, or anybody's self, but a selfhood of one's own—this the plea not for a room but for a self of one's own.[7] Surely, some of this is about the politics of interiority, but I do not want to make the mistake of merely proclaiming the prevail of interiority—of self-claimed definitions of self—as the solution; that is too tautological, too easy, too unachieved. Instead, there is a greater tussle between what is interior and what is not, a sense of how the interior is already exteriorized and what that means: how to express an imagination of the interior that is neither threatened by nor immune to exteriority.

Maybe Teresa de Lauretis's early version of an oft-cited essay "Upping the Anti (sic) in Feminist Theory" can be helpful in trying to variegate this essentialism.[8] In the essay de Lauretis makes the case that the essence in feminist discourse might be a conceptual rather than a real one, a lexical distinction she borrows from Locke. She argues that the conceptual essence is

> a totality of qualities, properties, and attributes that such feminists
> define, envisage, or enact for themselves. . . . This is more a project,
> then, than a description of existent reality. . . . In other words, barring
> the case in which women's "essence" is taken as absolute being or
> substance in the traditional metaphysical sense, . . . for the great
> majority of feminists the "essence" of woman is more like the essence
> of the triangle than the essence of the thing-in-itself: it is the specific
> properties . . . qualities . . . or necessary attributes . . . that women
> have developed or have been bound to historically, in their different
> patriarchal socio-cultural contexts, which make them women, and
> not men. (310)

De Lauretis's claims are interesting because they reassert patriarchy as an essential even as they reject any other definitiveness. I guess such is the problem with identity politics—that each stakes a claim to an essential while eschewing all others, each possessing an indefatigable integrity. If this is the best the conceptual vocabulary will allow, then I will give Chandra Mohanty the final clarifying word here. Talking in her introduction to *Third World Women and the Politics of Feminism* about "imagined communities" of struggle, Mohanty says that "the idea of imagined community is useful because it leads us away from essentialist notions of third world feminist struggles, suggesting political rather than biological or cultural bases for alliance. Thus, it is not color or sex which constructs the ground for these struggles. Rather, it is the *way* we think about race, class, and gender—the political links we choose to make among and between the struggles" ("Cartographies of Struggle" 4). Such is a politically relevant anti-identity structure.

Discourses of the Self: Identity and Subjectivity and the (Un)yielding Politics of Black Femaleness

Part of the difficulty of engaging essentialism in a poststructuralist context manifests in the use of the term *identity*, a term whose connotations regularly interfere with and impede its clarity. *Identity*, like the word *metaphor*, has both an umbrella meaning as well as a specific one. For example, the term *identity* refers generally to the discourses of self, but it also is a specific referent for those aspects of selfhood that are politicized, that are defined by and resisted within a recognizable social order, this inflection of the term being a contradistinction of its poststructuralist and more attractive kin, *subjectivity*. In teaching cultural theory, I have been trying to think of a new way to explain these two terms, *identity* and *subjectivity*, to my students. I invited them to think of the roots of both words: *subject* is more a fluid term (than, say, its counterpart, *object*), a thing whose indeterminacy is both freedom and peril (as in to be subjected to); and *identify* is about placement, a sense of repeatability, a way a thing is put into a place.

In the world of theory the difference between the two terms—the difference that their roots suggest—is similar to the difference between a person saying, "I am blue" or "I am water," and a person saying, "I am a Black man." The first pronouncement—"I am blue," "I am water"—is more clearly what a subject is and, even more cleanly, what a subject's access to and conceptualization of its body feels, is, does; its pronouncement is a stand-in for its subjectivity, an (im)precise fluidity that changes, is unreliable, and tells you everything you need to know, or can know, about the subject's be-ing. And, still, "I am blue" is not a description, nor is it intended to say that the subject is blue permanently or even definitively. Instead, it invites a consideration of what *blue* means, as well as specifically what blue means for the subject who is feeling, being, living, as blue, which is why it is indeterminate, because *blue* or *water* are, after all, imprecise: we understand them as concepts through a system of agreement, but they are not the familiar signs of self and fail under articulation's daunting weight. As such, even my attempt to describe, define, outline *subjectivity* as a term here must fail.

The enunciation of identity—"I am a Black man"—is what the subject is called, how it is marked, what is expected of it, as well as the subject's agreement (in a larger system of words and ideas) to being this set of things. Of course, the idea of being a Black man is no more familiar or precise than blue or water, but the former has a history in the Western world, for example, as a marker of some traceable and notable subject (or subject traits) that is widely enough accepted to be both useful and utterly useless as a term. The phrasing is many things, but it is surely an acquiescence, for it parades a fiction of knowability and reveals a complicated agreement between a subject and his others. Such is the case with all identities: their existence as ways of placing, of setting, of marking, in well-known and largely agreed-upon systems of order, a dynamic that means they inevitably say less than more, even as they announce themselves with thunderous clarity.

The tendency of my students is to want to favor one term over the other: *subjectivity* seems the more attractive valence because of its wildness and its disregard for systems of order without (as well as within) the subject, even though *identity* has a well-respected history (in terms of identity politics, for example) that would seem to indicate a level of freedom, even if only material. In fact, it was hard for many students, as it is sometimes for me, to think that identity can only be so rigid, especially for this reason: they and I need to think that identities can be and are empowering.

Of course, neither one is better than the other. For sure, *identity* (and its cohorts—*modernity*, *capitalism*, and so on) cannot be allowed merely to order and rule, and *subjectivity* cannot be imagined to be politically, socially, and materially immune. This is one of the difficulties of theoretical imagination—it offers abandon but often at the price of political and ethical tepidity. That is not sufficient; instead, I want a brokered solution that conceptualizes the two terms, *identity* and *subjectivity*, in a dialogue, a dance that considers the subject's relationship to its own unending and yet finite constitution as a delicate balance, a play of willfulness and compromise, wildness and patience. As such, "I am a Black man" is irresolute and ludic, and "I am blue" accounts for the bounds of race and gender; both become (in)capable expressions of a subject, are identities of one body's (un)becoming. I choose to use the two terms interchangeably, a revised poststructuralist configuration that maintains the cultural relevance of *identity* and the theoretical savvy of *subjectivity*—my opening gesture toward considering the impact of Black women's cultural production on poststructuralism.

Part of the generic absence of Black feminist imaginings from the architecture/corpus of contemporary critical theory—and by *absence* I mean not only how Black feminisms deploy theory's ideological principles but especially how such feminisms inform and reform these principles, a more active encounter—is motivated by the consideration of the Black subject (and its intellectual discourse) as preemptively illiterate and atheoretically invalid, impotent. Another aspect of this void is that race, and Blackness more precisely, is a consuming enunciation, one that makes the subject that is marked as Black *only and always Black*, at least first and foremost, if not always. It is the trouble noted by Frantz Fanon's "Look, a Negro," James Baldwin's stranger in the village who is hardly a stranger, Ann DuCille's occult of Black womanhood that unerringly haunts white women.[9] In truth this trouble is a many-edged sword: partly a side effect of antiracist struggle, it is a descendant of the emphasis on race that is so necessary. As Blackness has been armed in the projects of nationalism, so has it disarmed its own potential fluidity, its coveted "subjectivity," becoming and embracing the absence that Du Bois's construction makes evident. Of course, I am not laying fault but pointing, instead, to what is untenable about nation and even of self.

In fact, Black female subjects are in a more pronounced conundrum, for the essential Black subject is rarely female and is never feminist, as it is that the essential female subject is rarely Black and never antiracist. This means that Black women have little (or no?) access to whatever benefit political essentialism may bear. Black female subjects mostly materialize as figures of difference in someone else's complicated subjectivity (which is why Barbara Smith's self-centeredness is so radical). In fact, if the intersectionality that binary identity systems make necessary is definitive of Black women's experience of subject, then it seems almost ideologically and theoretically impossible for there to be a Black female essentialism: the subjectivity is too piecemeal, too deployed in something other than itself, too much an afterthought of Black men's or white women's totalization of race or gender. On the terrain of identity Black women do not manifest at all (which is why Sojourner Truth and Anna Julia Cooper are laboring so hard for visibility) so they cannot be essential.

I am being dramatic intentionally, for surely this is a playful extreme. At the very least my conjecture would suggest that abjection is the essence of Black female identity, abjection itself being an essence. But that seems too dour and too incapable (as well as politically irresponsible). My theoretical play was intended to highlight the particular and unyielding intersection of Black women in the very fibers that are poststructuralism and, in doing so, to lay some of the groundwork for introducing my ideas that will not always walk the theoretical party line. In fact, some parts of Black women's cultural production disturbs poststructuralism, frustrating if not preventing its descent into playfulness and a limited freedom. Such disturbance is at the heart of Teresa de Lauretis's useful essay on essentialism: that it is the Black female subject (as enunciated in cultural feminism) who seemingly interferes with poststructural feminism's potential achievement of freedom from the limits of the body.[10]

The obstruction that de Lauretis notes and criticizes occurs because these Black women who are encountering poststructuralism are also at a deep unease with their poststructuring, especially its intellectual arrogance, its attempts to complicate what is simple and lived, its disregard of the necessity of politics, its sometimes ahistorical posture. Theirs is not a "race for theory" but something finer; they are architects of a new cultural ideology that is aware of the irresoluteness of poststructuralism in general but especially of the never-resolved tension between their abjection and its prominence.[11] They hold on to the contradictions and refuse to let go of their Blackfemaleness, whatever its assumed simplicities. They echo Pat Parker's words from her poem "For the White Person Who Wants to Know How to Be My Friend," a poem that at once is an expression of the Black aesthetic and embraces a post-structuralist impulse: "The first thing you do is to forget that i'm Black. / Second, you must never forget that i'm Black" (99). They negotiate the crisis of self by holding firm the irreconcilables and are determined to have a "bottom line black[female]ness," one that is informed by but not beholden to the politics of "post-identity and anti-essentialism."[12]

These poststructuralists do not believe that precision in and of itself can be a goal of their ruminations, but they are also interested deeply in the greater clarity of self. In this spirit let me try, then, to be a bit clearer by engaging a quotation from Toni Morrison's *Sula:* it is a passage that I discuss extensively later in this book in relation to specific concerns about identity, but here I want to cite and use it differently, to support this point about the balance between guarding against essentialism and reveling in a sense of something that is definitive, soothing, a thing against reckless dissolution. Near the opening of the novel Shadrack is in a veteran's hospital, suffering from war dementia. His hands shake continuously, and his body is on the whole unreliable; it seems to be against him:

> Like moonlight stealing under a window shade an idea insinuated itself: his earlier desire to see his own face. He looked for a mirror; there was none. Finally, keeping his hands carefully behind his back he made his way to the toilet bowl and peeped in. The water was unevenly lit by the sun so he could make nothing out. Returning to his cot he took the blanket and covered his head, rendering the water dark enough to see his reflection. There in the toilet water he saw a grave black face. A black so definite, so unequivocal, it astonished him. He had been harboring a skittish apprehension that he was not real—that he didn't exist at all. But when the blackness greeted him with its indisputable presence, he wanted nothing more. In his joy he

took the risk of letting one edge of the blanket drop and glanced at
his hands. They were still. Courteously still. (13)

The "Blackness" Shadrack encounters in the toilet water is *indisputable* but
not precise; in fact, it is arguable that this Blackness lacks precision because
it occurs in a dark toilet water, and what Shadrack probably sees, feels, and
senses is the *impression* of himself, an outline of his face that, however it comes,
communicates a sense of reliability and self-centeredness that soothes and
steadies him. Similarly, I am interested in this work in the starkness of such
an impression, whatever the limits of precision may be. Sometimes the
poststructure is vague, but that will have to suffice, for it is the best that language permits. I am not being uncomplicated here, but it is as simple as this:
some things cannot be expressed better than to say, "to be loved, to be held,
to remember."

In a Year's Time

Around 1970 two significant cultural explosions occurred that changed both
the surface and substance of academia, one being the importation of
poststructuralist thought into mainstream U.S. scholarship and the other the
proliferation of writing and other cultural production by Black women not
only in the United States but also in Canada, the English- and French-speaking
Caribbean, and West and East Africa. Of course, the identification of this
single year, a round one at that, is somewhat performative, especially as ruminations of each explosion manifest before and propel beyond my marker of
choice. Still, there was a substantive realization of Black women's diasporic
literary productions between 1965 and 1972: first or significant works by now-
luminary Black women appeared during those years, including Ama Ata
Aidoo, Maya Angelou, Toni Cade Bambara, Angela Davis, Buchi Emecheta,
Nikki Giovanni, Rosa Guy, Bessie Head, Merle Hodge, June Jordan, Audre
Lorde, Paule Marshall, Toni Morrison, Flora Nwapa, Jean Rhys, Nawal el
Sadawi, Efua Sutherland, and Alice Walker.[13] Coupled with the ferocious interest of critical theory, this postcolonial / post–Civil Rights groundswell determines that the body of Black literatures, and dare I say contemporary
literatures as a whole, from this moment on, becomes indisputably inflected
with Black women's ideologies; these women are a critical mass, not homogeneous in intent or result but nonetheless defining and definitive. They are
not singular; the sheer multitude of their residencies is a corpus of torque-like
difference, a "postmodern blackness" if there ever was one.[14] They are subjects of disruption as well as its articulators, the intersectionality of cultural

feminism that is ready-made for poststructuralist affiliation. And this work covers a broad sample of them: Bambara, Gayl Jones, Morrison, and Walker (United States); Lorde (Grenada / United States); Michelle Cliff (Jamaica / United States); Aidoo (Ghana); Jamaica Kincaid (Antigua / United States); Marshall (Barbados / United States); Dionne Brand (Trinidad / Canada); Marlene Nourbese Philip (Tobago / Canada); and Myriam Warner-Vieyra (Guadeloupe / Senegal). Hence, anything but wild vagary would be unbearable.

Methodologically, I have taken Mary Helen Washington's invocation as guide and decided to center Black women, a critical posture that Truth and Cooper and the women of the Combahee River Collective also propose to the cultural imagination.[15] My book, then, aims to engage the specific and general implications of Black feminist cultural thought on and in relationship to poststructuralism. Although I am interested in theory, my deference, where there is one, is always to the subject, always to the body that is deployed in theory's play. For me there is a quiet and steady need for responsibility, a need for acquiescence to human life and its urgent but simple yearnings. If I err, I would rather that humanity prevail over my own intellectual flourish, for I take Barbara Christian's arguments seriously: mine is not a race for theory but an expression of something close-to-accurate about life, instructive and complicated, even as it necessarily fails in the face of living.[16] Left with no better choice, I defer to living and the body whose living is my subject, a body that is always more *and* less than my musings need or can sustain.

This humility is inspired by my awareness of my position as a Black man in this textual world of Black women. In the development of these introductory arguments, my identity has been sly but not silent: my use of Du Bois and Morrison's Shadrack, for example; my revelatory "I am a Black man" as the signal example of an identity claim, for another. I do not want to belabor the landscape but also want to acknowledge the difference, itself a manifestation of the comments about essentialism and Black feminism's poststructure. So, how to say it clearly and simply? These ideas are some of what I have learned from engaging Black women's cultural and intellectual work, theirs being a serious gift to my life. Their feminism is neither exclusionary nor apolitical, and my consciousness is neither burdened nor aloof. This is unsteady terrain, my speaking and theorizing *with* (not *for*, not even *about*) Black women. I am intent, despite nudging from an early reader, to maintain this preposition *with* as my ideological compass. The reader wanted me to be more forceful in my scholarly preparedness to write this book, but there is no way to do so without assuming a position of supremacy—without falling into the cycle of opportunity that a male-centered academia would afford me. The binaries and their hierarchized disposition are set; theory over literature, men over women, novel over story. Still, there is one clarifying truth—whatever my presence in the text, whatever my disposition, I cannot be and am not the sole authority. This is a struggle, a lovely one, toward my and their manifesting as viable subjects of this work. This book is and is not about me. It has to be both. And more.[17]

Specifically, I imagine the work in three sections, divided around self, memory, and language. The first three chapters use the notion of "girlfriends," a key and repeated cultural metaphor in contemporary Black women's creative work, as a site from which to theorize Black female selfhood. From textual examples and definitions of what constitutes a girlfriend, the chapters engage the idea of otherness as a locus of identity and posit a model of identity that oscillates between a "me" and "not me." The achievement of this investigation of selfhood is an identity that is spiritual, fluctuating, and multiple as well as singular. This section's conclusions about identity are the structural center for the succeeding chapters and their considerations of memory and language.

The second section argues that, in Black cultural contexts, memory is a body—either a literal fleshy, self-contained entity, or an attribute of a body. This corporeal imagining of memory bears implication for the process of selfhood and identity articulated in the first section and further argues that, if memory is a body, then the process of coming to a relationship with memory is ontological, a process of being and becoming . . . a practice. This process of becoming at once constitutes and disturbs notions of home and nation, two concepts that are important locations of Black collective identity and which are therefore central to how a subject experiences and encounters her subjectivity.

The final section begins with the problem and contradiction that language (English) represents for Black people in diasporic contexts. Specifically, the imposition of English is a cultural standard and a colonial violence, yet the acquisition and "mastery" of English offers creative (and self) expression. This ambivalence of language inaugurates a dilemma for the Black woman artist, who must work with a language that is sometimes working against her. The section grapples with postmodern attitudes toward wholeness and explores how Black women cultural producers complicate the rhetoric and role of the narrator, creating an intimacy between what is objective and subjective and revealing the gaps that both make and unmake the text and, ultimately, its language.

What Becomes . . .

Denise Riley, in her gorgeously written *The Words of Selves*, suggests that there should be an anti-identity politic, a place where the neat coalescence of self can disarray (11). I admire that suggestion and uphold it and, as an act of flattery to Riley, offer my own revision: an anti-identity politic that is not anti–Black women.

This book will trace such, these Black women who surrender to (un)becoming as a process, a thing that is itself and its opposite, who sustain both a political ethos and a fantastical surrender. They articulate what at once becomes and is undone . . . this their cultural ambling and their articulate theoretical (un)structure.

They whisper to me this: for all of the self's fluidity, there is something still undeniable. Call it will, agency, even foolishness—it propels the subject through the world, often ungraceful, often tripping, but with her urge intact: to be loved, to be held, to remember.

Chapter 1 The Other Dancer as Self

Notes on Girlfriend Selfhood

Near the end of Toni Morrison's *Beloved*, Paul D returns to find Sethe in bed, exhausted, beaten, and almost hopeless from her struggle with Beloved, memory, and slavery. Paul D begins an exchange of words about their—his and Sethe's—tomorrow, but Sethe is still focused on the twice-lost baby girl, whom she pronounces her best thing. Paul D's response is generous, loving, and enchanting: "You your best thing, Sethe. You are."

His rejoinder is complicated because it does not preclude Sethe's claim of her lost daughter (or her alive one) as her best thing, even as it suggests that there is a something that Sethe possesses, has, evokes, an intimate invisible textuality that also must be claimed. The incantatory "you your best thing," especially as a signal moment in a novel of *Beloved*'s literary proportions, foregrounds the issue of subjecthood that is central not only to the world of this novel but also to the many other works and lives it echoes. What or who is this "you"? What are the names and properties of this intimate? What are its boundaries, its failings, its unsustainable integrity; how does one know one you from an/other? How is an awareness of this you, as a process of becoming (a) subject, achieved and facilitated, especially for Black women who historically do not figure as subjects and who are commonly imagined as and expected to be selfless?

The central consideration in this chapter is the issue of selfhood, a consideration of some significance, for, as Zora Neale Hurston asserts, self-revelation is "the oldest human longing."[1] Although the discourse of self is widely (if not over-) articulated in contemporary cultural thought, I want to focus on the relational aspects of selfhood evidenced in some contemporary Black feminist narratives. In these works subjectivity is a struggle of community, a negotiation of and balance between a subject and the other subjects around her. The argument is this: through a discourse of otherness some Black women scholars represent selfhood as the dynamic relationship between one woman and her other, her girlfriend. This relationship is dynamic particularly because the boundaries of self, metaphorically but also literally, are disrupted, severed, transcended; the self and its girlfriend become contiguous and sometimes indistinct subjects. This selfhood is a volatility, occurring via two levels of identification between self and other: identification *with* and identification *as*. The continuous movement between *with* (in which a subject materializes comparatively) and *as* (in which the subject materializes metonymically) also represents disidentification, because the subject is always being dislodged / always dislodging herself from a settled identity with her other.[2] In this context subjectivity is an "ungoing unsettling process" that makes chaotic grace of the material and spiritual edges that normativities would to calcify.[3] A subject's desire and impulse toward an/other is political, aware of but not overdetermined by the legacies of race, gender, class; it is sisterhood as "political solidarity between women."[4] This solidarity is not a state of achievement but, rather, a process, and it extends beyond its own specificity such that the power of negotiating otherness between two Black women is both a model and conduit for a Black female subject's (un)becoming in relation to others who are not, in name, Black women but with whom she shares an ethical and political affinity. Whatever the vagaries, this much is sure and clear: the solidarity of girlfriend subjectivity is explicitly committed to centering the lives and experiences of Black women, a kind of self-centeredness necessitated by the social imperative for Black women to be selfless. It resists essentialism while respecting the indelible realities of Black female selfhood.

In putting forth a model of selfhood that locates identity relationally, I am engaging and broadening the Black diasporic cultural value of finding who you are in other people as well as specifically encountering work that Black feminists have produced in the last thirty years.[5] From the practice of consciousness-raising groups and the use of coalitional models in political strategizing in the 1960s and 1970s to the articulations of "sisterhood" in the explosion of writing by Black women in the 1980s and 1990s, it is clear that community is a particular location of power and self-identity for Black women. In this chapter, more than chronicling incidents of community and sisterhood, I want to explore *how* subjecthood is theorized: how selfhood is achieved via community as well as how the two are antiphonal. I am interested in the specific ways that Black women identify with themselves, with one another, and how such identifications are an articulate theory of subjectivity.[6]

In many ways the discourses of white supremacy and patriarchy presume to overdetermine all considerations of Black selfhood as either an intercommunal tension (with whiteness) or an intracommunal tussle (between men and women).[7] Here, then, lies a key divergence: the aesthetic of the girlfriend subject obsesses neither on white masculinity nor heteronormativity but, instead, centers a Black female subject and her permutations, a model of subjectivity that operates from her sometimes plural and always volatile self-center.

This investigation of selfhood is also immersed in the conceptual vocabulary of psychoanalysis; I am determined, however, to explore selfhood in a context that will not always be compatible with psychoanalysis, especially its classic configurations.[8] For one, I am interested in subjectivity as a politic, as a domain that is relevant to civic and historic matters. As Erich Fromm argues in "Politics and Psychoanalysis," much of classic psychoanalysis fails to account adequately for identity politics, resulting in a discourse of identity that sexes subjects and evaluates their familial relevance but which barely calculates for gender, race, ethnicity, or the impact these indices have on an individual's identity formation. And, though I am somewhat swayed by Terry Eagleton's defense of Freud in *Literary Theory: An Introduction*—suggesting that Freud's work "makes it possible for us to think of the development of the human individual in social and historical terms" (163)—I am undeterred in needing to interrogate the question of politics further.[9] In some ways my anxiety about psychoanalysis is summarized by Claudia Tate's assertion that little has been done to make psychoanalysis relevant to Black cultural production. Specifically, I am worried about the legacies of psychoanalysis as a discipline and those of the subjects that I am putting in its purview. But, buoyed by critical studies by Tate, Hortense Spillers, and Evelyn Hammonds that validate the use of psychoanalysis as a frame for thinking about Black female subjectivity, I move forward, somewhat anxiously and with a promise to engage the matter more closely in a later passage.[10]

Girlfriends, Sisters, Cousins: Metaphors of Black Female Relationality

If the process of subjecthood manifests as an oscillation between identification "with" and identification "as" (and the requisite disidentification), then the narrative construct that correlates to this shifting is the girlfriend, the other Black woman who is a subject's girl. Poetically, Andrea R. Canaan defines a girlfriend as the following:

> You know, the kind of woman friend you
> can be a girl with.

You know what I mean a woman you giggle
with one minute and can be dead serious
the next. . . .
The kind of friend that you usually
tell all to and when you forget to tell
her some secret that you have been holding
and casually mention it to her, you are
surprised that you hadn't told her.
You know, the kind of friend that you can
go out with and it's not always dutch. . . .
I mean the kind of woman who always honors
what is private and vulnerable for you.
You know, I mean girlfriends.
(302)

The aesthetic described by Canaan is that of a woman-centered engagement, two bodies in embrace and grip, a friendship of substance and sustenance. "A woman who loves other women, sexually and/or nonsexually. Appreciates and prefers . . . women's strength. . . . Loves struggle. . . . Loves herself. *Regardless*" (Walker, "Womanist" xi–xii). A girlfriend, an othermother, play sister, god sister, cousin, or sisterfriend—all terms of the nonfilial, visceral bonds of sisterhood between adult Black women.[11] These are the ties that bind, shake up, shake loose, the ones that hold and undo, become and unsettle. And, though it is arguable that such couplings are not exclusive to Black women's culture, the term *girlfriend* has a particular evocative connotation in Black women's cultural discourses.[12] The girlfriend is this other someone who makes it possible for a Black female subject to bring more of herself into consideration, to imagine herself in a wild safety.[13] A woman is encouraged by her girlfriend to be herself radically, even as the heft of doing so might be too much for their connection to bear. This a rare but necessary moment of the practice of Black female selfishness.

As a discursive conceit of Black women's identification, girlfriend selfhood not only foregrounds the binary of self and other but also challenges the constitution of each term as distinct and separate entities. In her essay "Beauty: When the Other Dancer Is the Self" Alice Walker offers an anecdote that narrativizes this idea of merger: telling the story of how she lost sight in one eye as a child and tracing her struggle to a positive sense of self after that loss, Walker remembers the moment when her young daughter first notices the scarred tissue that is her eye. She (Walker) is afraid of what act of repulsion and scorn her daughter might respond with, for Walker has become used to her eye being the site of an uncommonness that clearly marks her as other.

But her daughter surprises her, and, instead of scorn, she cups Walker's face in her small hands and proclaims, "'Mommy, there's a world in your eyes.' (As in, 'Don't be alarmed, or do something crazy.') And then, gently, but with great interest: 'Mommy, where did you get that world in your eye?'" After this gentleness Walker writes that, "for the most part, the pain left then" ("Beauty" 370). Rebecca's act of sight and love sends her mother into a potent moment of self-reverie and celebration, one in which she meets her self: "That night I dream I am dancing to Stevie Wonder's song 'Always' (the name of the song is really 'As,' but I hear it as 'Always'). *As I dance, whirling and joyous, happier than I've ever been in my life, another bright-faced dancer joins me. We dance and kiss each other and hold each other through the night. The other dancer has obviously come through all right, as I have done. She is beautiful, whole and free. And she is also me*" (370; emph. added). Walker here unites with her other self, a self she experiences spiritually but also materially. This meeting of the self is joyous, an act of mutuality that suggests that the human yearning for companionship is fulfilled in the meeting of a self that is one's self but also not oneself—this other dancer is both a distinct self from Walker but is *also* her.

Walker's image of a twirling companion corpus is an effective metaphor for reading Sula and Nel's process of subjecthood in Toni Morrison's novel *Sula*. The two women are dancing others, girlfriends who love each other under the rubric of an "always." Their meeting occurs in a moment of subconscious twoness that is characteristically similar to Walker's dancing reverie: "it was in dreams that the two girls had first met. Long before Edna Finch's Mellow House opened . . . they had already made each other's acquaintance in the delirium of their noon dreams. They were solitary little girls whose loneliness was so profound it intoxicated them and sent them stumbling into Technicolored visions that always included *a presence, a someone, who quite like the dreamer, shared the delight of the dream*" (Morrison, *Sula* 51; emph. added). This presence, this someone, is the girlfriend, the other who is so much the self that the boundaries between the two become fluid and sometimes collapse. The delirium of their meeting mirrors the fantastical quality of Walker's dance and evokes a similar joy. It is an ecstatic experience, one that is simultaneously in and out of the material body, conscious and not.

The description Morrison offers of Nel and Sula in their youthful days further expands this idea of the presence of a someone:

> When Nel, an only child, sat on the steps of her back porch surrounded by the high silence of her mother's incredibly ordered house, she studied the poplars and fell easily into a picture of herself lying on a flowered bed, tangled in her own hair, waiting for some fiery prince.

He approached but never quite arrived. *But always, watching the dream along with her, were some smiling sympathetic eyes. Someone as interested as she herself* in the flow of her imagined hair, the thickness of the mattress of flowers, the voile sleeves that closed below her elbows in gold-threaded cuffs. (*Sula* 51; emph. added)

Nel's falling into a picture of herself is a surrender to companionship, her embrace of the coveted mutuality and the other eyes that would be "as interested as she herself" in her (Nel's) living breath. "Similarly, Sula . . . spent hours in the attic behind a roll of linoleum galloping through her own mind on a gray-and-white horse tasting sugar and smelling roses *in full view of a someone who shared both the taste and the speed*" (51–52; emph. added). Sula is Nel's fiery prince, as Barbara Smith argues, and Nel is that someone who sees Sula's actions and is enough (like) Sula to experience the pace and texture and thrill of the ride.

The continued description of their girlfriendness evidences the political imperative of becoming: "So when they met, . . . they felt the ease and comfort of old friends. Because each had discovered years before that they were neither white nor male, and that all freedom and triumph was forbidden to them, they had set about creating something else to be." This is the specificity that race and gender apportions to their lives that neither totalizes nor is minimized by the vagaries of their desire and love. The subjectivities they bring to each other both sustain and supersede the identity margins their bodies are framed by. They are girlfriends, dancers, each other's something, the other red-hot body that subjecthood needs—the body that makes possible the tension and unease of at once being a one and a more-than-one, of being a two: "Their meeting was fortunate, for it let them use each other to grow on. . . . they found in each other's eyes the intimacy they were looking for" (52). Their intimacy is self-centered; it facilitates each girl's process of me. They look at each other, and they tremble knowingly not because of what they see but largely because what is felt there, in the looking and the seeing—the slippery colors of dreams, the viscerality of yearning and fearlessness. They know each other to be the other piece, the self they have been looking for, even missing. Their friendship develops not just as a bonding of two people in a union but as a being in the company of one's own self in the way that Walker meets her (own) beautiful, bright-faced dancing body.

In a key moment in the novel Sula and Nel are playing in the yard, digging holes, working "until the two holes were one and the same" (58). This mutuality is characteristic of their friendship, which was "so close, they themselves had difficulty distinguishing one's thoughts from the other's" (83). The need for self-distinction is momentarily muted by the deliberateness of their union, the political character of two young Black women who choose to be together against the impossible of the world around them. But deliberateness is not everything, for, though their union is chosen, it is also surrender, like the falling in sleep—it is a calling, a sway, a seduction, as well as a measured purposeful strut. Poetically, their meeting is a choiced submission to the girl-friend: a meeting of one's (other) self at the river, a meeting made possible by first choosing to go to the river as well as choosing to be open to the encoun-ter of one's (other) self. This openness yields to an outstretched hand and then another hand, a holding that is intimate and political—an act so powerful that it propels (each) body to love even when she has long since left the river and is in a place where loving is normally very hard. It is a chosen meeting, a looking not because she has to but because she chose, chooses, to. It is the practicing of what looking (and seeing) brings forth.

The integrity of Nel and Sula being both like each other as well as *being* each other is not compromised by the necessary disruptions in their coupling. "She [Sula] had clung to Nel as the closest thing to both an other and a self, only to discover that she and Nel were not one and the same thing," the nar-rator writes, as both women attempt to make sense out of Sula's momentary affair with Jude (119).[14] Perhaps the central example of disidentification amid them is Nel's marriage to Jude, an occasion that interferes with the self-centeredness Nel had embraced as necessary to her relationship with Sula. In fact, it is Jude's failure to find work and his need to consume someone that prompts him to marry Nel: "it was rage, rage and a determination to take on a man's role anyhow that made him press Nel about settling down. He needed some of his appetites filled, some posture of adulthood recognized, but mostly he wanted someone to care about his hurt. . . . The two of them together would make one Jude" (82–83). And so there it is—Nel's loss of self in a whirl of Jude's selfishness that is neither reflection nor thrill.

That the coupling of Nel and Jude yields only one Jude is antithetical to what results from Nel and Sula's volatile twoness: as Nel "raised her eyes to [Jude] for one more look of reassurance, she saw through the open door a slim figure in blue, gliding, with just a hint of a strut, down the path toward the road" (85). That the woman who is leaving is unnamed suggests that she is an icon of self. Surely a literal reading acknowledges that she is Sula or even that she represents the dissolution of Nel's union with Sula as a casualty of marriage. This woman might also be interpreted as Nel, as the textual appa-rition of the submission to Jude-ness. But the namelessness of her blue body is evocative and affords me the license to fantasize her as an entirely other body. She is a third term, an/other woman who manifests from the generosity of Sula and Nel's twoness and who each woman can claim, if she wishes, for herself. She, this third woman, this icon of the subject, is the (un)reliable body against and with which a woman can (self-)manifest. This gliding blue is a repeating and multiple subject who generates from Nel and Sula's dissonance to become the icon of (their) selfhood. Their coupling produces even as it fissures.

Reading the gliding blue as a third woman is crucial to the productive and nonbinary character of girlfriend subjectivity: it is not Sula herself or Nel's relationship with Sula that is subjecthood for Nel; instead, it is the third woman who represents material selfhood, this third woman who is, for Nel, Nel, and for Sula, Sula. This woman is the always, the reassurance that does not overwhelm nor demand succumbing; she is the *you* of Paul D's loving incantation, "You your best thing." She is the you who arrives in the tussle between a Black woman and her an/other, in the interstitial of girlfriend subjectivity's with and as.[15]

This model of subjecthood is conversant with Walker's *The Color Purple* in which Celie's achievement of self is the result of a long series of identifications with and as other women. Her sexual experiences with Albert offer an early moment of girlfriend identification that brings Celie closer to her self/ selves: "I lay there thinking bout Nettie while he on top of me, wonder if she safe. And then I think bout Shug Avery. I know what he doing to me he done to Shug Avery and maybe she like it. I put my arm around him" (13). Celie thinks first of Nettie's safety even as she is experiencing an act of violence, then she thinks of Shug, a woman who is her girlfriend in every sense of the word. This meditation on Shug brings Celie closer to her own body as she recognizes their sameness. And, though it occurs as a slight moment in the novel, this connaissance traverses significant psychic and material terrain for Celie. The gesture of affection she makes is not toward Albert, who is barely an object in her reverie, but instead toward herself, toward Shug, and toward the growing union between her and Shug. Celie is acting like, even becoming, Shug in putting her arms around Albert (performing the sassiness that she, Celie, is not allowed to exhibit) as well as pretending to put her arms around Shug (imagining Shug as the body that replaces Albert's). And, considering that fantasy is a realm of totalized selfness, Celie is also performing a more significant act of self(ish)ness and agency as she puts her arms around the product of her own imagination. This small scene in Walker's novel is a multivalent moment of (un)clarity between at least three subjects (and none of them is Albert): self, an/other, and the self that quite literally materializes from this process between self and other. An (un)becoming.

There is a similar aesthetic that manifests in contemporary Black women's photography, especially works by Lorna Simpson and Carrie Mae Weems. Two

Lorna Simpson, *Easy for Who to Say*, 1989. *Courtesy Sean Kelly Gallery, New York*

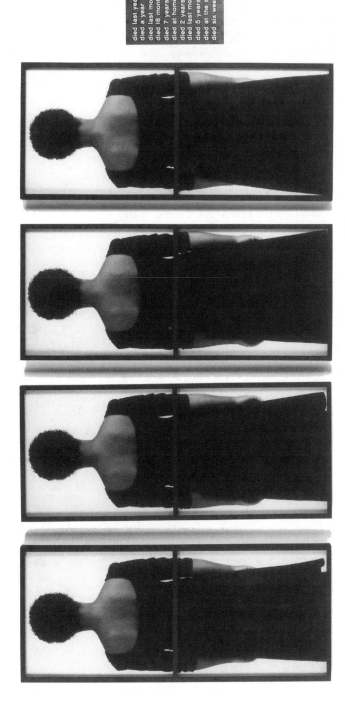

died last year
died a year ago
died last month
died 18 months ago
died 7 years ago
died at home
died 2 years ago
died last month
died 5 years ago
died at the same time
died six weeks ago

Lorna Simpson, *Time Piece*, 1990. Courtesy Sean Kelly Gallery, New York

pieces from Simpson's 1989 series reveal a sense of Black female subject sameness, of repeated bodies. In *Easy for Who to Say* Simpson centers five Black women as vowels. The images are of the same woman but five different versions of her—not exact copies of one master photograph but numerous subjectivities of the same subject (for example, the hair in each is slightly different, as are the places where the image is cropped and framed). Simpson's captions for the series pronounces a changing sameness in the explicitly political character of these subjects' relationship to one another, their subjectivities varyingly (mis)represented as "amnesia," "error," "indifference," "omission," and "uncivility," as well as by their plainclothed facelessness (which I will address later). A second slide from the same series, *Dividing Lines,* even further evokes political solidarity and a sameness that is not the same: the subtle difference in posture of the two women who are in a line-up, backward to the viewer— one woman's body is more erect, evidenced by the presence of her shoulder blades; the other woman is more slouched. Their solidarity, their girlfriendness, is in the repeatable hold of/on their bodies. In a third slide, *Time Piece,* the poetic side bar makes death across various states of time the condition of Black female unity.

Two years later Simpson's work focused on Black women's hair, but her aesthetic principle of connection, similarity, and solidarity remained constant: in the slide *Same* she positions eight Black women in pairs, each pair tied together by hair braids. Again, there are subtle yet signal differences between the images, though the subjects are the same one Black woman. The singularity of the slide's model is hard to ascertain decisively, and the unity between each Black female subject and her other self is partially disrupted by the frame of the photograph; hence, the connecting braid is not at all a clean and straight umbilical. The caption lines could well be the narrative of Nel and Sula: "they pronounced water the same way; were disliked for the same reasons; they pronounced machete the same way; read with the same accent; were not related; worked for the same pay; read the news account and knew it could have easily been them; knew illness; didn't wear their hair the same way; were let go for the same reason; had never met." These examples of Simpson's work use, as Coco Fusco argues, ambiguity and juxtaposition to "tease out . . . [multiple] interpretations" and represent the "uncanny dissonance" that is key to girlfriend subjectivity (6).[16] They are evidence of an aesthetic of poststructural twinning that yields a one, a two, and more. Uneasy and unencumbered.

The presence of this an/other woman is an intermediary structure that makes possible a Black woman's willful selfish love within the cultural and social imperatives against self-centeredness and the danger that self-love is. Through this third body the inherent and totalizing love of the other that is

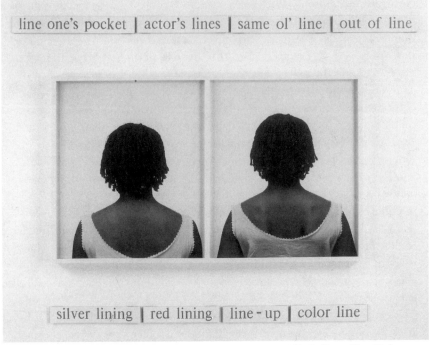

line one's pocket | actor's lines | same ol' line | out of line

silver lining | red lining | line-up | color line

Lorna Simpson, *Dividing Lines*, 1989. *Courtesy Sean Kelly Gallery, New York*

expected of women manifests, instead, as a love of not only an/other woman but as a love of self. The with and as identifications develop as a series of repeating moments in which there is really no other woman except one's ability to *be* that other woman. In this context a self-centered subjectivity develops as a subject moves between an identification *with*, which sustains the individuation of corpus, and an identification *as*, in which the self (dis)integrates into an amorphous textuality that is less boundaried but no less precise in its ethic.

This subjectivity is wary of the responsibility Black women have had for everyone else before themselves, their being "the mule of the world." It is against the background of Black women's expected selflessness that Celie's slow engagement of herself is selfish. Yet no character of the works discussed thus far behaves more selfishly than Sula, who understands profoundly that her self-love is neither encouraged nor sanctioned in social culture. When Jude is complaining about the attacks made on his subjectivity as a Black man, Sula rattles off a list of reasons why Black men are widely "loved," a term she uses loosely and somewhat humorously.[17] Sula here is asserting her relationship with Nel

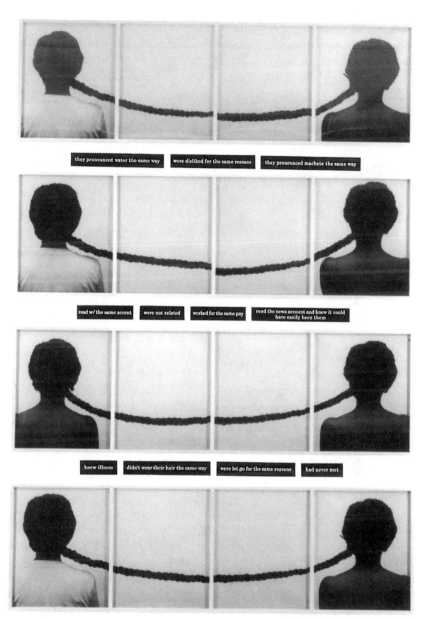

Lorna Simpson, *Same*, 1991. *Courtesy Sean Kelly Gallery, New York*

by signifying on and ridiculing Jude. But she is also giving attention to the invisible destructiveness of Black women's selflessness—the same Black women who are, in her description, "worry[ing] themselves into bad health just trying to hang on to" Black men's cuffs (103). Sula's argument is relevant not only to the world of Medallion but to the larger social reality of Black women.[18] And, as such, for Celie to love Shug, and Nel Sula, requires an act of will, even willfulness; there is hardly any social reward for such love. The identification that generates from this love is powerful and self-reflexive, an embrace of an/other as an "ongoing unsettling process" toward one's embrace of one's own volatile self.

The girlfriend alliance, which is unconscious as well as conscious, is neither a foregone conclusion nor a stable process. It is not predetermined by race or gender politics and unallies as much as it allies, demanding of the subject *agency*: first to choose the alliance and then to be able to not rely on it (figuratively, to "unchoose" it). An example from The Color Purple helps to express this more clearly: Celie's earliest comments are about how she feels about men, particularly Albert, whom she is afraid to look at for what the look might invite. Of women Celie writes, "I look at women, tho, cause I'm not scared of them" (7). For Celie women represent a possibility of being engaged by an/other that does not violate and render her abject nor fill her with fear, as do relationships with some Black men and most white people. Celie's act of "looking" at women requires her own (self-) engagement; looking is an act of discernment, and Celie has to make sense of what she discerns, which is the beginning of her choosing to connect with Shug, Sofia, and other women—a moment of self-intimacy and self-interest that represents and nurtures the agency to be uncoupled.

In this way Black woman loving Black woman is serious business, dangerous, rigorous, and necessary business. Revolutionary business.

WHAT CELIE, SHUG, SULA, NEL, and Walker's "other dancer" represent is a phenomenal dialectic between self and other, an oscillation that becomes a process of Blackwoman-centered identification. It is an (un)becoming, a gathering and scattering of affiliation, an arrival at and refusal of one's own. That this model exploits a binary is conversant with contemporary theory, especially psychoanalytic and postcolonial discourses. The work of Jacques Lacan, a French psychoanalyst and philosopher, is perhaps the most cited and most relevant to my discussion of subjectivity. In "The Mirror Stage" Lacan suggests that the struggle for selfhood is evocative of the impossibility of language.[19] Here he argues that the young child moves from object relations identification (primarily with its mother) to identification with the image in the mirror as itself narcissistically. This identification in the mirror is misguided and inaccurate, for it projects a unity that the child itself does not experience in the body; hence, the image and the experience are fantastical and imaginary as is the unity between signifier (word) and signified (meaning). Subjectivity, then, is constituted by the endless recognition of the failure of language.[20]

Lacan's essay is both a useful warning against the easy correlation between self and other, a solipsism that can offer a false sense of wholeness at violent cost to others as well as to one's own self, and a good source for critical theory's fascination with a discourse of multiplicity and fragmentation. Still, there are two concerns with Lacan's analysis as it relates to my discussion of subjectivity: one, Lacan here fails to race the subjects of his discourse, and, since those subjects are clearly gendered (not just sexed but gendered), then they ought to at least also be raced; and, two, his discussion of fragmentation ignores the impact that social institutions have on the condition of people's lives, another example of the apolitical posture of psychoanalysis that Erich Fromm notes. Both of these contribute to a larger problem with Lacan's discursive premises that warrants longer engagement here: the Lacanian mirror relies heavily on the relationship between a subject (child) and an object (mirror/image), foregrounding the subject's *image* as the primary attribute of its sense of self. Such valorization of the image, especially in the absence of political and cultural analyses, too readily perpetuates the role the visual sign has played in modern Western history in erecting discourses of inferiority, particularly for women, people of color, and especially those who fall into both broad categories. In fact, the idea of the image (and its perceived normalcy—its beauty) might be one of modernity's most essential and insidious characters; I would venture so far as to suggest that, metaphorically but also literally, the mirror, the image, and beauty form an unholy trinity of widespread violence.[21]

As a discourse, beauty reinforces Black female selflessness, literally positioning her as a nonsubject and a nonentity—as one who is without an identifiable and sovereign self. If we momentarily revisit Lorna Simpson's work, it is not accidental that her subjects are faceless: their faces are either deleted or obstructed, and many of her pictures are photographed from behind the subject, revealing another way to look . . . sometimes suggesting slyness and agency . . . sometimes evoking a sense of self-defense, a shielding. When the faces are erased, as is the case in *Easy for Who to Say*, they are replaced with a symbol of the erasure that, for these women, are part of their everyday encounter with culture (in this case, a white oval and a vowel to match the word of social disregard). In many of Simpson's works the unrevealed face seems to imply that the subject's action—in this case her relationship to water and to sustaining the discounted narrative—is more important or at least more a location of agency than her face, her image. Another contemporary Black woman photographer, Carrie Mae Weems, delivers a striking argument against the utility of the mirror, beauty, and their cultural savagery. In one piece from her 1987–1988 exhibit titled *Mirror, Mirror*, Weems gives us a Black female subject who intends to find in the mirror her beautiful self; instead, the mirror is harsh and returns not her self but a witch, a fairer-skinned woman than the subject who reminds the latter what mirrors symbolically mean to Black women: "Looking into the mirror," the caption reads, "the Black woman asked 'Mirror, mirror on the wall, who's the finest of them all?' The mirror says, '"Snow White you Black bitch, and don't you forget it!!!'"[22] Although the mirror is held close, the subject has to turn her head away from the intensity of a reflection that is not her, that is not her girlfriend.

The privileging of image as an eminent textuality of human subjectivity is one problem, and the absence of attention to how race and gender function in the valence that images carry in the social order is another. And, still, the function of the image as a measure of self-reflection is potent and indispensable—even for the subjects of Black women's narratives. I want to be careful not to overstate my critique of Lacan such that the mirror appears to be only irrelevant or disturbing to Black female subjectivity. In fact, it seems that the mirror's function in Lacanian psychoanalysis—to initiate the exploration of language and introduce the subject into a (futile) process of identification—is performed, albeit differently, by the other self, who mirrors the girlfriend in Walker's and Morrison's narrations of selfhood. That is, in place of the mirror and its cold and inaccurate reflection is an/other woman whose abilities to reflect the girlfriend's self might be no more accurate than the mirror's but whose presence is a subject (with flesh and other attributes), not an image or an object. Not a sign that has to be taken for wonder but a subject that is itself wonder. In this girlfriend model of selfhood it is not the image in the mirror that holds the self's gaze; instead, the self's gaze, or its entire being, is held and engaged by an/other self. A model of identity in which self and image are negotiated through an object is profoundly less dynamic than the volatility of identity negotiated through two subjects, as Homi K. Bhabha suggests in "Signs Taken for Wonder." Bhabha's essay is a clever postcolonial rereading of Lacan that disrupts the exclusivity of the binary of child and object and highlights instead the two subjects of the discourse (in this case the Indian native and the white colonialists). In reading Bhabha's essay, I have come to make a distinction between being "othered" and being "other." *Other* describes a nominative subject position and sometimes a place of agency, while *othered*, an adjective, is metaphorically a (dis)placement, an imposition of identity. In this way the other is a subject (position) less static and less marginal than the othered.

Against a mirroring system that leaves Black women widely unaccounted for, girlfriend subjectivity suggests that *everyone* is other, that every subject comes to identity via a process of being (and loving) an/other: identity is relational, and there is no "I" without an/other, which is what is suggested by Walker's other dancer, Sula and Nel's relationship, and Celie's attending to self. This process of selfhood operates from a negative or a deficit position—that of being (considered) "an other"—such that the deficit is neutralized or at least made normative. Subjecthood is all (un)becomings, losing and holding, fading and appearing; it sways and trails, is sturdy and fragile—even inexistent. Mae G. Henderson makes a similar argument about otherness in her essay "Speaking in Tongues":

> What is at once characteristic and suggestive about black women's writing is its interlocutory, or dialogic, character, reflecting not only a relationship with the "other(s)," but an internal dialogue with the plural aspects of self that constitute the matrix of black female subjectivity. The interlocutory character of black women's writings is, thus, not only a consequence of a dialogic relationship with an imaginary or "generalized Other," but a dialogue with the aspects of "otherness" within the self. The complex situatedness of the black woman as not only the "Other" of the Same, but also the "other" of the other(s) implies, as we shall see, a relationship of difference and identification with the "other(s)." (17–18)

Henderson's articulation identifies otherness as a key theoretical location for thinking about Black women's identity and simultaneously resists the idea of otherness as only marginal. As imagined and constructed through various Western discursive systems (especially Hegel's), identity is a power struggle that privileges one subject in relation to the *other*. Yet for some Black women identity is fashioned through a process of selfhood that does not merely invent an other for the self's (dominating) sake but instead inhabits otherness as the name of the marginal self, as its possibility. Otherness, then, is a more capable location of subjectivity, a site realized not only because it is marginal but the opposite—that to *be* an other is a universal experience, the moment of vulnerability that every human subject encounters and that pulls her off center at the same time that it confirms that she is, her own, center. To be an/other is also to *be* (in the intransitive sense of the word)—to manifest, to desire, to covet, to surrender, to fail, as well as to impel movement. My representation of the term as *an/other* is intended to imply unity and disruption, subject and object, self and (not)self, and what lies between. Both and all and sometimes none. To be an/other is to be, quintessentially, a subject (un)becoming.[23]

Let me try to further resuscitate the centrality of the image in the process of subjectivity by beginning with a narrative scene that somewhat awkwardly involves a Black man (with a promise that the awkwardness will be resolved later in the chapter). In an opening moment in *Sula* it is anything but a mirror that offers Shadrack a sustaining sense of his self. Shadrack is searching for his reflection, for something that will let him know he exists, a moment that seemingly mimics the dilemma of Lacan's child; this search is motivated by his fragmented sense of his self, his body, which shakes repeatedly and becomes to him more grotesque as new deformities manifest—all a condition of postwar dementia. Of Shadrack's struggle Morrison writes:

> Like moonlight stealing under a window shade an idea insinuated itself: his earlier desire to see his own face. He looked for a mirror; there was none. Finally, keeping his hands carefully behind his back he made his way to the toilet bowl and peeped in. The water was unevenly lit by the sun so he could make *nothing* out. Returning to his cot, he took the blanket and covered his head, rendering the water dark enough to see his reflection. There in the toilet water he saw a grave black face. A black so definite, so unequivocal, it astonished him. He had been harboring a skittish apprehension that he was not real—that he didn't exist at all. But when the blackness greeted him with its indisputable presence, he wanted *nothing* more. (13; emph. added)

Morrison's careful use of *nothing* frames the "indisputable" something that Shadrack sees; "nothing" is its name, not a description of its essence (as is the case with otherness). That Shadrack finds an unshakable sense of self in dark toilet water (and not in a mirror) is important, especially since he hardly sees an image there. Instead, what renders his once-tremoring hands "courteously still" is not a precise image of his face but the *impression* that his face makes upon his other sensibilities—an impression, a sense, a feeling, a textuality, that is less visual and more tactile. Perhaps he sees a line near his eyes that reminds him of a grandmother's smile or a war wound that gestures toward his survival or an outline that looks murky and spiritlike. Whatever he sees, though it is not precise in form, it is precise in impact. His process of selfhood in this moment forgoes the precision of the image in exchange for an intensity of the other attributes (the an/other bodies) that constitute self.

The other of girlfriend subjectivity is a subject who mirrors in fuller textuality than an image or its representation in language can. This mirroring that an/other provides is not the fragmented, flattened, or reversed image of self that Lacan's mirror offers but, instead, is the potent (even when flawful) act of looking at, and seeing, an/other. The choral refrain of the song "There Were No Mirrors in My Nana's House" by vocal group Sweet Honey in the Rock is an apt definition for this mirroring: "There were no mirrors in my nana's house . . . and the beauty that I saw in everything . . . was in her eyes." A grandmother's eyes generate a reflection that complicates the subject's sense of individuation, forgoes the racial and gender problems of mirrors, and initiates a process of "looking" that disrupts the violence of visual culture. This is a selfhood in which the subject is more than othered, more than the object of marginalization, more than displaced. And, though this girlfriend beholding is in part reliant on the presence of an/other subject and hence as likely to offer mis-reflection, such is offset by the commitment to the self's (un)becoming—that being beheld in an/other's eyes is ultimately a process of being beheld in one's own hands and the unsettling this all is.[24]

THE THIRD BODY CREATED in the wake of subject-to-subject relation suggests that borders of corporeality have been crossed. This body, which functions as an/other to the self and her girlfriend, is literally a transgression and represents the domains of subjecthood that have been traversed, shared, complicated, and disturbed, revealing all the while the high value that movement, mobility, and motion have in this practice of selfness. It is as if "the discovery of human behavior . . . happen[s] in motion. . . . [as] a process of moving from the self to the other and the other to the self" (xxxii).[25] It is no accident, then, that Walker's an/other is both a dancer, a subjectivity of movement, and also partly a phantasm, a corpus of unstable and shifting materiality. The (un)becoming of girlfriend subjectivity requires reckless movement, hence motion and mobility—represented as dance, migration, gregariousness, dreaming, fantasy, for example—are repeated parts of its narrative literalization.

Movement so clearly defines this subjectivity because the dialectic between self and an/other yields a space for a subject to traverse without having literally to go too far out of her (own) self, too far away from her self-centeredness. It is a human impulse, and a healthy one, for a body to yearn for adventure, to desire to see the before-unseen, to want to wander, linger, even get lost: to be and to become *unfamiliar*. Yet the domains of adventure and travel are often masculine ones (and are heavily limited to women) and also have particular dangers: not only the danger of being hurt/violated by what is out there, a perpetuity that all women have to pay some attention to; but also the danger of losing one's self, of going too far, of being seduced by apoliticized centerlessness that perishes self and ethos as it feeds the necessary wanderlust. Such is the risk and agency of travel.

In girlfriend subjectivity the presence of an/other introduces a space between the self and her other self that can be traipsed, risked, lingered. And still this space of psychic travel does not replace the need for literal travel and venture; nor does the literal venture supersede the risk and intensity of the psychic journey and tension. In fact, the experiences of Nel and Celie, which hardly involve travel, would almost suggest that the psychic sphere is more crucial were it not that both women have Sula and Shug/Nettie as their counterparts, women whose penchant for and experience of travel Nel and Celie encounter vicariously. These alliances emphasize the need for a mobility that allows risk but which does not predicate masculinity; that is, a mobility that honors the vastness, the complicatedness, of interior spaces, what Angela Davis terms "the highly social character of interior lives." It is this space—the interior—that women most often inhabit and that most readily emerges in the psychic tussle between a self and her an/other.[26]

This mobility facilitates agency and creates a practice of negotiating oneself through space and time, of placing and shifting one's subject textualities in relation to an/other. That such travel crosses borders while remaining allied to the ethos of a self-center suggests that the process of girlfriend subjectivity is at once self-focused and self-specific and, by virtue of mobility, is also indeterminate and multiple (though not disconnected or fragmented).

There is a useful contradiction here between the subjectivity's specificity, its singularity even, and its multiplicity. The specificity is the self's commitment to an ethic of centeredness, the acceptance of the dangerous political work required for a Black woman to love herself selfishly, thoroughly, excludingly, flawfully, a practice that gives up the outside places of center. The integrity of this commitment is grand, an a priori condition of self-love. Yet it is in constant conversation, even compromise, with the multiplicity implied by the idea of a relational subjectivity, one that opens out, that is generous and collective, one that risks loss as it offers adhesion. Girlfriend subjectivity cannot only (exclusively) be specific and selfish, for it engages an/other, for the construct of the an/other is its foundation. This conclusion has a larger implication: even as the other initially described here, or even as represented in the identificatory trajectory of a character, might often be an/other Black woman, the mobility and transgression and variance connoted by the third character necessitates, ultimately, that the identity of an/other is not limited; it cannot be for it is always (un)becoming. The process of relating with an/other Black woman *might be* a certain safety, an initial gathering place, even a necessary field of exposition, but it is not guarantee; such a relation might be a ritual of beginning but can never be the only shore/sure. In fact the model of selfhood is also about risk, not only safety.

This matter gets more complicated, at least to articulate: the generativity of girlfriend subjectivity and its principle of mobility works against any exclusivity that is not that of the self; and the self herself is an exclusivity that is multiple, a fact that tempers what exclusivity can mean though the ethos of Black female selfishness is not ever compromised. Let me be more careful and more clear: the notion of being girlfriends, upon which the identification depends, is rooted in a political, ethical, and spiritual solidarity, not only a solidarity based on being, in some essentialist social order, a Black woman. In fact, it seems that the ultimate ethos of the identity is against reliance on easy coalitions and subjectivities granted and therefore policed through state and nation apparatus. The coalitioning is open to "sisters and those who love sisters"[27]—those who are themselves outside, marginal, and other and who are appreciative of the urgent need for a Black woman to center and love herself. In this way the act of a Black woman practicing coalitions with her girlfriend is a literal model for her coupling with other people (who are not Black women) in girlfriend relationships, relationships that maintain the integrity of the commitment to Black women selfishness. The model is not exclusive then and opens to anyone who is committed to justice and love and the survival of a Black woman.

I would not want this comment to suggest that the model of selfhood is suddenly depoliticized and available to any unspecified subject. The seeming contradiction between the model's specificity and its wide-openness is reflective of a recurring dynamic in Black women's articulations of themselves. For example, many Black feminist scholars have argued that one of the flaws of white feminist movements has been the call for separation from men, which is less productive for Black women, whose experience of racial oppression affirms a bond with Black men. This argument suggests that the goal of identity politics, at least for some Black women, is to articulate strategies and ways-of-being that are committed to Black women but also to other groups of people who themselves are committed to antiracist, antisexist, and other liberation activisms. Perhaps the best expression of this is Walker's definition of a womanist: "A woman who loves other women, sexually and/or nonsexually. . . . Sometimes loves individual men, sexually and/or nonsexually. Committed to survival and whole of entire people, male *and* female. Not a separatist, except periodically, for health. Traditionally universalist" ("Womanist" xi). Walker's definition asserts that a Black woman–centered model of identity can also be a model that enunciates a survival practice that can be engaged by those who are not Black women, though it is imperative that the commitment to "sisters," to "loving sisters," remain at its center. It is in the consistency of this latter qualification that the political integrity is sustained. A similar consideration applies to the sexual politics of girlfriend selfhood, which is *sometimes* specifically lesbian but is certainly *always* woman centered and woman loving. Because she offers a brilliant conceptualization of these (dis)junctures, let me cite Cheryl Clarke, who invites us "to imagine Black women's sexuality as a polymorphous erotic that does not exclude desire for men but also does not privilege it. To imagine without apology, voluptuous Black woman sexualities" (224). One could substitute the word *subjectivity* for *sexuality*—or simply acknowledge that the two are synonyms— and the yield of Clarke's statement is an expansive model of a subjectivity determined to be centered in the political impulses of Black feminism. Voluptuous Black woman identities.[28]

The coupling that I am suggesting here is as much a political choice as it is an emotional one. The girlfriends come together not out of convenience, in any sense of the word, but out of a *consistent (if unconscious) commitment to their own selfness.* The implications of their choice to be girlfriends becomes more (or less) as their identifications oscillate, but its politicized tenor remains. At the moment they find each other, Nel and Sula are against the rest of the world; they are young, female, and Black, and their bodies are already imperiled. In recognizing their state of otherness, they choose each other but also choose freedom and triumph. Their coupling, careful and haphazard, is not an erasure of the material and/or politically distinct other who the girlfriend also is. Instead, the coupling is a continuous engagement of the porous borders between self and an/other self, toward a collectivity that is political, liberating, and ultimately unsettled; it is simultaneously "the impulse behind [one's] excesses and the force that drives [a] quest for justice."[29] This coupling builds a coalition with a self and then another self and then other selves, until the practice of coalition achieves an embracing of all of one's selves, a simultaneous differentiation and integration of the self, a process of (un)becoming.[30]

This fluidity within girlfriend selfhood invites transgression (implied in the prominence of mobility between subjects) and challenges common social boundaries of gender. For one, the coupling of women as girlfriends, sexually or nonsexually, in an alliance predicated on Black woman self(ish)ness, dislocates heteronormative ideologies of race and gender that assume or demand

Black women's presence for the sake of others who are not themselves. It is a literal redefinition of who a Black woman is.

The coupling even directly impacts gender roles, as seen in *The Color Purple*, in which Celie describes a moment between her and Shug: "Shug say, Girl you look like a good time, you do. That when I notice how Shug talk and act sometimes like a man. Men say stuff like that to women, Girl, you look like a good time. Women always talk bout hair and health. How many babies living or dead, or got teef. Not bout how some woman they hugging on look like a good time" (72). Celie notes that Shug's behavior extends outside of the things women do and say, an extension that is also at the axis of Shug's being able to be Celie's other: not just teeth and babies but also a deep, committed look at and interest in Celie. This interest is followed by a daring (manlike) proclamation, "Girl you look like a good time," a proclamation that helps Celie to begin to see herself in an/other way. Shug's "good time" comment is free of the particular sexual (and violent) valence that the interest of men often bears. Instead, Shug offers to Celie what she, Shug, sees, which is not precisely who Celie is (or what Celie might feel like) but is part of who/ how Celie *might* be. Shug's offering opens a door for Celie to think of herself as abundant and joy possessing. Her spoken reflection of Celie (she is Celie's mirror) is strong enough to make an impression upon how Celie thinks of herself without reinforcing sexist and racist perceptions.

Walker's novel offers further commentary on gender-particular behavior. As Celie and Albert have a conversation late in the story, he asks her, "What it is [she] love so much bout Shug." "He say he love her style. He say to tell the truth, Shug act more manly than most men. I mean she upright, honest. Speak her mind and the devil take the hindmost, he say. You know Shug will fight, he say. Just like Sofia. She bound to live her life and be herself no matter what." Celie recognizes these characteristics as *womanist*, not masculine: "Mr. _____ think all this is stuff men do. But Harpo not like this, I tell him. You not like this. What Shug got is womanly it seem to me. Specially since she and Sofia the ones got it" (228). Celie deems that the behavior is the result of a commitment to a kind of living, not the result of gendered essence.[31] This clarification is important because it informs the coupling that can happen not only between women but between women and their *male* girlfriends. Shortly after Celie makes this point, she and Albert "keep . . . each other company under the stars" (230), reflecting the possibility that Albert can be and is becoming a part of Celie's beloved community, a community that previously had been only women. Celie at this point (and perhaps as a result of the work that she and Albert have done) is not "afraid" of men, and she makes this lovely nonmale assessment of her and Albert's relationship: "Us sew . . . make idle conversation" (240).[32]

What I have been describing then as pairings of one Blackwoman self with an/other is actually the coupling of self with many other selves, not only Blackwomen with Blackwomen and not only as a pair. The identification is an expression of new intimacies that challenges the kinds of relationships that Black women can have with other people, for example, Black men. The coupling of one Black woman other with an/other in girlfriend subjectivity is a model of mutuality and relationality that is open to other couplings that maintain the integrity of sisterhood, other couplings that are committed to the survival of a Black woman. This cultivation of a community of selves often exists between a small number (three or four), yet even this small coalitioned selfhood radiates outward to involve intimate connections with greater numbers of people. Girlfriend subjectivity, which begins as meeting and understanding the other as the self, is literally a gathering of community, one by one. In *Sula* the connection between Sula and Nel is often pronounced by Shadrack and his connection with Sula. In fact, the novel begins with Shadrack because he is key to selfhood in the narrative and is also a "girlfriend" of Sula's. After she has died, he misses her and thinks of her as "his visitor, his company, his guest, his social life, his woman, his daughter, his friend" (157). In fact, it is Shadrack who calms Sula in a rare moment of fear (after she and Nel have killed Chicken Little) with a promise of the "always" of herself, an assurance that perhaps only a girlfriend can make. The folks of Medallion marvel at his polite public gestures to Sula and speculate that it is only appropriate that Shadrack treat Sula with some modicum of respect, for they are "two devils" (117).[33]

As Nel is also Sula's other, the three, then, are a tripling as much as Sula/Nel and Sula/Shadrack are pairings. In one sense Sula, Nel, and Shadrack form two pairs that overlap in their search for revelatory self-love. It is an uneasy tripling because the three live different lives, yet they intersect in key ways, particularly in their awareness of and presence within the risk of headlessness and their urge toward a kind of fearlessness Black women are mythically known and heavily penalized for. Further, all three are part of Sula and Nel's epiphanies (the death of Chicken Little, Sula's at her death, Nel's at the end of the novel).

The triple facilitates and reveals other connections. For example, Eva Peace is also a mirroring of Sula (both women mutilate themselves as acts of survival) and Shadrack (both have awakening experiences in toilets that initiate an unwavering commitment to life). At the end of the novel, with Sula dead, it is an interaction with Eva that brings Nel back to Sula, a reverie that collapses time and space and occurs as Shadrack watches, wondering where he had seen her (Nel) before. This community that Nel, Shadrack, Eva, and Sula constitute is cultivated through coupling as a political unit of identification.

Girlfriend selfhood develops as an intimacy beyond the two—or three— and yields a cultivation of community, a gathering of sisterfriends who one can identify with as well as against. It is the dynamism of the oscillation be-tween (dis)identifications that creates the expansiveness of what is initially a self-identity process. Celie's coming to understand her place in the world through her relationship with Shug exhibits this expanding dynamism. In a key example Celie identifies Shug as her own self: "My ears perk up when they mention Shug Avery. I feel like I want to talk about her my own self" (20). In one sense Celie wants to join the conversation about Shug, a desire that is, for Celie, willful and womanish. In another reading of the statement, however the words *her* and *my own self* are appositives; they represent the same entity and could be separated by a comma. Shug is Celie's own self, a reading that is supported by Celie's earlier performance of Shug-ness in her sexual ex-perience with Albert. Later Shug comes to represent the possibility for Celie to explore her relationships with other women: "I work on her like she a doll or like she Olivia—or like she mama" (48). In the space of this description of washing Shug's body, Celie transforms Shug from her first girlhood compan-ion (a doll), to her daughter Olivia, and then to her mother. And still, Shug is Celie, and the woman Celie loves. The process of identification here is mul-tivalent and makes more voluptuous the nature of the connection between the two girlfriends. In fact, when Shug makes up a song for Celie and names it after her ("Miss Celie's Song"), she is both identifying with Celie (and her struggle) as well as being Celie (Shug the performer becomes the narrative "Miss Celie").

The expansive connections facilitated by the model of selfhood are pos-sible because the coupling is an alliance, a political and spiritual union.[34] In contradistinction to the decoupling of the Lacanian child and mirror image, the Black woman self of this model embraces the fuller subject of her an/other self, and in a dancing motion the two traverse the boundaries of flesh, self, and other to achieve a union that offers an indisputable sense of *something* and make possible the cultivation of a community with other selves. Michelle Cliff's description of the guerrilla warriors in *No Telephone to Heaven* offers an image of coupling as solidarity that is useful here:

> The people—men and women—were dressed in similar clothes,
> which became them as uniforms, signifying some agreement, some
> purpose—that they were in something together—in these clothes, at

least, they seemed to blend together. This alikeness was something
they needed, which could be important, even vital, to them—for the
shades of their skin, places traveled to and from, events experienced,
things understood, food taken into their bodies, acts of violence
committed, books read, music heard, languages recognized, ones they
loved, living family, varied widely, came between them. (4)

This diverse group, hesitantly bonded, is "in something together"; they are
solidarity.

Communal identification achieved through what is a selfish and self-
specific process is, for some subjects, revelatory; it encourages a self to recognize
just how many selves she (and, in some cases, he) contains; this awareness of
selffullness repairs the sense of being marginal and outside and small. *Selffullness*
is in fact a more accurate term for what I have been intentionally calling "selfishness" (intentionally, because I am remembering Anna Quindlen's comment
about feminism offering women a little healthy selfishness, and I am also thinking about the cultural assumption of selflessness for Black women). In this
selffullness the other is everything, or, better said, forming a self-defined relationship with otherness constitutes the expansive totality of subjectivity.[35]

Such self-centeredness is clarity and self-affirmation and is also potentially narcissistic.[36] The self of this model is metaphorically similar to the ravenous and far-reaching surface that Elizabeth Grosz describes in "Refiguring
Lesbian Desire," a surface that imagines its contours to be everything and in
touch with everything and is centered only by its being full of self.[37] The danger of narcissism is also the danger of appropriation—that one self's centric-
ity overwhelms, in a damaging way, the self of the other. It is important to
reiterate Trinh's claim that identity is "an ongoing unsettling process," because
the movement of girlfriend selfhood *is* unsettling and disrupts the stasis necessary for appropriation. This selfhood further frustrates appropriation by the
ecumenicity of its other—there is no self who is not other, therefore establishing a hierarchy is more difficult and less fruitful, though certainly not impossible.

Girlfriend selfhood is selffullness through otherness, an arrogant assertion
in the face of social imaginations that intend to limit Black women's right to
willful self(ish)ness. It is an (un)becoming, a gathering and scattering of one's
selves.

THE STRUGGLE OF girlfriend selfhood is to "capture the I in I," to achieve radical self-possession.[38] This self-possession is propelled by the political imperative toward repair: of making otherness a viable location of identity. The
girlfriend, then, is an/other whose subjectivity depends upon but also consti-

tutes her ability to facilitate the other subject. The model of girlfriend coupling is a representation of otherness not only as subjectivity but as the *agency* of a mobile self that is more than its image, full of contradictions, and more than its singularity. This repair is not a reversal but is literally a *re-pair*, a rejoining of the severed self with its other; the seeing recognition of a girlfriend who has been othered but who is truly one's an/other.[39] The re-paired coupling is not a single unit, but is a multipled textuality that is centralized in its self-fullness. The re-pair is not a clean healing but an attempt to engage subjectivity as an unresolved oscillating relationship between a self and its other— the chiasmic identification *with* and *as* that is a dynamic exchange and disengagement between two parts and which establishes a model for potential exchange between a self and (any) other self.

This model of selfhood normalizes the other as a radical and political subjectivity and situates love as an operational schema of identity.

	Self(full)ness and the
Chapter 2	Politics of Community

AT THE CENTER OF girlfriend selfhood is a coalitioned subject with a ravenous, wide-spreading, boundary-less disposition, a subject inclined toward and respectful of the communal. But the contradiction between the subject's willful centeredness and her multiplicity reveals one of the unabiding trials of collectivity: despite other intentions, communities are often hegemonic and are characterized by order, stability, and familiarity as well as imperatives for reliability and acquiescence, even selflessness. These qualities are intensified when the community of note has been or is currently oppressed, for oppression magnifies the necessity of unity. Hence, while community sustains as well as is the result of the coalition of selves that constitute girlfriend subjecthood, such a coalition in its self-centeredness is both threatening to and threatened by community's functional schema.

This paradox of community is a defining tension of girlfriend selfhood. Often, the girlfriend subject who embraces herself as other does so in isolation—she is a subject marginalized and outside, imperiled and in jeopardy. She is scarred like Alice Walker before her dancing reverie; undereducated and discarded like Celie; outside the human welfare of triumph and freedom. She, this Black woman, is the subject named other who *is* the center of (the) community but whose centrality is her otherness, her being othered in the imaginations of those who are potentially her an/other. She functions as their mirror, reflecting the fear and anxieties they do not speak nor can hardly remember. Her outsiderness is tempered by her usefulness as a barometer of normality as well as by the gifted insight her marginality and ubiquity come to symbolize.

Being both a member of the community as well as outside it, she is both claimed and disdained, awesome and awful. Her outsiderness is partly radical because it mediates the imperatives of community, yet it is also a regulation, her being cut off from resources or excluded from connections. Once marked as an outsider, she is subject to being controlled and policed and delimited. The mobility that she craves and needs—a mobility that often appears to others as freakish, infantile, even socially and psychically neutered—is counter to the stasis that satiates community. And, further, if few will claim or embrace her reckless volatility, then who will be her an/other—which bodies, phantasms, dreamers, will people her girlfriend wildness? Who will couple with her, and then who else will join the dance to yield the unstable, thrilling triple, the quad, the collective?

Girlfriend subjectivity oscillates between states of claim and abjection, of connection and disarray. In such self-fashioning the other is an/other, both a "me," a "not me," and a "part of me." This subjecthood is a "self-connection shared" and proffers connection with both oneself and one's an/other.[1] The central consideration of this chapter, then, is how girlfriend selfhood, which turns upon states of outsiderness, reconciles the tug of community, which materializes both as a cult of acquiescence and an intolerance for difference. In this the girlfriend subject struggles to live her *apartness*, which means to live as a part of a larger community of selves, as well as to live apart from the communal body. Her challenge is to sustain herself, even in its ultimate unsustainability, and to avoid overidentification with the community's identities as well as with the identity of the an/other. Her apartness both makes a viable subjectivity possible and impedes it at every turn.

Outsiderness

Because the model of selfhood is one of oscillation and unsettling, connection is as likely as is disconnection. Such dissonance and isolation is widely evident in the examples of girlfriend subjectivity explored earlier: for example, in *The Color Purple* Celie and Shug are on the outside of their social community; they are left to fend for themselves, and Celie's isolation is so extreme that she is almost psychically dead. Or in *Sula* Shadrack and Sula are the hyperrepresentation of the fears, anxieties, and possibilities of Medallion's townspeople, who nonetheless can hardly bear their company.[2] But it is Myriam Warner-Vieyra's *Juletane* that captures the extreme isolation that can happen in girlfriend selfhood. Warner-Vieyra introduces Juletane as a human island, a character with an abject self-concept whose sense of fracture and isolation increases as she migrates from the French Caribbean to Europe and then to Africa. Each move heightens the alienation that materializes on Juletane's body as she is propelled from place to place by loss, longing, and aloneness.[3]

Although the novel is largely an autobiography of Juletane's subjecthood, it opens with a third-person introduction of loss and severing: "They say a removal is as bad as a fire. That's not quite true. After a removal you can prune, choose to keep or throw out, uncover long forgotten objects, which may prove to be much more interesting than they seemed years before. After a fire, what is left in the ashes is almost never of any use" (1). The anxiety of this description parallels the ontological void that is Juletane's identity: she has no origin, is conceived in a period of "fast and abstinence," and her real name is not even known to her. She is "erased from the register of time," an orphan "lost alone in the world" (2, 15). Hers is a profound crisis of identity delineated by the seeming absence of identity—an absence that is further echoed by the distant third-person narration.

Yet Juletane's extreme disconnection is bountiful in that it yields the ability to move, to create, to invent. Because she has nothing to bind to, because she is largely unclaimed, she can establish connections that violate the norms of community and that satisfy her most original and self-constitutive desires. In many ways she is an individual who is neither marked nor markable as a member of a particular community in any of the places she lives. But this fluency is often ambiguous because Juletane *is* readily connected, and her identity, at least as others embrace it, is well defined: think of her as an island, a body that is in literal isolation and which still (often) has intricate relationships with neighboring islands, former or current colonial powers, as well as to Africa as a mythic motherland.[4] The potential wild agency that Juletane's disconnection could offer is tempered by the reality that she *is* marked: to many people she is an outsider, a madwoman, a Black woman, locations of otherness that function as social restraints and qualify her sense of (self-)legitimacy and authority.

In fact, Juletane's consciousness arrestingly develops in tandem with this sense of otherness. Not only does she largely encounter herself as alone and estranged, but her sense of self is overdetermined by her experiences of disconnection and by what disconnection is supposed to mean. She becomes desperate, thirsty, for an/other to be herself. After growing up as an orphan in the West Indies and moving to France, where she was mostly confined and isolated, Juletane overidentifies with Mamadou, who in a flash of flirtatious grace "became [her] whole world" (13). On the promise of marriage, she moves with Mamadou to Africa, where she quickly finds out that he has another wife, Awa. Although Mamadou proclaims his love for Juletane, he necessarily maintains a relationship with Awa, who is the mother of his children, and, when an accident causes Juletane to lose their child as well as her ability to have children, Mamadou's affection dissipates, and a third wife, Ndeye, is brought into the house. Awa at least has the distinction of being the mother, and Ndeye is the third wife, the beauty and socialite; Juletane is a nothing, the crazy second wife, a foreigner to the culture and customs, a barren woman who materializes as part specter, part elderly relative. Juletane casts looming shadows upon the household, reflections that influence all of the relationships in the house. She is acknowledged as a powerful force, but that acknowledgment does not generate social power. Instead, she is communally dispossessed of the joys, rights, and responsibilities of adulthood. Her most severe dispossession, however, is of herself; she lacks a critical sense of herself as a subject, the ability to think and feel herself outside the parameters of contaminated feedback from Mamadou and especially Ndeye. It is only in her writing that Juletane comes to appreciate that she is in fact wildly possessed with many connections to other people, connections that vibrate and challenge and illuminate her subjectivity, her sovereignty. Writing becomes her practice of redefining community, and even after she dies her writing figures largely in Helene Parpin's own process of self-(re)possession.

Although Juletane often imagines herself as a stranger without relative or relation (43), she is not a stranger to Helene, who, after reading the first section of Juletane's diary, "lit a cigarette, inhaled deeply and savoured the smoke which she blew out through her mouth skillfully pursing her lips, as she breathed *it* in again through her nostrils" (17–18; emph. added). The satiated and anxious smoking act is juxtaposed against Juletane's writing, such that the referent *it* remains intentionally ambiguous. In fact, a few lines later it is the writing that is being breathed in again: "This evening, reading these lines, fragments of her own life came back to her and forced her to make comparisons" (18). Helene is already seduced, already exposed and laid bare, by Juletane's story. The narrative continues: "The more Helene read the more she felt drawn towards this woman. She felt her suffering and the difference between then. She was sure she could never love a man to the point where she lost her reason over him." Helene tries to maintain a comfortable readerly distance, to set careful and reasoned space between her own meticulous and well-managed life and Juletane's reckless and abnormal one. Still, Helene's life already has remarkable parallels to Juletane's story of marital vexation: "Two months before the wedding day Hector had sent his best friend to announce to Helene that he had been married the previous day to a French girl who was expecting his child" (27). Helene and Juletane, at least in regard to unfulfilled marital promise, are permutations of each other. They are each other's relations.

Warner-Vieyra establishes a dynamic tension between Juletane and Helene, a coupling that is facilitated through Juletane's writing. Helene is the self-determined and heart-closed woman who, "until that Friday afternoon in February, ordered her life as she saw fit, giving priority to 'me first'" (1). She is seemingly Juletane's opposite: Helene is an attractive, intelligent, and ambitious psychiatrist who also migrated from the French Caribbean to Paris, about to marry a man ten years her junior, and who is captivated by her enormous sense of self; Juletane is a young orphan girl who left her island at age ten to live with her godmother in Paris, where she meets Mamadou, who seduces her into a polygamous marriage that literally diminishes her already fragile sensibilities. Both women are outsiders, separated from family, powerful in ways that are sometimes socially debilitating (and unacceptable for women), and Warner-Vieyra uses their otherness to link them to each other across time and condition. Their connection does not actually materialize for Helene is reading and befriending Juletane's story some time after Juletane has died. In fact, the opportunity for them to connect had been missed when Helene was invited to visit the crazed Juletane, who flatly refused her visit. Nonetheless, Juletane's persistent desire and ability to connect to a someone, even in unyielding communities that resist and partialize her efforts, is what ultimately propels Helene's reconsideration of selfhood. Juletane's trials of self-connection help to reveal Helene's own troubled selfhood and interrupt her poorly constructed self-assuredness. As Juletane's narrative becomes her own girlfriend, it also trans-temporally becomes Helene's girlfriend.

Juletane's identity oscillates among the selves she constructs in her diary, and her sense of fragmentation and isolation is revised: "thanks to my diary, I discover that my life is not in pieces, that it had only been coiled deep down inside of me and now comes back in huge raging waves." The diary is the girlfriend an/other whose intimacy and depth is an invitation and a landscape on which Juletane can enact subjecthood: "It had never occurred to me that putting down my anguish on a blank page could help me to analyse it, to control it, and finally, perhaps to bear it or reject it once and for all" (30). Juletane's process—to analyze, control, and then claim or disclaim—is a necessary act of agency for a woman who first thinks herself dispossessed of a self and a community. In finding this self, she wants to know it and then make a considered assessment of its usefulness to her. She dialectically identifies with and as her diary as well as leaves open the possibility to dis-identify with whatever shows up on its pages. This unresolved but surely resolute connection to writing facilitates other coalitions with people in her living space; for example, she forms a connection with Awa's children ("I love Awa's children, they are the children I would like to have had" [40]), especially to Diary, whose name itself is an echo of Juletane's girlfriend.

As she becomes keen to the potencies of her scribbling subjectivity, Juletane comments on the lost opportunities for connection among the women, noting that the "co-wives, or at least co-occupants of the same house," are not in coalition with one another, an insight that is only possible because her writing is beginning to engender a sense of selffullness, a sense of identity that is expansive and informative, a sense of possibility (42). Juletane is literally author(iz)ing herself—making her self a subject and an authority. She begins to revise the outsider status that characterizes her youth and early adulthood and refuses the label "madwoman": "To me, I am the most lucid person in the house" (9). Her proclamation of lucidity is an assessment made in and of herself and is contradictory to her earlier subjectivities. A few lines later Juletane writes even more poetically of her (un)becoming vitality in a moment of looking through her room's window: "I open my shutters to the cool of a fleecy blue sky in the rainy season. The rain and the storm have soothed my long sleepless night peopled with confused images of a former time when I was full of hope. Then, I used to love those long, late nights, for sleep and dream would blend harmoniously into dawn. For years now, my mornings, a succession of long monotonous hours, have stretched out interminably. Today, however, *I feel, I breathe, I am alive*" (9; emph. added). Juletane here is able to name herself (as) an origin, a place with the ontological stability to sustain her recognition that she exists and is alive. In a later explication of her window watching, Juletane describes the towering mango tree that is often the first thing she sees in the morning, a comment that further evokes a sense of selfness: "Like every morning, the first thing I do is open my window, scan the sky through the branches of the mango tree and watch the household getting up" (29). Her description of the window not only asserts subjectivity but also refigures the Cartesian equation of "I think therefore I am"; instead, Juletane's chord of self-decolonization and self-assertion centers feeling and breathing as indicators of subjecthood.[5] By representing Juletane's revitalization under the heft of her own writing, Warner-Vieyra emphasizes the role of authorship as a site of (un)becoming, a site that is now signally feminine and revelatory and about disconnections and alliances.[6]

Juletane's practice of self, and especially her comment about the missed opportunity among the cowives, triggers Helene's recognition that she too had missed the moment for camaraderie with Juletane: "[She] regretted that she had not been more insistent about looking after this young *compatriot* who had been in trouble" (43; emph. added). Later Helene plays Beethoven's Ninth

Symphony in memory of Juletane's suffering, repeating Juletane's earlier playing of Beethoven and further allying herself with this madwoman. Theirs is a
girlfriendship that is slow in realization and which happens literally between
Juletane's diary and Helene, as it was between Juletane and her own diary.
Helene's consideration of Juletane's exile brings her to realize her own empti-
ness: "Helene was discovering that her life was very empty . . . She had delib-
erately closed her heart to love, to compassion, for fear of the suffering it might
bring her, and as a result she was living a marginal existence." Juletane's diary
causes her to "reflect, to look back, to question her usual attitude" (56). These
two women are not opposites of each other but are manifestations of the same
love-seeking subject: Juletane, living in exile and the absence of love, and
Helene, similarly in exile and closing off herself in an attempt to keep abjection
at bay. The story, then, is as much about Helene's self-possession and recognition as it is about Juletane's.

The alliance of Helene and Juletane as subjects in each other's process of
subjectivity extends beyond the two women and toward connections with
other women who appear in Juletane's underwater dreams. There Juletane
makes an ascent and descent into a liminal subjectivity, into a community of
people similarly engaged in a journey of identity. In one of the earliest dreams
Juletane writes of her interaction with another woman:

> "Where are we?" I asked the young woman nearest to me.
> "Shhh! Not so loud, you mustn't disturb anyone. Everyone here
> is on an inward journey and goes where he wants to. Earth is only a
> stage which we pass through, man's body is dust." (70)

Juletane's companion in the dream attempts to allay her fears and affirms the
surrender to liminality, to an alternative state of consciousness and subjectivity that forgoes the familiar and normative ways of identifying. In this community Juletane is neither abject nor exile, but the pleasures of this liminality
are in direct conflict with her function in the above-water, nondream world.
As Juletane merges both worlds, living more and more in a waking dream-
fulness, a clash is inevitable. It is Awa's children whose bodies become the
sign of what is unbearable about community, and they are poisoned by Juletane
in what is part an error, part an act of liberation. Neither the death nor
Juletane's liability are fully ascertained, which confirms the novel's surrender
to Juletane's hazy clarity that is more dream and meditation than anything
else. And, still, the killing, even as acts of fantasy, represent a disavowal of
metaphors of the communal, a denouncement of the binds of connection that
do not—have not—cultivate sovereignty for Juletane. If the children are dead,

Juletane is not the only culprit, even if the poisoning was her doing. This is for sure a drastic and dramatic moment, but it also gives stunning relief to the haunt and unyielding of community. It is also an act of Juletane's (un)becoming—her surrendering of the one clear bond she had (to Awa's children), a bond that was in some ways her attempt to resuscitate her lost possibility of motherhood. These children were her one connective thread to an otherwise untenable household. Her grip on that reality—and perhaps any reality—is loosened by these killings, a flawful but perhaps also necessary act of self.[7]

The harsh effects of this experience of liminality give way to another: Juletane is committed to a psychiatric home for women. I am encouraging the parallelism between the two events to illuminate the threat of selfhood that such institutionalization is, a threat that is a near equivalent of the death Awa's children suffer. These women are dispossessed (of themselves) under the guise of social order, communal norms, nation, and patriarchy. But Juletane's selfness is remarkable, and she emerges as a vocal leader for her and their sense of sovereignty, igniting a transformation for these her sisters, who have been deemed to be without social utility and left for an unproductive life.

Armed with her steady self-reflective process, Juletane encourages them to think of their subjecthood, telling one patient (Oumy), "I am trying to remember my life and . . . she should do that same, because it helps to take stock of oneself" (76–77). That notion of "taking stock" implies a multiplicity of selfhood, a sense that there is more (of) self than one might be immediately aware of. As her role as sister to these women increases, Juletane's own writing becomes less important; as such, one girlfriend—her diary—fades as an/other manifests, both serving the purpose of revealing to Juletane just who she might be: "Yesterday," she writes, "I did not have time to write in my diary: the whole day was filled with group activities: cooking, housework, sewing. Plus the constant coming and going of the women in the afternoon. Besides I don't seem to have anything worth writing about" (77). The fact is that she continues to record her own life, but her need for writing matures into writing about the other women in the hospital, recording their lives and making her diary theirs. In one example she notes the similarity between her own experience of isolation and that of another patient: "Nabou's experience in Paris strangely parallels my life in this country. We both knew the loneliness of being the 'foreigner' who had nothing to do but turn over memories for days on end, who had only one voice to listen to, her own until it became an obsession" (78). This one obsessive voice is the subject disconnected from a community, a subject unable to capture her resonant multiplicity, unable to surrender to her own.

Juletane writes about the other women, connecting them to her, her to them, as well as to other women similarly pressed to the edges of themselves and the world by the imperatives of community. What Juletane's selffullness necessitates, is a redefining of community such that the ideology of Mamadou's polygamy is transformed as happens in the hospital where Juletane is the centered subject surrounded by other women who are her partners, her girlfriends. Surely, hers is not a polygamous situation in the strictest sense, for her self-centered practice does not foreclose and in fact encourages her others to also be(come) self-centered. But it is polygamy in its many-womanedness: a refigured polygamy that tempers and soothes her life of exile and which emboldens her vitality . . . her complicated and bittersweet subjecthood that is a well-earned (un)becoming.

JULETANE'S REPRESENTATION OF girlfriend subjectivity is in many ways a struggle with the impositions marriage as a communal institution makes upon a woman's self-centeredness. Despite being an outsider, Juletane has to resist the allure of marriage as self-completion as well as resist the impulse to identify with and as the community and its encroachment on her self-particularity. These struggles of community highlight the danger of overidentification, which is readily a part of girlfriend subjectivity. As a heteropathic model of identity in which one subject identifies with a subject not its own, transgressing and even violating boundaries between both selves, girlfriend selfhood demonstrates the risk of co-optation and selflessness. It is possible for one subject's selfishness to overwhelm her an/other and for the overall impulse of self-centeredness to be privileged in one subject's process more than in her other's. Furthermore, the commitment to willful selffullness is largely antithetical to consistently attending to and evaluating the experience of the an/other as such consideration would detract the self from her centeredness. That is, the likelihood that the two subjects involved will be perfectly matched is slim, though such imbalance cannot impede the progress of girlfriend practice. She must couple and love, in anticipation that such coupling, however flawed, will make other couplings more possible for her and will reveal her to be more useful to her own self. It is a selfish, selffull practice that carries a threat of narcissism and other-disregard.[8]

The threat of overidentification is especially significant here because the self moves always toward connection with its other selves, with its community. In this context the girlfriend subject's impossible charge is to be keenly attentive to the imminent erosion of self, a charge that is most crucial when she, rather than being marginalized, is anointed as a beloved member of the

community. Such is the case in Toni Cade Bambara's *The Salt Eaters*, a novel about a girlfriend subject who, rather than being an outsider, is an acknowledged and cherished community member. A novel that characterizes a southern U.S. Black community after the Civil Rights movement, *Salt Eaters* fantastically portrays the aftermath of Velma Henry's selflessness for a community she loves. Velma is the premier activist, an example of the typical Black female work that constitutes the backbone and life breath of liberatory struggle and, as such, is the quintessential insider who has and is expected to sacrifice herself for the good of the community, the "good of the struggle." And it is not the case that the community, as an entity or as represented by various individuals, does not care for Velma; in fact, Velma is well regarded, well liked, and considered indispensable. Still, for Velma interaction in community is both "feedback and contagion," and the coalitioned selfhood that her communal alliance represents is not an unfettered success (250). The central danger of community for this Black female subject is clearly represented near the end of the novel, as Velma slowly emerges from the healing coma and regains a worldly consciousness. In waking, she tries "to look around, to take in the healer, the people circling her, the onlookers behind. But there were so many other things to look at closer at hand" (267). Velma immediately begins to identify outwardly, begins to be overwhelmed by the abundant presence of people who are potentially her an/other, but, as Minnie Ransom, her healer and spirit guide, reminded her earlier, "the source of health is never outside" (220). Velma's self-disregard is characteristic of her role as the community's "superwoman" and is what led to her depression and suicide attempt. Literally, Velma has become an outsider to her own self, exiled from an ethos of selfishness, though she is generously peopled with the Claybourne community. Her struggle, then, is how to make the selfhood of interiority also a selfhood of community.

The novel opens with Velma seated on a stool, self-aware and being watched. Minnie is conducting the healing, and a group of interns, doctors, and townspeople gather at the room of the Infirmary, interested in Minnie's powers, Velma's ailment, and the fantastic hoodoo that they imagine is about to happen. Minnie repeatedly urges a catatonic Velma to "hold on," but "[Velma] could barely manage to hold on to herself . . . She tried to withdraw as she'd been doing for weeks and weeks. Withdraw the self to a place where husband, lover, teacher, workers, no one could follow, probe" (5). Velma is overwhelmed and is trying to enclose the self that had been so accessible to others that it became lost to her. Aptly, she is described as "Velma the swift; Velma the elusive; Velma who had never mastered the kicks, punches, and defense blocks, but who had down cold the art of being not there when the blow came" (4). Hers is a mobility of self that is elision and illusion, a self practice that all the while dislodges her from her.

Velma's healing is a communal process and incites those present to encounter their own narratives of loss and anxiety. In fact, Velma's ailment and life history is an archaeology that manifests through these other narratives. For example, while awaiting the healing session's start, Sophie Heywood, Velma's godmother, reminisces vividly about her own son, Smitty, and his death at the hands of anti-activist police: "A boy face down in the street, his book bag flattened. The police rushing the statue like a tank. . . . The blow that caught him in the shins. . . . Sophie face down in the jailhouse bed springs. Portland Edgers, her neighbor, handed a billy club. The sheriff threatening. . . . The boy gagging on his own blood face down in the street, the cameras on him. Smitty with a bull horn. A Black TV announcer misnumbering the crowd, mismatching the facts, lost to the community. Smitty. The blow that caught him in the groin. . . . The blow that caught her in the kidney" (14–15).

It is no accident that Velma's moment of reconciliation and transformation is so public or invites such communal reflection, for she is literally a metaphor for Claybourne. Despite her difficult adolescence marked with rebelliousness and impropriety, behavior that threatened to violate communal expectations for her (particularly whom to marry), Velma remains the icon of the community. She is literally its tensions, its definitive clashes between old and young, male and female, professional and folk. The community is frayed and fragile, its constituents unreconciled and dissonantly motivated after the thrill of the triumphs of the Civil Rights Movement. They, these people, are moving in varying and conflicting directions, each with her own agenda for revolution, each with anxieties, disappointments, and unarticulated regrets. Each is carrying the burden of Black possibility and is too aware of the cusp of the moment: it is 1978, on the eve of the Spring Festival, which will be a place of realization for the artists-activists, the activists-numerologists, the activists-politicians, the working activists, the organized and unorganized, those who wish to be entertained and those who wish to be inspired. This possibility, the weight of the moment, is too much to bear, and it is under siege, if not already surrendered. The year 1978: on the eve of the last quarter of the twentieth century, the dawn of the last chance to turn the conservative and fascist U.S. political slide of the last decade . . . a moment deep and breathful.

Claybourne itself is a mythic place built by freed Black hands and backs, an act of self-determination. Its mythos is perhaps best represented in the memoried lore of the Infirmary, laid down brick by brick and committed to affordable, even free, health care, bolstered by its etched mission, "health is your right," as well as by the towering Old Tree (145). The Infirmary and its tree are gifts to future generations from those that have passed and are also reminders of ancestry and legacy. Claybourne is a community precisely and historically aware of its past, present, future, and especially its viability; an insular and intimate community, a "major energy center, one of the chakras of this country" (163).

Velma is the metaphor for this potent place and its pulsing anxiety; Velma is all that is (im)possible with Claybourne, Black people, the United States, the Diaspora. When Ruby is trying to decide what is wrong with her and her community, she says, "Maybe it's something in the air. Maybe it's Velma . . . Malcolm gone, King gone, Fanni Lou [sic] gone, Angela quiet, the movement splintered, enclaves unconnected" (193). The significance of Velma to the community cannot be overstated, and her healing session is announced with a clamorous thunderstorm that shakes the streets and propels festival goers into hiding and reflection. With such prominence Velma's life is under intense scrutiny, which is why she longs to be sealed in, like an hourglass: "to be that sealed—sound, taste, air, nothing seeping in. To be that unavailable at last, sealed in and the noise of the world, the garbage, locked out" (19).

Velma's descent into suicidal consciousness speaks as much about her struggle with communal demands as it does about the community's own diseased body. Appropriately, what we know of Velma and her condition we learn from other people and through Bambara's use of free indirect narration. In fact, Bambara fleshes out Velma's depression through an elaborate description of Obie's sitting in a whirlpool: "Trying to maintain equilibrium, trying to find a balance between the longing for clarity and the dread of finding too great a challenge in reunion. His body too far down in the hot water one minute, and slippery as he was from the massage oil, slippery as his elbows were hooked on the rim of the pool, he could go under" (285). This equivocating state, this precipice, is the pathology of the communal expectations for Black women—superwoman, matriarch, mule of the world. She, this Black woman, is the ultimate insider, the measure and beat of the community. She remembers, records, nurtures; she marks the outlying edges of the community—its limits as well as its core. She cannot possibly forget, move on, let things pass, for things are never only her own, never only for herself. Hers is a profound responsibility: "things seemed more pulled together when Velma had been there. . . . It was all of a piece with Velma around" (92). Her splintered body represents the community at its "crossroads" but also sits at the crossroads offering resolution and suture (37).

The community has overidentified with and as Velma, especially through her work as an activist, which exacts a heavy toll. Velma clearly remembers the reality and toll of organizing: "Like work and no let up and tears in the night. . . . Like going to jail and being forgotten, forgotten, or at least deprioritized cause bail was not as pressing as the printer's bill. . . . Like being called in on five-minute notice after all the interesting decisions had been made, called in out of personal loyalty and expected to break her hump pulling off what the men had decided was crucial for the community good" (25). In fact, activism becomes a personal indignity and an inconvenience; it pushes up against her female self and its needs. Sitting in a meeting with male leaders, Velma and the other women resist their imposition, especially the disparity of the work. Velma is seated on a rough wad of leaflets, her makeshift menstrual pad. "She felt uncomfortable, damp. There'd been nothing in the machines—no tampons, no napkins, no paper towels, no roll of tissue she could unravel and stuff her panties with" (26). Still, she proceeds with the other women to interrupt the male political egos at work.

She is the activist extraordinaire, pulling together the disparate groups, doing the work of seven people, trying to negotiate between the ideological camps: the political, artistic, spiritual, diasporic, intellectual, materialist, relativist, capitalist. She is a mother, a sister, a wife; a favored daughter. She is the community, a full self of other people, the site of identity for Fred and Obie and Lil James and Ruby and Palma and Minnie and countless others. She is the sister, girlfriend, cousin—the arch metaphor of communion. These people are all a part of her and yet in some ways have dislodged her from the body that is her own, because, in all that she is, she is not Velma herself. She is a communal insider who is literally an outsider to her own self, so much so that Minnie repeatedly asks if she is sure she wants to be healed. Minnie's persistent invocations to Velma (especially "Are you sure you want to be healed?" and "Hold on to yourself") reflect the depth of Velma's outsiderness, and during the healing Velma necessarily wanders off, "tracking herself" (42).

Velma's condition represents the self-sacrifice that identification with community means for some Black women. This danger is apparent in Nel's surrender to Medallion, in which her marriage to Jude is her return to community propriety and property: "Now Nel *belonged to the town and all of its ways.* She had given herself over to them" (*Sula* 120; emph. added). But it is Sula's experience with community that helps to underscore the inevitability of Velma's suicide attempt: although Sula encounters neither the extreme isolation of Juletane nor the clamor and worship of Velma, the town of Medallion is nonetheless ambivalent about her, an ambivalence characterized by the community's extending and withholding acts of communion to and from her. Sula "simply helped others define themselves," a relationality that, when mutual, yields a dynamic selfhood (95). But there is no mutuality suggested here, for the community seems to identify more against a surface of Sula than with or as her; rather than engaging and then disengaging the vibrancy of Sula, they respond to an *idea* of Sula, a myth or type in their act of uncreative imagination, as she becomes a marker and standard of things that are "too much," as in too much willfulness, too much evil, too much manliness. Although they do not try to harm her, they keep her at a comfortable distance that undercuts the relationality of their gesture of identification; they make borders out of the space between themselves and her and use her largely to affirm whom they are not, a negative but not a reflexive model. And, though Sula's self-centeredness is largely unaffected, such tension exacts a toll. Velma's situation is similar: even though she is loved and admired, she is hardly known, hardly engaged. Her heart is in the right marriage and the right job, but she, Velma, is not in her own heart. No one knows her, so they cannot possibly even disown or disagree with her. She is a type—a reliable, a predictable, but not a volatile human subject. The core of the heartbreak and failure of Medallion to Sula, and Claybourne to Velma, is that neither community really knows either woman nor commits the energy to know (and unknow) her. Velma and Sula are metaphors, not real flesh and blood, and so their subjectivities are taken for granted, misused, misconsidered. Their cast-in-type is the stasis and reliability that community demands.

Although the ultimate achievement of girlfriend selfhood is a surrender to the fullness of one's community, the community in question is not merely that of one's birth but, instead, a coalition yielded uneasily from the rigor of girlfriend tension. The communities of one's birth can sometimes offer security and familiarity, but only an earned community—one built from the pairing of self with an/other self—can offer the grace of oneself. And, though this chosen community may look like the community of one's birth, it is also not that community precisely or vaguely. Community here is an achievement of subjectivity, earned and earning, not a birthright but a becoming, like work, like a practice, like love.

Sex, Colonialism, Motherhood

The examples from *Juletane* and *The Salt Eaters* reflect the unease community is for girlfriend subjectivity. In the rest of this chapter I want to explore three intersections between self and other that readily highlight the heteropathic anxiety of community, especially as such anxieties narrate gender and nationality.

Perhaps it is not common to think of sexual intimacy between two people as an act of communal subjecthood. Mostly, sex is imagined and practiced as a private unfolding, a moment of one subject's identities laid next to and mingled with an/other's. But (heterosexual) sex is clearly also a site of communal expression not only in its collusion with gender imperatives but also in its assumption of procreation—that an adult man and woman's sexual potential is crucial to the national agenda, iconized as a tenet of (group) preservation. Marriage, nationalism, family, modernity: all sex is juried against a utilitarian heterosexual normativity that serves to limit men and especially women. But what the body knows is that sex is a wild volatility, a vociferousness that is uncontrollable and excessive and, as such, even dangerous. Cataclysmic. It is a union of two (but sometimes more or less) that mediates an/other and explores the limits and boundaries of self; it is a complication, a risk that is part revelation but also part an apprehension that threatens willful selfishness. A coupling of "two halves of ancient fruit succulent and sweet and no cleaving on the horizon" (*Salt Eaters* 88), sex is a moment of the subject in flux with itself, its other, and the politics of sexual identity . . . an act of subjecthood that potentially yields the greatest intimacy as well as the greatest vulnerability. There might be no other human interaction that is as articulate of self.[9]

This characterization of sex parallels how Obie remembers his coupling with Velma. Obie is one of the few who has tried to see beyond Velma's surface, to engage with all of her complicated self-protestations. Sex between them was a multifaceted meditation on identity:

> How long would it take to know the woman, his woman? Two years
> living with her before he learned to identify the particular spasm as
> her coming? He would enter her throbbing, and she would close
> around him. And somewhere, as their hips swung, the bottoms of her
> feet stroking the fat of his calves, her thunderous buns rocking in the
> seat of his palms, a muscle would clutch at him, and he'd feel the
> tremor begin at the tip of his joint. Two years it took to *distinguish her
> tremor from his pleasure*, her orgasm from the vibration of his hands, in
> his calves, the quivering of his tightened balls. Two years before her
> calling out his name in that way would not catch him by surprise.
> How much longer would it take to learn all of Velma? (94–95; emph.
> added)

Obie yearns to know himself and Velma, to know the distinguishing pieces of their selfhood in this intimate practice. Velma is aware of his yearning, and she resists the domination it implies and which for her too closely parallels the community's totalitarianism: to have her overcommit herself to something/ someone other than her own self-centeredness. During sex, "Obie [is] whispering hoarsely in her ear about the moist coils of her tunnel drawing him in deeper. *And she wanting to deny him herself, to hold back, to deny herself, to withdraw* into the sheets tangled under her knees" (102; emph. added). In Obie's whispers Velma hears an attempt to tell her whom she is, to name her. Her withholding is astute to the politicized limits of a heterosexual sexual endeavor in which femininity is dominated and masculinity dominates.[10] And, still, because this is a coupling between two lovers, two an/others, her abstention is also an abstaining from herself—to *deny herself*. Furthermore, Obie's is one of the few thoughtful attempts to get to know Velma, however fraught with masculinist overtones. So, therein is the impossible: Velma's need to resist being swallowed by Obie's subjecthood runs headlong into her own need to surrender to the wildness of her an/other's sexual boundlessness and especially to what is, in some ways, a rare and sincere interest in her most profound intimacies.

For many of the women in these narratives, sexual interactions with men generate an out-of-body moment, a narrative apprehension in which the activity metaphorizes as a panorama that sets the two bodies in relief and highlights power, difference, and agency. Both a blessing and a frustration, sex also represents the possibilities of girlfriend subjecthood, even as extended to these men who sometimes are (not) committed to a Black feminist ethos. To the keen girlfriend subject the act of sexual coupling is an informative moment, a meditation that can proffer insight about herself and her relationship to larger narratives that dictate selfhood. Clare, the central character in Michelle Cliff's novel *No Telephone to Heaven*, has a moment that evokes such self-consideration. The narrative reads: "Clare could entrust her body to this boy she barely knew and watch herself as he fondled her and feel pleasure in her parts but still be apart from him. Feeling free, the word she put to it then. So apart, so free, she could walk away and be glad they were done with each other" (88). Although Clare hardly knows this man, the coupling still asserts and augments her sense of self-centeredness. Her surrender to the pleasure of his fingers is neither a surrender to him nor to the politics of heterosexuality. She is not dominated, but neither is she callous and unengaged; hers is a freedom similar to Sula's experience of "utmost irony and outrage in lying under someone, in a position of surrender, feeling her own abiding strength and limitless power." Like Clare, Sula uses sex as a self-space, mostly because her unions with men are unfulfilling. Sula amplifies her sexual experiences with her own (self-)exploration, meeting herself after, and sometimes during, sex: "She wait[ed] impatiently for him to turn away and settle into a wet skin of satisfaction and light disgust, leaving her to the post coital privateness *in which she met herself, and joined herself in matchless harmony*" (123; emph. added). This other self that Sula meets is "matchless," taking the place of Nel, who previously had been Sula's matchful other; Sula's girlfriend self is revitalized by postcoital meditation.

Sula's later coupling with Ajax seemingly violates this sense of a matchless harmony with self, as her deliberation on his skin and his elemental constituency merges with (and for a while consumes) her consideration of her own subjectivity. She momentarily loses her way, dis-identifies with herself, encounters one of the vagaries of what it means to surrender to an/other: "*I will water your soil, keep it rich and moist. But how much? How much water to keep the loam moist? And how much loam will I need to keep my water still? And when do the two make mud?*" (131). This is a breathtaking exploration of the tension of coupling and, in general, of community: What is too much? What borders of self, what acts of self-preservation, are necessary? When to withhold and at what cost, and when does the urge toward union collapse too many borders, demand too much of the self? When do these moments of "too-much" become Black woman self-lessness, the being for everyone else but oneself? And what are the politics of gender, patriarchy, and sex that often render women positionally and subjectively prone, and how do these politics relate to Black women sexing Black men?

Sula's relationship with Ajax is an interesting study in sexual intimacy that is at once pleasurable and lovely but which fails to offer her surrender without demanding domination. Ajax is not Sula's girlfriend; he is not committed to an open, oscillating union of otherhood with Sula; neither is Sula fully committed to Ajax as a girlfriend, for her true longing is Nel, her other self—she still hungers for the volatility of bodies-in-flux that her identity and identification with Nel represented. Under the intensity of this desire to be an/other, she falls into Ajax and "began to discover what possession was. Not love, perhaps, but possession or at least a desire for it." This possession is not the same feel or process as the giggling and irreverent and committed freedom that she had with Nel. Sula settles on Ajax, or, perhaps more accurately, Ajax settles (on) Sula: "First there was the morning of the night before when she actually wondered if Ajax would come by that day. Then there was an afternoon when she stood before the *mirror* finger-tracing the laugh lines around her mouth and trying to decide whether she was good-looking or not" (131; emph. added). Then the green ribbon—her tying her hair up in a ribbon not for herself but to make him think her attractive. Her progression from practicing reckless selfishness to being Ajax's other is quick and shocking, especially because Ajax is hardly engaged in the process of being Sula's other. Her sense of beauty—a sense that before was unequivocal, like Shadrack's blackness, a sense that is referred to in the novel's epigraph,[11] a sense that is her birthmark in its changing permanence—is surrendered to the unreliability of a mirror and a man whom she hardly knows. She dresses herself to keep and hold onto him, even as she forgets and lets go of herself: lying in bed, listening to him talk about the rigors of his day, "Sula . . . was flooded with an awareness of the impact of the outside world on Ajax. . . . 'Lean on me' she whispers" (133).

This whispered love is a shift from her own awareness that she, Sula, is a Black woman and subject to at least as much danger as anyone else in the world. Instead, she hears only his woes and sees only the peril of his life, notably different from her earlier ridicule of Jude and his Black male whininess. Sula performs, dutifully, the demand that Nel's marriage had clarified—the making of one (male) subject, in this case, one Ajax, instead of nurturing the fertile mud as a joining of soil and water and loam, an amalgam that is not stable and that at any moment might separate into its own self-seeking parts. As affirming as he is to her mind, Ajax is not a girlfriend of hers, nor does he have interest in coupling with Sula in that way. He sees her clinging to him like this, and he leaves.

Ajax's absence is stunning, "an absence so decorative, so ornate, it was difficult for her to understand how she had ever endured, without *falling dead or being consumed,* his magnificent presence" (134; emph. added). Soon after his leaving, Sula realizes she never even knew his real name and that "when, for the first time in her life she had lain in bed with a man and said his name involuntarily or said it and truly meaning *him,* the name she was screaming and saying was not his at all" (136). The screamed name might well be her own, as well as Nel's, or, more precisely, the name that her connection with Nel allows her to call and claim in ecstasy.

Although the model of coupling dislocates the neat separation between sexual and nonsexual in respect to women, since coupling is based on open, generous, and radical relations between one woman and an/other, it is nonetheless important to note the expression of physical sexual relationships *between* women for two reasons: first, to do so is in keeping with the intent of writers who, lesbian or not, are interested in exploring the specificities of Black female selfhood through homo-sex; second rather than discount the importance of ambiguity, such discussion counters cultural practices that silence and erase queer sexuality whenever possible. Although girlfriend selfhood is not exclusively a model of lesbian identity, such identities and experiences provide insight into the negotiation of the anxiety of sexual surrender.

A return to an earlier discussion of Celie and Albert is useful here. Celie writes: "I lay there thinking bout Nettie while he on top of me, wonder if she safe. And then I think bout Shug Avery. I know what he doing to me he done to Shug Avery and maybe she like it. I put my arm around him" (13). Celie's thoughts move from Nettie's safety to Shug's sexuality to her own participation in a sexual union. The moment announced by Celie's arm around Albert's shoulders is not Celie's desire for Albert but, instead, is her precise desire for Shug, whose sexuality is, for much of the novel, the only kindling that incites Celie's erotic sensibilities. Celie's thoughts and action hint toward the possibility of a sexual union with Shug, which, when it does occur, is a profound spiritual moment: "I wash her body, it feel like I'm praying. My hands tremble and my breath short" (45). Sex with Shug offers Celie an/other to surrender to, something to have faith in that is her but also not her, a body that she can touch as if it were her own because it is and is not her own. Celie becomes an agent in her own life, and their sex is an act of self-exploration for Celie and of communion and sisterhood for both women:

> Listen, she say, right down there in your pussy is a little button that
> gits real hot when you do you know what with somebody. It git hotter
> and hotter and then it melt. That the good part. But other parts good
> too, she say. Lot of sucking go on, here and there, she say. Lot of finger
> and tongue work. Button? Finger and *tongue?* My face hot enough to
> melt itself. She say, Here, take this mirror and go look at yourself
> down there, I bet you never seen it, have you? (69).

This scene evokes a political subtext in regard to women's health coalitions—how one woman often helps another discover and take care of her body. Their union helps Celie to touch more and more of herself, to use a mirror as an apparatus that does not supersede her subjectivity but, instead, becomes part of her self-understanding—a thing manipulated by and for the good of a Black woman's self-awareness. For Shug sex with Celie is a place to tell her own story, to give life to the pain and loss that have made Shug as "manly" as she seems. Shug responds to Celie's loving prompt by crying in her arms, realizing that she, Shug, had participated in the abuse of Celie. Although Celie is in need of nurture and self-revelation, Shug here is also learning about herself and reclaiming her place as a lover of women, sexually and nonsexually, which means being a lover of her self. Their sexual union is a surrender in which each woman becomes more her own subject, which sometimes means becoming the (an/)other's subject, but is not a totalitarianism, not to have and to hold as possession or property, and certainly not about propriety. The surrender that this love act reveals is a surrender that permits selfishness, a surrender that provokes self-revelation as much as it occasions giving into another.[12]

In Ama Ata Aidoo's *Our Sister Killjoy: Or Reflections of a Black-Eyed Squint* one of the central narrative couplings fails under the weight of colonialism and heterosexuality. *Killjoy* is the coming-of-age story of a young Ghanaian woman, Sissie, who is invited by a colonial organization to travel to Europe (Germany then England). Aidoo metaphorically represents Sissie's journey through selfhood as parallel to her country's resistance to European colonization, foregrounding the political and national relevance of this Black woman's coming to subject. Of particular interest here is the time Sissie spends in Germany and her attempt at coalition with Marija, a native white German woman. Early in meeting Sissie, Marija initiates the friendship by proclaiming, "I like to be your friend, yes," also asking if she can call this new friend by the name Sissie, an African communal nickname for "sister" (28). Marija's declaration of affinity for and with Sissie is quick and decisive but not entirely thoughtful—an attraction of promise and excitement, a lusting, but not a considered act of solidarity. Toward achieving a union, Marija performs acts of love, including visiting Sissie at the youth hostel, inviting her home, preparing meals, and carefully picking fruits for Sissie to take after each of her visits.

It is no doubt that theirs is a coupling: for example, although there is a language barrier, the two women communicate well, leaving others at the grocery store to wonder who does the translation (44). Yet Marija's attraction to Sissie is problematic in two ways. One, it is a manifestation of Sissie's being "something of a crowd-getter. . . . [That] the mere fact of the presence of the African girl was phenomenal." In public spaces, even with Marija, Sissie was "the African Miss. . . . look at her costume. How charming. And they gaped at her, pointed at her smile. Her nose. Her lips. Their own eyes shining." Although Marija's friendship with Sissie is an attempt to circumvent her own marginal status in her community, Sissie is spared no objectification in this community to which Marija belongs. Marija's subject position as a white German woman renders her affection as counterpart to her people's objectifying gazes, at least until she acts against these violences. In fact, the townspeople implicate her, claim her desire as their own when they wonder "who was this Marija Sommer who was *monopolizing the curiosity that provided such fun just by being*" (43; emph. added). While their account of Marija's connection with Sissie is not sufficient to dismiss the relationship as only colonizing, their accusation does point attention to Marija's failure to recognize some of the political implications of her gesture of coalition—not a mere yearning for friendship but, instead, a complicated choice that necessitates an interrogation of (her) self, (her) community, and (her) country. Her white and female social identity informs both her status as other as well as her ability to be this Black woman's an/other, and, in absence of such consideration, her overture is partly misguided and partly flawed. But Marija is unaware of the colonial

trajectories that populate her desire; hence, her friendship with Sissie appears
to be merely a convenience of their mutual status as outsiders in a patriarchal
white German culture.

Sissie also explores this union in a flawed way—she is not fully open, honest, or trusting. Sissie arrives in Germany and senses her otherness but is not
quite sure how to respond to the subjection. In the recent past she has raged,
gone silent, even withdrawn from oppressive situations, all with limited success. And especially now, on this venture through Europe, Sissie experiences
being "an exile," which is for her a new subject position. Sissie's exile is not
banishment from her country as much as it is an experience of being condi-
tionally forced to leave one's country: the reality that a European education
might offer her more opportunities to be useful to Ghana's development.[13]

In her exiled state, which is also a place of deep ideological and ethical
conflict, Sissie halfheartedly attaches to Marija's offer of friendship. But Marija
is not an/other to her, and the possibility of a selffull coupling with Marija, of
achieving girlish reverie, does not exist in Sissie's mind. In fact, Sissie is well
aware of some of the political dimensions of her coalition, and her union with
Marija is cautious and expedient; she does not want to become an African
who falls in love with Europe (read: Marija), a self-colonization that she has
observed and critiqued among some of the men who have left her country.
Still, Marija's companionship is the only nonviolent gesture, on a surface level
at least, that a German native has made to Sissie. Even further, Sissie is genuinely intrigued to see what will come of this connection with Marija, her interest piqued by the new and odd and potentially dangerous liaison—her own
version of desirous fascination.

Sissie's and Marija's disparate fascinations suggest that neither woman is
yet committed to being each other's girlfriend, that neither is ready for the
weight coupling might carry or demand. Furthermore, though both women
are others, the imbalance between their status as othered, Sissie's own conflicted relationship to Europe (and hence Marija), and Marija's uncritical engagement of her nationality (as a site of othering) all interrupt their ability
to couple.

The evidence of the disunion is revealed in Sissie's thinking about, and
Marija's trying to enact, their union: "Once or so, at the beginning of their
friendship, Sissie had thought, while they walked in the park, of what a deli-
cious love affair she and Marija would have had if one of them had been a
man. . . . Especially if she, Sissie, had been a man" (61). Not only is the
homosocial subtext of the friendship highlighted here, but it is done so in relation to narratives of colonial and national power that intersect with race
and gender. Sissie recognizes that she is, in some way, already othered in rela-

tion to Marija, a white German woman; the only way to counter this ineq-
uity is to have their union be heterosexual, thereby making it familiar and
normative, as well as for she, Sissie, to be the man. Considering Marija's earlier coveting of "the African Miss," both women still recognize and work *within*
masculine and statist constructs of power; hence, trust and surrender cannot
exist in their relationship. Sissie is trying to resist becoming Marija's othered
as well as to avoid being subsumed under Marija's desire to own a piece of the
empire. Not only does Sissie not trust Marija with her (Sissie's) self, but she
also distrusts the colonial narrative as it is written on both Marija's body and
her own: that is, she is attentive to and apprehensive about Marija's subjugation
as well as her own.[14]

The gender fantasy is located in a discourse of colonial desire for and of
the other. In some ways Sissie's wish to be the man points attention to the
absence of social histories and theories that explore relationships between European and African women, especially ones in which African women are not
objectified, disempowered, or marginalized. Sissie therefore evokes a more common narrative, that of the African man and the European woman, and inserts herself in the position that, at least on the individual level, is potentially
more powerful. Even as Sissie later criticizes these relationships for their political insipidity, they are at least familiar and their dangers are more readily
known. She is on unfamiliar territory with Marija, and, because there is no
trust, she is attempting to normalize the union as well as secure her safety by
envisioning herself as the man.

The masculine fiction further materializes when Marija kisses her and,
"as one does from a bad dream, impulsively, Sissie shook herself free. With
too much effort, unnecessarily, so that she unintentionally hit Marija on the
right cheek with the back of her right hand" (64). Sissie and Marija are performing man and woman, and Marija's kiss results in a violent response. Interestingly, the way that Sissie remembers the incident reflects the conflicted
quality of her struggle to make a union with Marija:

> It all happened within a second. Two people staring at one another.
> Two mouths wide open with disbelief.
>   Sissie thought of home. To a time when she was a child in the
> village. Of how she always liked to be sleeping in the bedchamber
> when it rained, her body completely-wrapped-up in one of her
> mother's akatado-cloths while mother herself pounded fufu in the
> anteroom which also served as a kitchen when it rained. Oo, to be
> wrapped up in mother's cloth while it rained. Every time it rained.
>   And now where was she? How did she get there? What strings,
> pulled by whom, drew her into those pinelands where not so long ago

human beings stoked their own funeral pyres with other human
beings, where now a young Aryan housewife kisses a young black
woman with such desperation, right in the middle of her own nuptial
chamber, with its lower middle-class cosiness? A love-nest in an attic
that seems to be only a nest now, with love gone into mortgage and
holiday hopes? (64)

There is a difference in the way the event is remembered by Sissie—populated with the language of home and familiarity and poetically ambiguous—
and the earlier prosaic starkness of the narrator's telling. Metaphorically, this
difference is what is unreconciled between Marija and Sissie. In her relationship with Marija Sissie's yearning for a love that feels magical and dreamlike
does not merge with a similar yearning for a love that is political and revolutionary. Sissie can sense the two tensions in the friendship, like two parts of
herself that remain unwhole and unpaired.

    This unpaired quality is significant, especially because it is not inevitable.
Later, when Marija asks Sissie her birth date, we learn that

they had been twins.
Their mother was three months pregnant
Before the great earthquake, and
They were 10 months in the womb.
(68–69)

The referent *they* remains unattributed but could refer to a kinship between
Sissie and Marija, whose birth dates might have been the same. Or to the fact
that Marija might have been a twin, or Sissie. Or all three possibilities. The
introduction of the generic "they had been twins" certainly indicates a desire to
return to twin-ness, whoever "they" are. Yet Marija is not Sissie's other, not Sissie's
Sissie, a point that Sissie makes clear in one of their final conversations:

"Our people have a proverb which says that he is a liar who tells you
that *his witness is in Europe.*"
    "Vitness? Vas is Vitness?"
    "Like in court, *someone to speak for your side.*" (74; emph. added)

    That Marija does not know the term *witness* suggests that she is too
uncritically European to be Sissie's witness, that her friendship is not witness
to freedom. She cannot speak for Sissie's side, for she has yet to claim her
own side in the politics of colonization. As Sissie leaves Germany and Marija,
she has yet to embrace fully what her failed coupling with Marija means in
relation to her process of selfhood. When she makes plans to leave and does
not inform Marija, the latter is understandably upset. Sissie feels like a "bas-

tard. Not a bitch. A bastard" (75). Yet, true to the maleness of her role, "she was enjoying herself to see that woman [Marija] hurt. It was nothing she had desired. Nor did it seem as if she could control it, this inhuman sweet sensation to see another human being squirming. It hit her like a stone, the knowledge that there is pleasure in hurting. A strong three-dimensional pleasure, an exclusive masculine delight that is exhilarating beyond all measure. And this too is God's gift to man? She wondered" (76). Sissie's awareness of colonization propels her to perform "man" to Marija's "woman," a performance that brings her fleeting delight. Sissie is well aware that her dissolution of the union is flawed and that, were she more at ease with herself, she might have engaged Marija differently. Theirs was a friendship too entangled by unarticulated colonial imperatives, a friendship that largely evidenced anxieties and which was driven by the fear to retain small bits of power in a world where both women were already fundamentally without real access to power broking. What Sissie longs for is the merger of the political and spiritual, for an ethos that will restore her community and soothe her soul. In her journey through selfhood Sissie seeks something other than a small stake in worldly madness, something other than a communal and national role that is more shackle than freedom: she seeks to be enough herself to be an embraceable other, to be able to surrender whatever the failings of her an/other.

A THIRD NARRATIVE MANIFESTATION of the tension between reckless surrender and willful selfness occurs in the relationships between mothers and daughters and the consideration of motherhood; that is, the relationships between two women as well as the relationship one woman has to the idea and experience of being/becoming a mother. As an experience, motherhood is one of the social constructs that regulates womanhood and is both a subjection and a subjectivity—a cultural commodity determined and regulated largely by men, even as its condition materializes in and on women's bodies.[15] Hence, motherhood is a site of tension between individual women, on one hand, and cultural and national communities, on the other.[16] The choice (or not) to be a mother, as well as the condition of being (or not) a mother, is individual and personal, but it is also social, legal, moral, philosophical, and epistemological. Part of the potency of *mother* lies in the permutations of this dichotomy between individual and communal: while every person has an experience with a mother, not every person can be a mother (in the nominative case, though the term is also a verb, as in *to mother*). Further, the term's social currency is sometimes conflated with the word *woman*, a conflation that often serves as a form of policing.

As social currency, motherhood can be rejected, discounted, legalized, revised, idealized, and celebrated with whimsy and abandon. For Black women, in particular, motherhood is further imbued with social and institutional narratives because of the impact of race, class, and colonialism on the delineation of what a mother is.[17] Appropriately, motherhood is an amazingly political and ambivalent site for many Black women: in the United States, for example, choosing to give birth in a legal system designed to restrict and control Black women's reproduction is an act of political significance and resistance; conversely, choosing not to have a child in a context where Black women's bodies are imagined as reproductively prolific is also political, resistant. This vexed quality of motherhood acknowledges both the material appraisal colonialism imposes on Black women's children and the (de)valued commodity that Black bodies become.[18] It is this latter consideration that especially makes Black mothering an impossibility, a hard-to-bear responsibility that begins with inevitable despair and failure: if being a good mother is to secure the best for one's child, the Black mother cannot be a good mother and can hardly be a mother at all. This sentiment is evoked by the lament of an anonymous African-American mother in 1904: "I dread to see my children grow, I know not their fate. Where the White boy has every opportunity and protection, mine will have few opportunities and no protection. It does not matter how good or wise my children may be, they are colored" (Lerner 158).[19] One could also add, to that final sentence, "nor does it matter much how good a mother she may be." This impossibility is further evident in the cultural archetype of Black women as great nurturers to children not their own.

The impossibility of mother is an oppressing and oppressive social location that exists throughout the Diaspora, as noted in Mariama Bâ's widely translated comment on the African mother as icon: "The nostalgic songs to the African mother that, in moments of anguish, conflate her with Mother Africa are no longer adequate" (Nnaemeka 1). Bâ's comment warns against empty valorizations of *mother* that solidify the term but which rarely give specific or general attention to the conditions of the woman as a mother or person, to say nothing of facilitating her access to social power.[20] As a site of such tension and cultural (mis)consideration, Black motherhood is difficult to talk about clearly. For one, the cultural restrictions against interrogation and criticism are strong.[21] Nonetheless, because motherhood is conflated with and essentialized through female gender identity, it is a key site of consideration in exploring Black women's identity and selfhood.

One central example of motherhood as a site of female subjectivity is codified in classical psychoanalysis. Being a mother is what young girls become, and in fact the separation of mother and daughter is a key pivot of Freud's early work. The mother is hardly a subject, a human-faced being, but, instead, she is constructed relationally, not in regards to other women or others of her choosing but in regard to a socially determined other (for example, the child's self, the society's identity); in this context the idea "mother" is a location of otherness, an abject identity both marginal and powerful. Still, conceptually, mother is also another vibrant location of relationality between a woman and an/other—the particular relationship between mother and daughter. Alice Walker offers a useful representation of motherhood as a space of tension between a self and an/other self, two subjects who are sometimes distinct and sometimes not, even after the birth of the child: "when you give birth to a child, . . . you are really making a commitment to the agony of having your heart walking around outside of your body" (*Anything* 213). At least for a period of time (that before birth) mother and child's lives are one, inextricably linked and mutual, and every aspect of the pregnant woman's being—her thoughts, her desires, her fears, her joys, her flesh—is inflected by the presence of the child; the reverse is even more true.[22] And after birth, even in cases in which mother and child are separated, there is at the very least the residual impact of having been one body—or having lived in one body—and, in most cases, there is the agony and heart tug that Walker notes. This alliance, then, between mother and child articulates tensions between self and an/other self that parallel those in the model of girlfriend subjectivity.

Although the tendency is to think of the relationship between mother and child as one of adulthood and youth, I want to consider the specific relationship between mother and daughter as adults, as a relationship between one woman and an/other woman. In this context of adult relationality, motherhood (for the mother) can be thought of as a consideration of the creative power of one's self, the ability to have made an/other self, and the engagement of the failure and successes of this making; for the daughter (her experience of) motherhood is a consideration of relationality, of having been made in part by an/other, and also gestures toward her own creative power to make an/other (her own future child but also the way in which she has shaped her mother). While the relationship between mother and daughter in much psychoanalysis is one of separation, I side with Giselle Liza Anatol, who argues that "it is the connection between mother and daughter and not the separation that ought to be the source of critical inquiry."[23] In fact, while the historical relationships between Black mothers and their daughters have exhibited tension and separation, there is also a strong cultural value and history of alliance between mothers and daughters that has been ignored by dominant psychoanalytic discourse. As Patricia Hill Collins notes, there is a tradition of power and collaboration between Black mothers and daughters, including the passing on of a legacy of survival and the shaping of an identity.[24] Or, as

Dionne Brand says it, "No Caribbean woman writer can resist the knowledge that the mother is her own future" (44).[25]

Brand's overstatement is intended not only for dramatic flair but also to indicate the intimacy between mother and daughter in Black feminist narrative contexts. This sense of seeing one's mother as one's future spurs what Adrienne Rich has termed "matrophobia," a fear or rejection of the mother (and of her oppressed condition).[26] Yet, more than being her future, girlfriend identification as it exists between mother and daughter reveals the power in developing volatile matrilineal intimacies. Mother and daughter negotiate the tensions of being each other, becoming each other, loving each other; as girlfriends, both mother and daughter can identify and embrace a creativity that is not only having and raising a child (which for the daughter is a possibility) but also the wild creativity in their being girlfriends—two adult women who go outside the boundaries marked for their gender and who embrace their own and each other's otherness. Their practice is a process of subjectivity, involves the possibility of heartbreak, and is of political, social, and individual significance; it is an expression of a new politic of woman identification situated outside of the social and institutional appendage of mother. To be clear, the mother-daughter relationship is not the central Black female relational selfhood but is nonetheless crucial to such a discussion. What I am intending here is to explore how mothers and daughters become girlfriends, how they explore and inhabit a connection that breaks and frays and heals. What is most interesting to me about representations of mothers and daughters as girlfriends is how they highlight the import of choice: outside of and even against the familial and social confines of their relationship, mothers and daughters have to choose each other as girlfriends. This identification with and as and against each other extends beyond the boundaries of family and is an adult choosing, a process of becoming each other's selfish selfhood, a thing that goes against a deep grain.

In Michelle Cliff's *No Telephone to Heaven* the coalition between mother and daughter is situated within a locality of racial categories such as mulatto, sambo, and cooley that are intended to delineate and determine social position and to dictate alliance. But for Clare Savage neither the density of these categories nor the legacy of Jamaica's colonial history overwhelm the specificity and heft of her chosen relationship to her mother. In fact, Clare's matrilineal identity supersedes the colonial legacy of racial and class stratification, and she chooses to be "on the side of with,"[27] which is the side of the marginal, of the other—the side that one's an/other is on. This tension between (m)other and self is necessarily articulated against a backdrop of various struggles for national identity, because the idea of being a mother is as much national and communal as it is personal; hence, the anxiety of community evident in girlfriend selfhood manifests also as an expression of nationalism, an expression of an individual's relationship to a national identity.

The novel opens with a passage I have already cited—a backdrop of "men and women . . . dressed in similar clothes, which became them as uniforms, signifying some agreement, some purpose—that they were in something together." This alikeness is not frivolous; instead, it is a manifestation of and has helped to produce their solidarity: "This alikeness was something they needed, which could be important, even vital, to them—for the shades of their skin, places traveled to and from, events experienced . . . varied widely, came between them" (4). Or could come between them. They choose to ally, to recognize and re-cognize each other as "people you knew should call you brother, sister" (5), even amid the distinctions of class and color that permeate the individual and sociocultural consciousness of many Jamaicans, particularly the distinctions between dark-skinned and fair-skinned that reflect economic status, family history, and social and political position. The issue of choice, of bonding outside of the bounds of one's social archaeology, is key to Cliff's narrative landscape, which is abundantly populated with signs intended to designate racial position and thereby limit social alliance. But, rather than only limiting identity and coalition, these signs permit self-composition, allowing an individual to re-sign her- or himself. Boy Savage, Clare's father, who is fair-skinned enough to pass, denies being Black when his family arrives in the United States, partly because he acknowledges the incredibly violent racial topography he is now in: "He was streamlining himself for America. A new man" (57). When a white and racist store owner in Georgia questions his racial heritage because of his accent, Boy quickly retorts that his people owned slaves, aligning himself, in some ways, with a legacy of racial hatred. This uneasy alliance is part of Boy's approach to survival in the United States, avoiding, as he calls it, "unnecessary struggle." When his wife, Kitty, returns to Jamaica and later dies, he remarries an Italian-American woman, one of the "newly" white Americans, further cementing his commitment to re-signing himself as not-Black. While Boy's realignments make necessary mockery of U.S. racial typography, his rejection of Blackness also parallels his allegiances with fairer-skinned people of higher social and economic classes in Jamaica and reflects a definitive political expression.

Kitty, who is "fixed on these signs" and has aligned herself particularly with dark-skinned women since her days in Jamaica, makes different choices of racial coalition (59). In one of her first jobs when they arrive in New York, Kitty works at a laundry room, writing and stuffing friendly service notes into dry cleaning packages. The identity she is forced to assume as the voice of these notes is Mrs. White, a white matronly woman whose comments profess ease and comfort, offering bits of advice that maintain a sense of order and normativity. The conservative (and even repressive) politics of these notes offend Kitty's sensibilities as she copies them one by one and inserts them in with cleaned laundry. After a few weeks Kitty begins to rescript the messages to offer her own advice, and, eventually, she re-signs herself as Mrs. Black, a figure that she claims has killed Mrs. White. This is a decisive political act that not only threatens the establishment that Mrs. White represented but also attempts to ally Kitty with the two Black American women who work in the laundry. Yet the two women are fired because of Kitty's obstinate notes, and her attempt to re-sign herself as Black American is thwarted because her color and nationality are coded favorably in relation to her coworkers, who the boss presumes is responsible for the contrition despite Kitty's protests. Even the coworkers are *resigned* to their "black" fate, which further depresses Kitty's sense of the fluidity and solidarity that identity play can make possible.

Clare Savage, then, experiences two divergent perspectives on racial identity, both of which populate her own effort to reconcile her outsider subjectivity and her yearning for a sense of belonging. Much of the novel chronicles Clare's attempt to re-sign herself, to pair up with her an/other self. Although she initially chooses her father as her primary coalition, Clare soon begins to understand that she is not like him. In a pivotal moment in the novel Clare identifies with and as the four young Black girls killed in the Birmingham church bombing, an alliance with Blackness that is juxtaposed against her father's commitment to avoiding unnecessary struggle:

Boy takes up golf. Trades in the '52 Plymouth for a '61 Chevy. . . .
Through all this—this new life—he counsels his daughter on
invisibility and secrets. Self-effacement. Blending in. The uses of
camouflage.
    September 16, 1963. The girl Clare sits on a high stool in front of
her homeroom, chosen . . . to read the morning paper to the class. . . .
    In thick dark letters, stark: SUNDAY SCHOOL BOMBED . . . A picture
accompanies the letters. . . . Clare reads the text, the names, the ages
attached to the names. She monotonizes her voice for she is afraid of
being moved—and this news has brought her dangerously close. (100)

Clare's reading about these young Black girls is at first an act of recognition, an identification of who they were. But she is already aware of the more intimate identification that is inevitable with these, her sisters, and she tries, somewhat desperately, to dull her voice, to pay no attention to what she is reading. Some forgetting seeps in, but their frail bodies are laid against her own: "She has already forgotten the names, but the ages persist. She is older than all of them" (101). Even as Clare tries to be inattentive to four dead bodies, she is deeply disturbed by her classmates' own inattention (their moving of papers and passing of notes as well as the teacher's recording of attendance). In disgust of the absentia that surrounds Denise, Caroline, Addie Mae, and Cynthia, as well as that around her own self, Clare folds the paper in half and apologizes to the teacher for being unable to continue. But her process of identification with the dead girls does not end there: "The next morning on her way to school, she put a nickel in the blind man's plastic dish at the mouth of the subway and picked up a copy of the *News. On the front page was the picture she needed to see. A girl in a coffin*" (101; emph. added). Clare needs to see this picture not only to "put a face" with an incident but also to put the face with her own. She cut the picture out, put it in her wallet, and looked at it constantly.

During the weekend when she and Boy watch nonstop coverage of President Kennedy's murder, Boy inquires about the picture that has so captivated her attention. Although young, Clare nonetheless recognizes the difference between the social relevance of the president's death and that of four young Black girls and is looking at a picture of one of the dead girls during the nation's elaborate mourning of Kennedy. When she finally shows Boy the picture, he lectures her about being an American now and not laboring "forever as an outsider"; in this lecture Boy inadvertently lays the foundation for Clare's exploration of her relationship to her mother: "You are too much like your mother for your own good," he says as he takes the picture from Clare and turns to mourn the dead American president in a way he had not mourned his now dead wife. Nonetheless, the picture has left a firm imprint on Clare: "It did not matter that the picture was gone—it was in her mind. Connecting her with her absent mother" (102).

Clare's hesitant identification of four young Black girls quickly develops first into an identification with these young bodies ("they are like me") and then an identification as them ("they are me"). The dis-identification imposed upon her by Boy's comments and his removal of the picture leads, ironically, to a stronger identification with a girlfriend subject closer to her own—her mother. This recognition initiates Clare into a literal and psychic journey, a colonial retracing of her ancestry and a sometimes futile searching for home in a somewhere that ultimately only exists in the community of girlfriends she creates, a coalition that ultimately is with and through her mother. "Her story is a long story. . . . There are many bits and pieces to her, for she is composed of fragments. In this journey, she hopes is her restoration" (87). Her mother, herself.

When Kitty moves to Jamaica, leaving Boy and Clare in New York, Clare feels somewhat abandoned and resentful. Yet Kitty has not forgotten Clare and writes to her of the imperative of self-composition: "A reminder, daughter—never forget who your people are. Your responsibilities lie beyond me, beyond yourself. There is a space between who you are and who you will become. Fill it" (103). Kitty's reminder generously implores Clare to form a community that sustains without encroaching on her centeredness. That is, Kitty does not demand that Clare become Kitty, to live as Kitty had; instead, Kitty's comments gesture toward the unimaginable wonder that Clare's selfness can create. These words from Kitty highlight Clare's agency, her ability and responsibility to choose her coalitions, her mobility to traverse the borders between self and not-self, racially and otherwise. As she remembers her mother's urging, Clare makes a significant choice of self, proclaiming, "My mother was a nigger . . . and so am I" (104). This moment of embracing the U.S. racial sign, *nigger*, represents an attempt at coalition and an as yet unfulfilled commitment to the *solidarity* of who she, Clare, is, to her constituencies. It is a moment of radical self-possession (radical because she is in fact crossing borders, since she does not *look* like a "nigger") that exists against the self-dispossession that her father practices and which furthers her mother's own failed effort to forge community with those two Black laundrywomen.

But this coalition is premature, for Clare is not quite ready to claim her mother as a girlfriend. Instead, she leaves New York and begins a restless journey that will eventually end in Jamaica. Her journey through colonial lands is her quest to find home and reveals the profundity of the phrase *motherland*—it is a twofold travel to homeland and girlfriend, both articulated through the myth and reality of her mother and which leads ultimately to Clare. It is the tension of community exemplified through the struggle for national consciousness—how to claim home when it does not exist, how to reconcile a sense of nationalism with a commitment to Black female selfishness.

While traveling, Clare seeks to couple with various others in an act of cross-nationalism: in London she lives with four young women who are also displaced—women from Cyprus, Nigeria, Australia, and Leeds. Together, they are five women on the outside of British culture, though none of these relationships develop the intensity that Clare seeks. Removed from and ambivalent about the only homes she has known (Jamaica and the United States), Clare is a wandering other, an embodiment of Black female diasporic otherness. This subjectivity manifests on the streets of London as she looks at a brooch in the market when the vendor rudely suggests that she buy it or leave. Clare turns and leaves, and, as she does, "another woman, tribal scars cutting diagonally across her cheeks, [takes] Clare's place" (112). These two women are interchangeable even with their different warrior marks; this other woman is one whom Clare has chosen to become when she proclaims herself "a nigger" and whom Clare is looking for but perhaps not seeing; this other woman is her access to a Black female–centered national consciousness. This other woman is whom Clare is awaiting, the presence to fill and complete her: "Whom had she awaited? . . . No one . . . unless it was the woman on the tube. . . . The day before she had given a light to the woman sitting next to her on the tube. The two had chatted and the woman asked her to be her guest at the ballet that evening. . . . Had she expected the woman to seek her out. Did she want this?" (115). Clare is in full search for a sister, a someone to be her an/other, a someone to be in self-centered solidarity with. She tries identifying with/as Jane Eyre: "The fiction had tricked her. Drawn her in so that she became Jane. . . . Yes. The parallels were there. Was she not heroic Jane? Betrayed. Left to wander. Solitary. Motherless. Yes." Then, realizing the differences between her and Jane, she rejects Jane and, instead, imagines herself as Bertha:

> No, she told herself. No she could not be Jane. Small and pale.
> English. No, she paused. No my girl, try Bertha. Wild-maned Bertha.
> Clare thought of her father. Forever after her to train her hair. His
> visions of orderly pageboy. Coming home from work with something
> called Tame. She refused it; he called her Medusa. Do you intend to
> turn men to stone, daughter? She held to her curls, which turned
> kinks in the damp of London. Beloved racial characteristic. Her only
> sign, except for dark spaces here and there where melanin touched
> her. Yes, Bertha was closer the mark. Captive. Ragout. Mixture.
> Confused. Jamaican. Caliban. Carib. Cannibal. Cimarron. All Bertha.
> All Clare. (116)

Later, in Paris, Clare identifies with Bobby, a wounded U.S. Vietnam veteran who experiences postwar hallucinations that leave him violently indifferent to others. But her coupling here is no longer self-centered, as she determines to "appl[y] herself to [his] wound," literally trying to become his pain and salve (144). This is a moment of extreme self-sacrifice, the kind of selflessness that is dictated by the politics of race, gender, and heterosexuality: Bobby is not capable of being Clare's girlfriend, nor is Clare herself functioning in a self-loving capacity as she self-effacingly promises never to leave him.[28]

In these attempts at coalition Clare crosses borders of time, space, nation, corporeality, and gender; still, she exists alone and as an outsider, unfulfilled and without a communal body of her own. It is only on a brief trip to Jamaica that she finds herself interfaced with an embracing (though frightening) national consciousness—her "face was the dead stump of Kitty," and people on the island remind her constantly, "You are the daughter of your mother" (118). Clare's relationship with her dead mother unfolds slowly as

she forms a relationship with another Jamaican outsider, the transvestite Harry/
Harriet, who becomes, for a while, Clare's girlfriend.

After their first meeting during Clare's visit, Harry/Harriet writes letters
to her while she is off in Europe, keeping her abreast of the situation in Jamaica; in doing so, he literally becomes her connection to Jamaica, which is
also her connection to her mother and herself. Narratively, Harry/Harriet is a
self-composition, a young dark-skinned boy who grew up poor, raped by a male
police officer, and often working as a helper inside the homes of people more
well-off. Defiantly and lovingly, Harry/Harriet chooses early on to seize his
outsider status—dark, poor, queer, effeminate—and to embrace himself as an
other. This achievement is a site of his keen understanding of the politics of
otherness and informs his ability to sustain empowering coalitions with other
marginal subjects. His reflection on his sexual violation is particularly revealing: "I have been tempted in my life to think *symbol*—that what he did to
me is but a symbol for what they did to all of us, always bearing in mind that
some of us, many of us, also do it to each other. But that's not right. I only
suffered what my mother suffered—no more, no less" (129). Harry/Harriet uses
his rape to understand the colonial condition, the exploitation of Jamaica by
European and American colonizing forces, as well as the neocolonization that
generates (from) greed and corruption among Jamaica's ruling classes. But it
is his decisive comment about his mother, his realization that she too had experienced rape, that articulates a national consciousness befitting a feminist
ideology. Harry/Harriet's combining national political history with his mother's
(and his own) personal experiences argumentatively suggests that national
identity is female, that the achievement of a liberating national consciousness is inextricably linked to the female body, not just the idea of a "motherland" invoked by men who are inattentive to the particulars of women's
experiences of nationalism but a particular and specific female-centered sense
of collectivity. National collectivity is marked female through Harry/Harriet's
reflection, his composing his self through an alliance with his mother. Further, the failures and possibilities of nationalism are enunciated on Harry/
Harriet's dark-skinned transvestite body, a body that evocatively voices the
uneasy intersections of gender, sexuality, and nation(alism).

It is this sense of female-centered national collectivity that allows Clare
to connect with Harry/Harriet. In fact, she names herself his an/other in re-
sponding to his question of whether she thinks him strange: "No, I don't find
you strange. No stranger . . . no stranger than I find myself. For we are neither one thing nor the other." Here Harry/Harriet is both who Clare is not
and who she is; he is her me and not-me and offers up the dynamic tension
that she has been seeking. But Clare is still hesitant about claiming her iden-

tities as she inarticulately stammers her alliance with Harry/Harriet; in response, Harry/Harriet reminds her about choice: "The time will come for both of us to choose. For we will have to make the choice. Cast our lot. Cyaan live split. Not in this world" (131). This urging echoes her mother's earlier comment about filling the gap and is a principle that Harry/Harriet eventually commits to practice when he gives up his hyphened existence and becomes Harriet. Although he cannot afford, and therefore does not have, sex reassignment surgery, he chooses and becomes she: "the choice is mine, . . . is made" (168). Harriet refuses to have her identity be subject to material politics and the limits imposed by a colonial economy. Harriet's decision suggests that not only are seemingly immutable identities (gender, physiology) mutable but that the steadfastness of a choice, of a decision to coalition, is liberating and revolutionary.[29]

It is Harriet who convinces Clare to come home, to find her place in the national landscape. Interestingly, her return to Jamaica comes shortly after she loses her unborn child as well as her ability to have children, which she notes as "another reprieve from womanhood," her prayers answered (157). Clare is rightfully ambivalent about motherhood, for without its possibility she is able to search for and become her mother's girlfriend, an identification that imitates the responsibilities and heartbreak of motherhood but which also modifies motherhood as a woman-defined site of subjectivity and national consciousness.[30]

Her transnational journey characterizes the relationship between mother and daughter as also a struggle for national identity. When Harriet asks her about her childhood, she offers a synopsis that centralizes her mother: "[First I] pretended I was Pip in *Great Expectations*—my favorite book. Pretended I was Sidney Carton. Peter Pan. Even Columbus, God help me." Then: "'I explored the country. First with my mother. She felt about this place . . . it was where she was alive, came alive, I think. She knew every bush . . . its danger and its cure. She should have stayed here. In America she was lost [. . .] .' As she spoke, picturing the two of them, the recent past invaded . [. . .] 'I was fortunate I knew her here'" (173). Clare re-members her racial and national identities on the axis of her relationship with her mother. This conflation of the female with the national corpus is evident also in Kitty's relationship to her own mother:

> When [Kitty] dressed her mother's body—being the only blood-daughter left on the island—when she dressed her mother's body, it was the first time she remembered seeing her mother's nakedness. *This secret thing which had been hidden from her for thirty years became hers, for she was the only member of the family entrusted to it.* The breasts full—the nipples dark—were stiff with lifelessness, and she caressed

them. From somewhere came an image of a slave woman pacing aisles
of cane, breast slung over her shoulder to suckle the baby carried on
her back. (71; emph. added)

These fleshy secrets whisper urgently to Kitty and give firmament to her embrace of the struggle for sovereignty. This moment of becoming her mother is
a beyond-death girlfriend coalition that pulls Kitty back to the land; similarly,
it is an after-death reverie that facilitates Clare's decision to become familiar
again with the place of her birth, the lives of the people, and herself. In giving prominence to Clare's identification with and as and against her mother,
Cliff implicitly asserts that the mother-daughter coalition is the lifeblood of
Jamaican nationalism.

    This girlfriend nationalism is most evident in Clare's central act of re-
claiming her mother, which is also an act of mothering her own identity—
when she interviews for a place with the guerrilla revolutionaries. During the
interview Clare is asked a series of questions by women who are, in their interests and dispositions, also her mother, also her an/other. The questions and
answers from the interview are presented in short, staccato lines, resulting in
a dialogue that is partial and thorough, a mosaic of what becomes and what
undoes a self:

> Tell us about yourself.
>   . . . I am Jamaican. My mother is dead. My father lives in New
> York. We are not in touch. . . .
>   To whom do you owe your allegiance? . . .
>   . . . if anything, I owe my allegiance to the place my grandmother
> made. . . . My grandmother believed in using the land to feed people.
> My mother as well. (189)

Clare's responses give name to her mother and her mother's mother: these
women are her subjectivities; her intimate tussles with them are what holds
and what disintegrates. This is the assessment Clare makes of her journeys:

> It says here (glancing at a folder on the table) that you did graduate
> work in England . . . the Renaissance . . . am I correct? . . .
>   . . . Tell me, why did you do it?
>   Because it did not concern me . . . I was looking for something to
> take me out of myself. (193–194)

The critique is harsh, maybe even too easy, but its impulse is careful, studied,
and poignant: what she was looking for was the texture and thrill of a girlfriend, a thing she achieved in embracing her mother. This realization of the
potential gifts of motherhood—of the agency of self and an/other fostered via
this dance with a mother inspires Clare to reconsider what she had previously

thought to be a burden, to imagine motherhood but with a commitment to female self-centeredness:

> Would you kill if your child got polio, and you knew this was a result of government policy, and you knew exactly whom to blame?
>
> I don't have any children.
>
> Imagine that you did.
>
> Yes. I'll try. (Thoughts of missed motherhood flooded her; facts, myths she had heard. Weren't women supposed to accomplish superhuman feats when their children were endangered? Would she? Had her own mother? . . . Would she have such a keen sense of justice and the strength to carry it out? Had she known the blood clots [her own] were the beginning of a child with half a brain would she be angry?) Yes. I think I would. I am trying to be honest. (191–192)

As the interview progresses, Clare's responses are more a self-conversation, the engagement of her own vagaries. This is the context in which she can imagine motherhood—as a process of self-identity and as a self-determined site of national liberation; she is even able to consider teaching as an act of mothering. Cliff's construction of the interview as narrative allows for the lines to collapse, for the rapid-fire question and response to bleed into one sustained and irresolute consciousness.

Clare's achievement of self evidences the power of alliance and reconstructs motherhood as a location of one woman's self-centered practice of national consciousness. She engages the anxiety of community by embracing the community that she already is: "the woman who has reclaimed her grandmother's land. She is white. Black. Female. Lover. Beloved. Daughter. Traveler. Friend. Scholar. Terrorist. Farmer" (91). She is all Clare, full of her selves.

Chapter 3   Liminality and Selfhood
Toward Being Enough

W HAT IS TENDER, undeniable, fluid, like winter, memory, or hunger: this practice of pairing with an/other and oscillating between states of (dis)identi-
fication yields a liminal identity, a subjectivity that is material and corporeal
but which also transcends the limits imposed by corporeality, visual culture,
and colonization—a selfhood that challenges the normative constructions of
"self." This liminal subjectivity is not exactly an achieved state; instead, it is
a series of uncoverings—like the ever outward concentric circles made by a
pebble's break of pond surface, circles that also progress ever inward. What is
uncovered is not a new identity but, instead, a self that was always *there*: the
girlfriend subject in her full humanity had always been a multipled subject of
remarkable depth, and her practice of coupling with an/others is subjectivity
as revelation. These revelations mark an/other part of the "waiting" self, the
self that was and is always there, a self that was, is, and (un)becomes.

The liminality of girlfriend selfhood is a liminality of otherness, a surrender that embraces what it is to be other, a practice of tension between two
essential principles: "I am (a) me" and "I am someone's an/other." This recognition of both an indisputable me and an indisputable us is an invocation
of spirituality, an awareness of the fluctuating dimensions of identity. It is a
movement toward a self whose limits are self-motivated and which disturbs
the imperatives that demand Black women be focused singularly on either race
or gender. Those are places of social order, useful in organizing but hardly ever
places where people live their lives: the feel of the body is more about hunger
and thirst and desire—even as those expressions are inflected by racialized or

gendered culture; these impulses, then, are what (in)forms and unforms the subject. If girlfriend selfhood has an ur-principle, it is a commitment to profound love of self: that the self is only, entirely, her capacities to practice and engage and grapple with her love for and of herself. Self-love is self-origin and self-authorship.

The liminal, the self-centered, the self-created: these are bodies of divinity and this practice is one of spiritual subjectivity. As in Walker's dance with her other self, the girlfriend pairing sometimes exists in a liminal space, in space that is not materially or dimensionally real, even as the ramifications of the coupling bear material significance. This marriage of real and imagined, of the lived and the dreamed, acknowledges that the political urgency of girlfriend selfhood necessitates a material and tangible coalition; and, still, that coalition occurs when a self extends beyond her inherited material and social boundaries, refusing to be bound. This subjectivity turns on potentiality and (the pleasures of) negation.[1] It is a discourse of self that possesses more an urge for its unstable presentness than for the all-consuming stricture of its past. It is Nietzschean in its agency.

The subjects of this chapter are meditative, engaged in an articulate spiritual ambulation. They, these Black female subjects, amble toward a graceful awareness of their fullness, of their enoughness. They can be disrupted and disturbed; they experience anxiety. Still, they are, always, women alone, subjects (un)becoming, women who are their own plentiful company. It is, as Ntozake Shange notes, to find god in oneself.[2]

The Liminal Divine

The liminality of girlfriend subjectivity exposes and complicates the binaries that constitute a socially accepted notion of reality, especially of how bodies are imagined, marked, and controlled. This struggle over the body is an important one for Black women, whose subjectivities within dominant discourses have been largely limited through body politics. This, then, is the necessary reclaiming of the viability and integrity of her physical body as well as the articulating of a Black female selfhood that encompasses nonphysical permutations. Velma Henry's descent into healing, for example, enters a dreamscape, a place where her memories of things experienced are inflected both by images from literature and folklore as well as images of what she had wished for, what she had longed for. Bambara's representation of the healing exploits the border between "this side" and an other, revealing the selves that people Velma, these bodies running, dancing, standing, and writhing in a psychic and material landscape. Further, the triplet of Velma, Minnie, and Old Wife is a gathered liminality, each woman a reflection of the other and bearing (their) likeness on many planes of existence. The three women are engaged in the dance of healing, careening into one another, through one another, generating a fabulous light that falls upon those watching the ceremony and ultimately all the people of Claybourne. Old Wife and Minnie especially exploit the limits of the corporeal body (which Old Wife cleverly calls the "corporal body" as a comment against the incessant policing bodies endure [50]), moving between the here and the there. Their mobility is radical, sometimes reckless, and couples the flesh and the spirit in a process of subjectivity.

The focus on immateriality further highlights the potential to coalesce with bodies that are not one's own. Such embrace produces the stranger, that third woman who is both self and an/other self, but also is the union of self with an/other self; that gliding blue woman who is seen leaving Nel's wedding who is Sula, Nel, Sula-Nel, but also an/other woman, a new and lovely mystery. As Velma is dreaming and remembering her communities, she thinks about a woman who is next to her but whose presence is that of a stranger, an unfamiliar familiar: "She [Velma] might steal a glance sideways at the woman next to her and study the elegant shoes, the red and gold and white sequined ruffles at the hem of the extravagant gown, the hands clasped with three wedding bands shining on the ring finger—before she wrenched her eyes back to the safety of her swollen feet. There might be an answer. But she would not look up from her feet" (259). Velma does not know who this woman is, though her studied attention and hesitation to ask her question—who are you?—suggests that this woman is a familiar someone and that the question is not only about the stranger's identity but also Velma's own. "It was a woman all right next to her, trying to get *familiar*. She used the same brand of sandalwood soap too. She *felt* her more than anything else. A *glow*, as if she were beaming at her, not daring now but *inviting* her to look! She didn't risk it" (259; emph. added). Although Bambara uses words such as *familiar, felt, glow*, and *inviting* to suggest the connection between this woman and Velma, she also heightens the sense of ambiguity and liminality with the same words. In fact, the specificity of the self being spoken of is complicated by Bambara's use of *her* and *she* without caution, so that the subject and object are conflated, exchanged, and merged.

This clever narrative ambiguity, in which Velma's self is also this woman's self, and indiscriminately so, continues as Velma's dream moment incorporates "real" people and situations into her other-consciousness in an attempt to identify this woman: "What was her name? M'Dear never used a name. The mailbox probably read Mr. and Mrs. Lot. Period. Surely she'd gotten the flyers, she was on the mailing list. Seen the posters, read the papers, knew what they were trying to do to effect change. *Maybe the thing to do was invite the self by for coffee and a chat.* Share with *her how she herself* had learned to believe in ordinary folks' capacity to change the self and transform society" (259–260; emph. added). This woman becomes Velma's meditation; she thinks that maybe the only thing to do is to invite the self for coffee and a chat. But which self—her own? This other woman? Both? The language here mirrors Walker's meeting of her other self in a dance, a suggestion of the palpable and (almost?) material intimacy that can exist between a woman and her other self. This woman that Velma is imagining and dreaming is also perhaps a someone she has encountered in real life as well as a part of Velma's self, a part of her coalition of selves. This woman is, in the worst case, another burden for Velma's subjectivity, but she can also be a salve, a lyric, a calm. Whomever she is and however she arrives, she is Velma: When Minnie's healing ritual is almost complete, Velma thinks that "she could be coming apart, totally losing her self." But then she remembers this woman: "That woman in the park, who was that but *another her, a part?*" (262; emph. added).

That this dreamed-up woman could be Velma's other self, and an indispensable other self who holds her together at the moment she is most susceptible to coming apart, denotes just how crucial imagination is to girlfriend subjectivity. Sula and Nel find each other in a similar moment of imagination, as Walker does her dancing aesthete; Juletane encounters an underwater community in her breathing and dream space in her diary; and Clare finds her girlfriend mother in fantasizing about literary characters and the lushness of the Jamaican landscape. Yet, because the realities that necessitate coalitional selfhood are in fact all too real and material, the gift of imagination is itself not sufficient. Still imagining one's connectedness is a necessary part of expanding the kinds of coalitions one can have with other selves, with one's own self; imagining one's other self, in the absence or presence of a real material other, provides the girlfriend with an/other for measure and meditation. Imagination helps to sustain the tension and tussle that is subjectivity's only appetite.

In a 1998 essay titled "Strangers" Toni Morrison narrates her own encounter with a stranger woman, an encounter that closely parallels Bambara's explication of Velma's intimacy with the dreamed (of) self. Morrison's essay begins with her meeting an old woman near the edge of her neighbor's garden. The woman does not live there but claims to be fishing with the neighbor's permission. The two women have a pleasant, sisterly conversation, "about fish recipes and weather and children." "When we part," Morrison writes, "it is with an understanding that she will be there the next day or very soon after and we will visit again. I imagine more conversations with her. I will invite her into my house for coffee, for tales, for laughter. She reminds me of someone, something. I imagine a friendship, casual, effortless, delightful" (68). But the woman is not there the next day or the next or subsequent days. She never returns, leaving Morrison to make sense of the feeling of loss she feels, the anticipation she had experienced, and the love she had imagined. "I feel cheated, puzzled, but also amused, and wonder off and on if I have dreamed her." And, though Morrison tries to minimize the power of the woman's presence, in an effort to soothe the loss, there is still loss: "A certain view from my windows is now devoid of her, reminding me every morning of her deceit and my disappointment. . . . I try to understand the intensity of my chagrin, and why I am missing a woman I spoke to for fifteen minutes. I get nowhere except for the stingy explanation that she had come into my space . . . and had implied promises of *female camaraderie, of opportunities for me to be generous, of protection and protecting.* Now she is gone, taking with her my good opinion of myself, which, of course, is unforgivable" (69; emph. added). Morrison marks the loss of her imagined other, this woman who momentarily insinuated herself as a girlfriend and whose presence helps Morrison to sustain a good opinion of herself—an/other self who is indisposable to Morrison's (process of) selfhood. Did Morrison fictionalize the insinuation as part of her own process of selfhood? She leaves both open to possibility, even as the ambiguity does not soothe the real loss of a coalition.

This woman stranger exists at the intersection of self and other; she constitutes a selfhood that is centered in mutuality, pairing, and coalition. The trope of the stranger is almost by definition a metaphor for liminality—the stranger is a spirit self, a self that exists as an idea, a force, an energy, as a less-than-material self—like the body of gossip or whisper, sly and silklike, tenuous and tenacious. This liminality represents a transformative context in which subjectivity literally materializes through engagement with immateriality (the girlfriend's imagination) and emphasizes again the mobility that is so crucial to girlfriend selfhood.

Earlier, in chapter 1, I discussed this mobility as it relates to the achievement of a coupled self; here I would like to extend the discussion to include corporeal disintegration into immateriality, examples of transcending flesh that characterize girlfriend selfhood. Looking more closely at *Juletane* might help to elucidate this idea: textually, Juletane is a stranger, out of place in a land that is not her own, and is "ostracised by the whole community" (23). Juletane's presence as a stranger is complemented by her madness, and in the absence of a home Juletane locates herself in herself, surrendering to her own self and spirit. It is the only self that she is initially able to hold on to: "Like every morning, the first thing I do is open my window, scan the sky through the branches of the mango tree and watch the household getting up. . . . [In the shower] the water is cool on my skin, like a gentle caress. It is a good feeling; I forget about myself, I am lulled into *sleep, I dream* about streams and water-falls. I am back in *my island*, a child again, on the banks of a clear-running stream. I wade in, my weariness dissolves in the cool water. My heart swells with happiness" (29; emph. added). Juletane identifies with the growing wonders outside her window as well as those of her imagination, and her material adult body yields to her childhood, to a sense of cool, to the dissolving of a subject-hood that has failed her. She is both imagining the experience and experiencing the imagination. This dissolution is a self-embrace, and soon Juletane is transformed into a desperate craziness and moves like a ghost, her "clothes floating about [her]" (38). She literally becomes an/other self, her corporeal body transformed into ghostly stranger. This transformation facilitates her later connections with the underwater spirits and the other "ghostly" women in the psychiatric hospital.

The transformation to liminal subjecthood extends the body outside of the boundaries imposed by its self, boundaries that sometimes impede coalitions between self and other (self).[3] The liminal subject is simultaneously deep within and far outside of the body. The need for transcendence does not imply that the body itself is inherently limited but, rather, that the body is so severely and consistently policed that its presence as an intimacy of self is hardly promised, sometimes compromised, often in peril. Furthermore, corporeal mutability—in its recognition of the multiplicity of one's own self, of one's ability to create (and destroy), of the all that is self—parallels godliness and asserts the lovely limitlessness of the human animal. This precise relationship between transcending the body and embracing godliness is evident, for example, when Sula severs the tip of her finger as a deterrent to the young boys who want to harm her and Nel. Sula's self-mutilation, in forgoing pain and normativity, evokes a sense of power that seems unimaginable, that startles the young boys into a very unmasculine scamper. What scares those boys is her fearlessness, the strength and limitlessness articulated by her behavior that is certainly not girlish and is even a bit inhuman.

The engagement of liminality is, as a practice, synonymous with finding god in oneself, a self-divinity that is a key aesthetic principle in the African Diaspora. Self-divinity personalizes the relationship between a girlfriend self and her god, such that god becomes her an/other, becomes a part of her practice of self-articulation. Hers is not a relationship with God as a social institution but, instead, is a relationship with and to god as an intimacy, as an expression of one's selfness. Of course, such is always the intent of god-concepts, but rarely do the bounds of organized religions resist imposing doctrine where human agency should be.[4] The sanctity of the intimacy between girlfriend self and god is evoked in *Salt Eaters* when Bambara writes, "[Sophie] would no more break discipline with her Self than she would her covenant with God" (153). The word *her* is a modifier of the capitalized entity *Self*, a term that in its capitalization (and hence properness) is an equivalent with *God*. Bambara's sentence echoes Shange's "found god in myself," which suggests that the communion with a higher spirit is also a communion with self.

At the center of Walker's *The Color Purple* is the fellowship between Celie and God, who is the addressee of her letters initially. Early on Celie identifies her relationship with God as her community of solace and reliability: "long as I can spell G-o-d I got somebody along" (18). Similarly, when Nettie doubts whether her letters will be read by Celie, she invokes God as a reliable someone: "I remember one time you said your life made you feel so ashamed you couldn't even talk about it to God, you had to write it, bad as you thought your writing was. Well, now I know what you meant. And whether God will read letters or no, I know you will keep on writing them; which is guidance enough for me. *Anyway, when I don't write to you I feel as bad as I do when I don't pray*, locked up in myself and choking on my own heart" (110; emph. added). Like Celie, Nettie's invocation suggests that God is her other self, is the girlfriend she can talk with and to. But it is also noteworthy that Nettie implies a reverence for Celie as subject of prayer, gesturing toward the god whom Celie is in Nettie's imagination. Nettie's metaphor levels the field between God and Celie as well as arguably makes godliness more attainable for herself via her identification with Celie (when she says, for example, "Now I know what you meant," which is a statement of alliance).

This hint of self-divinity in Nettie's comment permits a bolder claim later in the text, when she acknowledges the misuses of Christianity and moves closer to proclaiming her own relationship with the divine. Describing the arrival of Olivia and Adam with a white family, Nettie puts quotation marks around *God*: "And then they say 'God' sent them Olivia and Adam." Nettie's anger and disillusionment at the invocation of God in support of violence against Celie inspires her to revise God's mantra of immanence such that she becomes the marker of her and Celie's self-divinity, a subtle but definitive movement away from somebody else's God and into their own: "But on the other hand, if you can believe I am in Africa, and I am, you can believe anything" (112). Nettie proclaims her presence in Africa as immanence (the irrefutable "I am") and declares Celie's belief in her immanence as omnipotence; in so doing, she restores the agency that belief in God is supposed to offer, by coupling such faith with a sense of selfness.[5]

Celie eventually changes the address of her letters from God to Nettie.

"I don't write to God no more," she notes at the start of this first letter, perhaps realizing that she had *always* been writing to Nettie and to herself. The salutation to God was a necessary gesture, a someplace outside her that was safe and sure; God manifested as a readily accessible symbol (within the realm of what little Celie knew at the beginning of her adult selfhood), and Celie makes him her girlfriend until she is able to establish an/other relationship with Nettie/herself.[6] The move from God is both a recognition of the complications of God worship ("the God I been praying and writing to is a man. And act just like all the other mens I know. Trifling, forgitful and lowdown" [164]) as well as her recognition of her own loving spirit. In this latter respect Celie's selfhood fits into the self-divine framework that Shug, the most conventionally Godless of all the characters, introduces. "Any God I ever felt in church I brought in with me," Shug says: "God is inside you and inside everybody else. You come into the world with God. But only them that search for it inside find it. And sometimes it just manifest itself even if you not looking, or don't know what you looking for" (165–166). This view of divinity institutes God as a trope of girlfriend revelation, and Celie's achievement of subjecthood is the realization of the God in herself. When she tells Albert that she is leaving, she signals her godliness with her words to him: "It's time to leave you and enter into the Creation" (170). As she gets up to leave, Albert attacks her with his words: "Look at you. You black, you pore, you ugly, you a woman. Goddam, he say, you nothing at all." But Celie, who throughout the novel hardly speaks, delivers an answer to Albert in a voice that is an incantation: "Until you do right by me, I say, everything you even dream about will fail." She invokes herself as the everything through which salvation is possible, in a voice that is newly hers. "I give it to him straight, just like it come to me. And it seem to come to me from the trees." And, when Albert lunges to physically attack her, "[a] dust devil flew up on the porch between me, fill my mouth with dirt." She Celie speaks a prophecy through the dirt, much like the biblical God speaking through the burning bush: "The dirt say, Anything you do to me, already done to you" (176).

This process of becoming one's own god characterizes the liminality of girlfriend subjectivity and forgoes the perceived limits of the fleshly body, especially death. When Celie receives the telegram about Nettie's death, she writes: "I sit here in this big house by myself trying to sew, but what good is sewing gon do? What good is anything? Being alive begin to seem like a awful strain" (216). Celie initially embraces Nettie's death as a profound loss that disrupts her own commitment to living; so overwhelming is her grief that she forgets herself, the power of the connection that she had with Nettie, and the life this connection made possible. Still, Celie's letter writing undercuts

her own despair: the letter, which is addressed to Nettie, exists as a space beyond Nettie's physical death. The integrity of Celie's connection to Nettie,
to herself, to life itself, is not interrupted by death. In fact, death is no longer
death; its significance and impact have changed. Celie later becomes defiant
of death and, in that same letter, writes: "I don't believe you dead. How can
you be dead if I still feel you? Maybe, like God, you changed into something
different that I'll have to speak to in a different way, but you not dead to me
Nettie. And never will be. Sometime when I git tired of talking to myself I
talk to you" (220). Celie imagines—and then wills—Nettie into another being,
another manifestation, which is possible because Nettie's and Celie's spirit selves
are malleable. Nettie's self, and her connection to Celie, is persistent, constant, dynamic, and forever, or for as long as they love each other that way.[7]

The coalition between god and self exhibits the integrity of girlfriend
selfhood where the psychic distance between self and other is almost nonexistent. The dissolution of differentiation, which is also the understanding of
the stranger as the self, is a spiritual process. The stranger—that familiar old
woman fishing at the edge of the fence, dressed in old men's clothing, and
inviting. She is missed, this stranger, her presence fleeting and furtive. In this
flash of her, the girlfriend subject sees her own self; the clamor for the stranger
is really a craving for some part of the self: "To understand that I was longing
for and missing some aspect of myself, that there are no strangers. There are
only versions of ourselves, many of which we have not embraced, most of
which we wish to protect ourselves from. For the stranger is not foreign, she
is random, not alien, but remembered; and it is the randomness of the encounter with our already known—although unacknowledged—selves that sum-
mons a ripple of alarm" (Morrison, "Strangers" 71). Not foreign. Sometimes
random, unexpected, even uninvited, but not at all really a stranger.[8] A
stranger as a metaphorical subject who helps the girlfriend to "put a space between those words [your/self], as though the self were really a twin or a thirst
or a friend or something that sits right next to you and watches you" (Taylor-
Guthrie 208). The process of communing divinely, communing with one's divinity, is also a process of making claim on those stranger selves and welcoming
them into a coalitioned self. They may have been, may even still be, raucous,
bodies unfit, but they are bodies of one's own, and they propel tension. When
Sofia returns from her in-house imprisonment, she is, in Celie's words, "the
stranger," "the one they can't quite find a place for" at the Thanksgiving din-
ner table (172). She is a self who is lost, beaten, battered, forgotten—or almost left for forgetting. Yet she sits at the table, a place is made for her, and
all the faces there must take her in, reconcile the her in them, the them in

her. Her sitting at that table represents all of the welcome that there could be. The stranger, too, is part of the divine self, and the act of reclamation is not appropriation but a political act of self-alignment. This act asks the question, Who do I have to be to let you in? a question that necessarily situates the stranger's place in the self. Who am I if I let you in? And how, just how, do I keep thee, myself?

Selffullness

The coalitioned subject originates with a dancing couple engaged in each other's embrace and (self) gaze. From this twoness tumbles a multiplicity of coalitions, a community of coalitioned selves that are a re-pairing and healing subjecthood. This selfhood is an ongoing unsettling process that operates on a principle of self(full)ness: a self that is uncompromising in its assertion of selfness as well as in its encompassing selffullness. The practice is one that acknowledges the tension between coupling, on one hand, and solitude, on the other—a me and an us, the will of the self and the surrender to the community, these two urgings that propel and exist in each other. Girlfriend subjecthood is not only the connection between two women but also the tension generated by the connection and the production of other selves by/in/through this tension. The third space, the space that exists between but which also yields self and other self, is generative and communal but is also, remember, propelled by the subject's choice of adhesion—a thing that is severely self-centered. Thirdness highlights the adhesion as well as the choice, the multiplicity and its furtive singularity. When Celie and Shug leave Albert, they are making a choice, on a level different than before, to connect with each other. "Shug say, Us each other's peoples now, and kiss me," Celie writes (156), noting the agency in this connection sealed with a kiss (156). *Choosing* to be "each other's peoples" is the work of community, like the sewing that Celie does that brings together her and Sofia (their quilt making), her and Shug (their reading of Nettie's old letters), and her and the community (their buying the pants she makes). Community here is not merely an expectation or a given; it is a choice, a commitment, the ongoing efforts of imagination. It is a creation and a politic.

As it reveals the multiple textualities that constitute one's own self, girlfriend selfhood confronts and reconfigures the seeming selflessness that community demands of Black women; rather than selflessness, communal identity is almost flawfully determined by the particularity of a Black woman's selfhood, whatever its threat or vagaries may be. It is not community that is, has, yields integrity but instead her, her own-ness. When the people of Claybourne gather together in *The Salt Eaters* at the Southwest Community Infirmary for Velma's healing, Bambara's language intimates selffullness, the many as the one, the one as the many: "The rest of the old-timers . . . remained in deep concentration, matching the prayer group in silence and patience. For sometimes a person held on to sickness with a fiercesomeness that took twenty hard-praying folk to loosen. . . . concentration was necessary to help a neighbor experience the best of herself or himself" (107). The achievement of the best of one's self, a phrasing that itself suggests self-multiplicity, is a communal process as much as it is an act of individual will. In fact, the idea of the individual as a modern lexical construct, one that has social and economic motives, seems hardly appropriate here, though I have throughout used the term. Instead, think of the idea of the "one" as it is referenced in Bambara's language and as a wide metaphor of singularity and multiplicity; the idea of one as a meditation, a distilling, a complication, a life's work, a state that becomes and undoes.[9]

Think, then, of community as a parallel to achieving this oneness, as an invitation to be filled and replenished as well as to be emptied and cleared, the coming to community as a kenosis.[10] In *No Telephone to Heaven* Cliff's description of the ruination that the landscape undergoes is such a clearing and filling. The land, an entity neither singular nor plural, "possess itself" (105): "lands [. . .] once cleared for agricultural purposes [. . .] have [. . .] lapsed back into . . . 'bush.' An impressive variety of herbaceous shrubs and woody types of vegetation appears in succession, becoming thicker and taller over the years" (1). Ruination is the name for Clare's journey to self, clearing the spaces of subjecthood that have been cluttered with selflessness, filling the selfscape with an abundance, with as many of one's selves as it can hold. Clare is radically self-possessed, a multipled one like the guerrilla revolutionaries she joins who "took rakes and hoes to [the land]. As the land cleared, it turned black—blackness filled with the richness of the river and the bones of people in unmarked graves" (11). They are a generative community of selves, selffull and singular.[11]

The idea of selffullness is represented by the statement "you are all you have" and its simultaneous indication of the infinite and the finite. "You are all you have" is both a call to celebrate the manyed-ness of you as well as a warning and reminder of the tenuousness of that which is not-you. This duality is the competing character of community, and it necessitates a Black female subject's commitment to her own self: no matter how imprecise and unreliable her selfhood may be, its integrity is its unending struggle to sustain selfishness.

Such self-centeredness depends upon being able to know oneself to be enough, to be able and willing to whisper to self this bit of affirmation. Shug's practice of selfhood gives voice to a sense of "enoughness" when she experiences herself to be everything, moving away from as well as through Godlike omnipresence: "My first step from the old white man [God] was trees. The air. Then birds. Then other people. But one day, when I was sitting quiet and feeling like a motherless child, which I was, it come to me: that feeling of being part of everything, not separate at all. I knew that if I cut a tree, my arm would bleed" (167). Shug's recognition of her fullness is not superficial but, instead, recognizes the environmental politics that give urgency to her meditation.[12] In fact, the threat of violence—psychic, physical, environmental—is one of the forces against which girlfriend selfhood allies, threats that often materialize against Black and female subjects even as (their) communities remain oblivious or disseminated.

Being enough is a struggle to maintain as well as a conflict with community. Morrison's *Sula* exemplifies this conflict as Sula's attempts at selffullness—represented varyingly by her refusal to marry or have children or her leaving Medallion—are rejected by the community as well as by her an/other. Even on her deathbed that sense of being full with self is unchanged, and it frustrates Nel, who has come to visit her and was hoping to find her more contrite and repentant. In their exchange Nel questions just what, other than her own selfishness, Sula has to show for the life she lived:

> "Show? To who? Girl I got my mind. And what goes on in it. Which is to say I got me."
> "Lonely, ain't it?"
> "Yes. But my lonely is mine. Now your lonely is somebody else's. Made by somebody else and handed to you. Ain't that something? A secondhand lonely." (143)

Sula's biting response is a warning against the lonely that community can legislate, a separation of self from center in exchange for the comfort of the community's acceptance and familiarity. When Nel later suggests that having a man is an endeavor well worth its cost in selflessness, Sula responds, "They ain't worth more than me" (143), which surely Nel knows because no amount of selflessness has produced happiness in her marriage with Jude.

Girlfriend subjecthood moves between "a me" and "an us," in which both represent subjectivities centered in that young Black girl in search of a mirror. Identity as represented in these narratives is being able to be the stranger's other, in recognizing oneself not only *in* but *as* the stranger—claiming one's own hyper-marginalization and becoming one's own other. The "us" is the practice of a self's coupling with an/other who is herself, is like herself; an/other who is sometimes imagined or dreamed as her other self; an/other who sometimes *is*, literally, herself. The process is one of heartbreak and risk as well as of uncompromised love.

Aidoo offers an exquisite narration of the struggle to be enough in *Our Sister Killjoy*. The novel's title chapter characterizes the absence and failure of connections through the news story of a successful heart transplant: "The evening papers had screeched the news in with the evening trains of the underground. Of how the Dying White Man had received the heart of a coloured man who had collapsed on the beach and how the young coloured man had allegedly failed to respond to any efforts at resuscitation and therefore his heart had been removed from his chest, the Dying White Man's own old heart having been cleaned out of his chest and how in the meantime the Dying White Man was doing well, blah, blah, blah!" (95). The narrator sarcastically enunciates Sissie's dis-ease with life in England, where she feels isolated, situated as she is among other Africans who have readily (or not so readily) embraced capitalism and, by extension, colonialism. These Africans have determined that they can make better money in England; that they are still, at heart, Africans because they send money home to their mothers; that, in fact, they are working to build homes for their mothers; that it is okay to have white wives (since most of her fellow Africans are men) and to be uncritical about the impact race, gender, and conquest may have on their personal relationships; and that her politics, her attempts to find ways to negotiate Africanness in England differently than they have, are naive.[13] Sissie has to break alliance with this community of her people, one of whom is her lover, her beloved an/other, because the solidarity of this community endangers and marginalizes her own selfness.

This severing is narrated in "The Love Letter," an epistolary chapter that merges Sissie's voice with the narrator's. The letter is written from an open and encompassing first-person perspective and is the only time that the novel is absent of the narrator's biting wit. It is reasonable to surmise that the narrator all along has been watching Sissie's coming of age and waiting to be able to claim her as an/other, while Sissie had been too afraid (and perhaps unknowing?) of her own self to surrender to such a coupling (as was the case with Marija, though under different circumstances). Whatever: the novel's tensions, represented variably by Aidoo's manipulation of sarcasm, irony, and narrative voice as well as her construction of unreconciled miscommunication between characters were all along manifestations of the identificatory tension between Sissie and the narrator. In fact, the tone and perspective of the letter is significantly different than what either Sissie or the narrator has presented throughout the rest of the novel, and in this way the letter evidences a merged and allied narrative voice.[14]

The shift to first-person also introduces the self-reflective quality of the letter, a "female coming into her own" (Owusu 353). Although written about the unfulfilled union, the letter's tone and comments articulates Sissie's claim on her own self as enough. In this way the letter is addressed as much to herself, to her girlfriend self, as it is to her boyfriend; its message is as much dismissal as it is welcome. "My precious something," it begins, a tender invocation that forgoes anger because no anger is needed; in fact, the clearing of an old relationship, one entangled in the limits of heterosexuality and patriarchy, has made room for the sister that is Sissie's own name. The letter generously recounts the political, spiritual, and affective gaps in the relationship between Sissie and her partner. Its language is soft and easy: "My precious something, all that I was saying about language is that I wish you and I could share our hopes, our fears, and our fantasies, without feeling inhibited because we suspect that someone is listening" (115). This desire to have a space where self and self could meet and share without anxiety reflects Sissie / the narrator's frustration with gender politics and colonialism, the way that language and voice are apportioned and appropriated. "That is why," she writes, "we have to have our secret language. We must create this language. It is high time we did. We are too old a people not to. We can. We must. So that we shall make love with words" (116).

The movement of the letter is toward self-expression, toward a dissolution and integration that centers this merged narrative voice. Soon after her opening, Sissie / the narrator claims her own self as the missive's subject, almost as if the lover himself were imaginary:[15] "When I started to write this letter, I thought I just wanted to say how much I have missed you. How much I still miss you. I know you will not believe it. Besides, what difference will it make even if you believed me? . . . But *your image is before me all the time.* Like the spirit of someone I have wronged. And yet, I have not wronged you, have I? Indeed, if there is anyone I may have sinned against, *it is me.* That desiring you as I do, needing you as I do, I still let you go" (116–117). Recentered as a subject—even one whose vulnerabilities leave much that is in question and flux—Sissie / the narrator critiques the self-effacement and silence that her lover and other African men had expected. Refusing to accept the easy narrative of women's place, Sissie / the narrator imagines her self-image differently: "See, at home the woman knew her position and all that. Of course, this has been true of the woman everywhere—most of the time. But wasn't her position among our people a little more complicated than that of the dolls the colonisers brought along with them" (117). This stands as a critique of the masculine bias of African politics and the misconsideration of a woman's subjectivity.

Aidoo's crafting of the letter's prose makes Sissie / the narrator's voice matter—both that it is considered and of import and that it materializes. Although Sissie has never been silent, her voice has not been valued in these conversations with men, and, rather than needing to develop a voice, she has had to "throw" her voice as a means to disrupt sexist nationalism and politics.[16] The letter, in its intimacy and subject matter, is a moment of such disruption: its aesthetic is personal and national, angry and quiet, and centered in the subjectivity of one, a Black woman. There, amid love and loss, are the challenges of colonialism; there, too, is its urgent and respectful argument for Africans to return home, to meet themselves again. It is not only a romanticized nationalism, a judgmental one-uppance in which self-authenticity is at stake; instead, the letter's girlfriend trajectory imagines the journey home as a journey to the self, to the shifting vagaries of a Black female subject. This argument supports her own thoughtful choice to return home, a decision that is less about going to Ghana and more about a turn into selffull commitment.

What is most remarkable about this letter and its achievement of selffullness is that Sissie decides not to send it:

> When she realised that she had been writing all the time they had been in the air, she was amazed. The letter was deservedly long. Over the next couple of stops, she read and reread it. Somehow, the more she read it, the more relieved she felt. That she had actually written it. Yet she felt somewhat uneasy too. It was definitely too long and anyway, what did she hope to achieve by sending it to him? . . . She sat quietly in her seat and stared at the land unfolding before her. . . . Suddenly, she knew what she was not going to do. She was never going to post the letter. Once written, it was written. She had taken some of the pain away and she was glad. There was no need to mail it. It was not necessary. She was going to let things lie where they had fallen. (133)

In the air on her way back to Ghana, with a commitment to a Black female subjecthood that includes nation, Sissie, whose voice is again distinct from the narrator's, realizes that the letter was a self-conversation, a volatile interaction between her and her an/other; she did not need to send it, for it had already served its purpose—to reclaim the self she had lost, put aside, or deferred, in a tussle with colonization. Instead, she clears the place in her spirit and sits there, restful and at peace and with her (other) self. She is enough with and her (un)becoming.

(Un)becoming . . . Being Enough

"Being enough" is not a reactive statement of self-protection. After Helene's fiancé marries another woman the day before their wedding, news Helene hears from his best friend, she decides that "she would use [men] for a while, then as soon as they seemed to becoming involved, she would stop seeing them without any explanation" (*Juletane* 128). Helene's disposition is at this point ruthlessly independent, yet her state of being enough is an outward and reactive one. It is protective, anxious, does not facilitate selfullness and generosity. Instead of being open to possibilities, which the practice of selfhood offers, Helene is closed, her heart frozen to others and to her own self; it is only in reading Juletane's diary that her heart melts and the fullness of her vulnerability and potential power become evident to her.

Being enough is at once quiet and wild, a peaced conundrum that does not assume the absence of violence but which earns self-assuredness from having understood how much one is the world's center, how much the world is one's center. Risk-full, yes but assured by its practice of being a me and an us—these two arcs of subjecthood that are not security but knowing, not knowledge but (un)becoming: disruptive, unreliable, puzzled and puzzling, and, still, they are the name of the self, full, capable, possible, a location of and inspiration for imagination and agency. The language is slipping here, the idea too, so let me turn again to the text. When Shug writes that she is coming home, Celie's calm is the steady of what being enough can yield—Celie is at once thrilled by and desiring of Shug's return and committed to her own self-affection. Of Shug's homecoming Celie thinks "If she come, I be happy. If she don't, I be content." This balance evokes a new subjectivity, a sense of what it is to know without certainty, the risk and thrill and surrender of being (able to be) open; it is what it means at once to be able to become and to be undone. Celie notes that "this [was] the lesson I was suppose to learn"—the value and valence of her own self(full)ness, her capacity to be and encounter satisfaction, joy even (*Color Purple* 240). She does not dismiss Shug's return; in fact, she claims it not only as a possible source of joy but also as a location of the selfhood she has learned to practice.

This being enough exists without a period, as in "I am enough". The period here is signally misplaced, because the statement of being enough is more open than not, more an invitation than a dismissal. Being enough is a recognition of the other as the self but not an exact replication, for exactness hardly matters. No—it is the recognition that the other has the same name, be it freedom, disappointment, girl, longing, tired, love. It is the recognition of the self herself.

The final letter of Celie's writing is addressed: "Dear God. Dear stars, dear trees, dear sky, dear peoples. Dear Everything. Dear God" (242). Celie writes to the fullness of herself, a universal body that generates from the particular, a selfhood that is grand in scope because it aims to be nothing more (or less!) than its own self.[17] Her salutation is an "I am enough," whispered quietly like Sula's last words or Nel's depthful cry, whispered to the self and echoed by the an/other who is also the self. It is the melding of a call and its response into one cry, like the "my precious something" of Sissie and the narrator's letter. The address of the "I am enough" does not beg for loud public approval; it exists in its quiet stating and is answered at the same moment it is spoken. And it opens out, like the ending of all of these novels, each ending with a beginning, a new place yet arrived at. The novels trail off the page, like the selfhood that they narrate—resisting closure and, instead, suggesting the constancy of the subject's (un)becoming. Nothing is sure, but all is possible.[18]

She, this girlfriend subject, is enough, her name always encompassing the other, just as the phrase *girlfriend subject* evokes a someone else, a journey of surrender and transgression, a traversing the borders of a social body. But it is not mobility alone that is her freedom: she has a certain integrity, a certain commitment, that helps manifest the multiplicity and the moving.[19] Maybe the integrity is love or something less vague: maybe it is Sula and Nel's recognition of Black femaleness and its attendant limits. Let's, for this moment, call it fearlessness: fear is a provocative psychic body with both exterior and interior constitutions—as an exteriority, fear is both used to police and control as well as can be initiated by bodies that control, but it is fear as an interiority that is more relevant here, the way that fear manifests and replicates itself in the wild interior landscape, and potentially institutes levels of control unmatched by what is outside. What if fear as an interior psychic body is an/other, one of the many dreamful dancing girlfriends to be embraced and disclaimed? What if fear is a precise doorway or a plush landscape through and in which to encounter an/other, fear itself? It seems that to fear fear is to fear the self, to circumvent its articulate body, the knowing that fear can offer.[20] The girlfriend subject feels fear, cultivates a difficult relationship with fear, but she cannot, does not, let it exist as a stasis within or without her.

She is unreliable. She is committed only to herself and her unwieldy passions and committed only to love. She does not harm, although interactions with her can hurt and cause pain. She knows what she loves, a knowing that is multiple, confused and confusing, and, in spite of such clarity, she is often unable to articulate what she loves, never mind how or why. And why should she? Her love is her own, not a possession but as if the word *is* were an equal sign and the phrase an equation. . . . her love is her own. She understands that, for her as a Black woman, to love and be loved often means to be expectant and expected, which she is neither. She understands that being expected and expecting means being able to be relied upon by some other as well as to be willing to rely on some other. Such dependency is directly connected to thinking that one can possess an/other as well as being thought of as one who can be owned. She understands that such practices of reliance are female projects, little ways that women are known in the world and which take her away from herself—from the small things she loves, covets, fears, desires, but especially from the big of her imagination. Who can bear the big of her? No one, she thinks. No one.

And, still, this lover is not a loner, is not a rugged individual. She is a one—intimately as well as infinitely connected to her others, her girlfriends who come to her through a process of realizing the me-/not-me-ness of her capacity to connect with and love an/other person. This process is the difficult and sometimes frustrating realization of the word *selffull*—at once self, at once other; full of one's self as well as of one's other selves. She, this lover, like Sula or Juletane, is an unreliable commune.

She is a social trespasser, trampling race and gender, creating intimacies that foreground her own viability.

She is a mobile spirituality and a body still: she, this Blackwoman, is Oya—peace and passion, turbulence and calm, centered in her self(full)ness. Oya, the river, a Yoruba dance(r). She is also Oshun, an/other river, an/other dancer, a movement of facility that suggests not only ease but ambulation. She is the center and its edge. She is a dancer, this selffull Black woman; like Judith Jamison in Alvin Ailey's *Cry*, she is "an ecstatic state of grace."[21] This is the subject as ritual, a ritual that is more than a performance and, instead, a spirited and complicated engagement of repetition and play, constant and (un)successful integration of parts material and not. This girlfriend selfhood is about rediscovering oneself: encountering what you thought you knew, who you think you are, an encounter that happens through tensions. It is not discovery with a restorative or corrective bent but just to see, just for possibility's sake. Of course, it is also not against restoration, and, in fact, the sense of a "just to see" is already corrective of the social order's imposition on Black female selfhood. No matter its ambiguity: it is a reclamation of selfhood's agency from the policing fictions of social identity.

This movement of subjectivity is a dance, after all, is what happens when one human body encounters another: the subject always imagines, for a moment and quite unconsciously, that the other body will be an exact match, will mirror and complement her own precisely . . . that this other body will cover and enter and totalize her own, not as colonization but as a mutuality that is only imaginable in the momentary luxury of new contact. Soon enough that promise of matchfulness fails: the other body, as is the case with all bodies, is not a match, now or ever. Sometimes the slip of the promise of matchfulness occurs in what is said or not said; sometimes it is in a glance or an item of clothing worn differently, awkwardly. Whatever it is, there is a profound and sometimes painful awareness of the impossibility of exact matchfulness, an awareness that hardly ever fully disarms the subject from imagining and coveting the same in a future moment, for the impulse toward matchfulness is a human one, recurring and impossible. So, here she is, this girlfriend subject at this impasse, realizing again and anew that it is the engagement of this now awkward and sometimes inelegant dance with a matchless other that yields her subjectivity and agency, a movement that offers the practice of proximity and abandon with this imperfect other, that offers disappointment and loss and risk. Her subjectivity is a twirl, a choreographic ambling, that sustains and breaks alliances with the other, unmatchable; it is part will and surrender, part agency and faith, not about control or possession, not about endless flailing. A dance. Her subjectivity is a struggle, yes, but also a rapture, a pleasure of selves—a shaking loose of the web of identity and its impediments. A reverie; yes, a reverie unreliable and unrepentant.

The Western and conventional wisdom about devotion (say, in marriage or in religion) suggests that the most sublime experience is to lose oneself in loving another—to give up oneself in the love of another. Such surrender is complicated because it at once exacts an erosion of self while promising a more that potentially reinstitutes and restores the self; such is also complicated because the nature of the surrender is linked to markers of social identity. But it is not enough to dismiss the sublimity of surrender; the truth is there is something sublime in loving an/other, engaging the profound volatile dynamic between self and other. Instead, girlfriend subjectivity proposes a surrender that, for a Black woman, is not only loss, denial, or sacrifice—a devotion that is selffull rather than selfless . . . abundance rather than lack. A reverie.

> When a window sealed for too long finally opens, it offers a sigh, a breath, that escapes, arises, falls—all at the same time. We can call that breath love, or missing.
>
> It is that expiration, in its softness, the way it glides over broad spaces, and always gestures towards the open and the possible . . . it is that expiration which reminds me of the difference between you and me—that you are not me, nor me you.
>
> (We can call that recognition pain.)
>
> It is also this expiration that reveals our choosing: this you, this me, who choose to meet at that place in the river; there, with our

hands extended towards each other, we gather our selves and claim
the face across the short way that is also ours as well as not ours.
    We choose and the choosing is as a breath; it gives life.

The faith in the connection—in the chosen relationship between a woman and her girlfriend, the moving between "a me" and "an us"—is the integrity of the self. What is sacred about the self, where the self has unflappable integrity,[22] is (in) its capacity to love—to choose and make coalition with an/other, to use that coalition as a model for achieving further connections that ultimately reveal one's own divinity and re-center the sufficiency of the full self. This subjectivity is about developing other ways to interact with love, risk, generosity, and self(full)ness and without fear and domination; it is, as mentioned in the opening chapter of the section, a new intimacy. This couple, this woman and her girlfriend, her beloved, her (an/other) self, together, in a slow, sweet dance. This woman and herself are the merged subject of Lucille Clifton's untitled poem, and their merger is an invitation, a relationality:

won't you celebrate with me
what i have shaped into
a kind of life? i had no model.
born in babylon
both nonwhite and woman
what did i see to be except myself?
i made it up
here on this bridge between
starshine and clay,
my one hand holding tight
my other hand; come celebrate
with me that everyday
something has tried to kill me
and has failed.
(*Book of Light* 25)

This nonwhite person, this woman person, stands hand in hand with herself. She and her an/other self are a "they," a they who are, as Bambara writes, "ready to speak the unpronounceable. On they stand with no luggage and no maps and ready to go anywhere in the universe together on just sheer holy boldness" (265). The she who is this they is her own enough and accepts the challenge of living offered in this model: a challenge to living (as) / loving oneself (an/other), the beauty and consequence of rightful living. This commitment to (un)becoming is the subject's only promise.

| | An Indisputable |
| Chapter 4 | Memory of Blackness |

I N A VILLAGE of West Africa is a community of people whose successes, materially and spiritually, depend on their faith in the prayer that the community elder, an aging woman, performs once a year. When this elder passes on, a new elder is chosen and celebrated and now has responsibility for the village prayer. This new elder remembers part of the prayer ritual well, for, though the ritual is never fully disclosed to anyone other than the one performing it, the elements are widely, if not well, known—there is a chant, a place, and a time. He can only recall the time and the place; whatever traces of the chant were there are now gone. No one else in the community has recall of the chant either; they only remember that there used to be a chant.

After some consideration and much communal discussion (and also because the time of prayer is nearing), the elder decides that he will, at said time, go to the praying place on the east side of the mountain; he hopes that this act, though flawed, will bring forth prosperity as in the past. And it does— the community continues to thrive as it had before: children are born and loved; young people are nurtured and ritualized into adult responsibility; adults work, laugh, struggle; and the elders are beheld. Crops grow, weather is weather, and spirits continue to flourish.

When this elder passes on, his successor faces a dilemma similar to the one he had faced, although few remember the repeated situation: while she can remember the time for prayer, she cannot recall the exact place (to say nothing of the long unremembered chant). As before, the community gathers, trying to piece together just where that beloved place was—the mountain's top? Or maybe its base? Or was it near the river? These places, though all lovely in their own ways, fail to trigger the recall that the group is searching for.

And, as before, the elder makes a decision after the community's extensive consideration: she chooses to mark the praying time right where she is at that moment, hoping that this act will be enough.

It is, and the community thrives once again as it had before and in new ways, as communities do when they become older.

When this elder passes, the new prayer man, along with the people of the community, cannot recall anything of the praying ceremony. Many years have passed, and pieces of things slip off, fade away. What they do remember, and remember quite vividly, is that there once *was* a chant, a place, and a time for prayer; they remember this bit with brilliant faith.

This memory and its faith were all they needed to enact the power of the prayer. To this day their community continues to thrive.

THIS NARRATIVE IS my retelling of a folk story I have heard in various contexts. My memory of the story is somewhat imprecise and inexact and hence is a poignant metaphor for my topic at hand. I do not intend to engage the story fully but, instead, want the story's presence to evoke and linger, to manifest as a literal embodiment of the (chapter's) subject. Think, then, of memory as the body of a woman and her contested claims to subjecthood, similar to the pronouncement that Guyanese poet Grace Nichols makes with her title "I is a long memoried woman." Here the subject at once is vagaried and concretized, and the "I" is both a memory and a female body. It seems reasonable, even self-evident, to assert the relationship between subjectivity and memory, to propose that a subject arrives in memory's trace and fade. But what about femaleness; why a woman? How does the body memory become or be christened "she"?

In this chapter I want to argue that memory is fashioned and imagined in corporeal terms; that is, memory is either a body in full—a literal, material corpus—or is a central attribute of a body, of how a body is constructed, engaged, and identified. As a corporeality, memory not only figures as a psychic component of identity but also is a literal other, an entity whose character and fleshy constitution informs subjectivity. Corporealized memory is a stunning contradiction: on one hand, it is an undeniable almost essentialized girlfriend whose presence demands attention and characterizes definitive articulations of Black female experience; on the other, its body is *unreliable*, a shifting corpus that makes subjective its own essence. In this way memory is at once both an indisputable and controvertible manifestation of Black female subjectivity—it is an essentialism whose integrity is its pervasiveness but also its variability. Memory, I will argue, is a Black female cultural body, a product and process that everyone forms a relationship with, an omnipresent and illusionary girlfriend.[1]

"There is no Deed but Memory"

This citation from the close of W. E. B. Du Bois's *Autobiography* suggests that memory might be the most highly appraised conceit of Black cultural discourse (443). Such status arguably accrues from the potential that recovery holds to counter the legacy of erasure, the loss and losing that is colonial history. In most Black contexts memory is a political practice linked with consciousness and decolonization, its urgency effectively summarized in the South African Freedom Charter's proclamation that "ours is also a struggle of memory against forgetting." This, then, is memory's Black subjectivity: it is an essential and defining corpus, a quintessential characteristic of personal but especially collective identity.[2]

Although the term *memory* is most commonly used as a noun to indicate an object, a thought, an image, or an expression, it always implicates the action of remembering, the verb, the process that produces but also depends on the memoried thing. The negotiation between product-memory and process-memory is especially important to Black culture, as Genevieve Fabre and Robert O'Meally argue in *History and Memory in African-American Culture*. Fabre and O'Meally suggest that memory is a volatility, a series of expressed and sometimes conflicting narratives that gain status through acceptance and refutation, through timing and personality, and under the influence of political and social needs determined by the pulse of cultural centers. Their argument makes notable use to the phrase *lieux de mémoire* from philosopher Pierre Nora, which translates as "sites of memory." Such sites, Nora argues, exist "where memory crystallizes and secretes itself at a particular historical moment, a turning point where consciousness of a break with the past is bound up with the sense that memory has been torn—but torn in such a way as to pose the problem of the embodiment of memory in certain sites where a sense of historical continuity persists" (cited in Fabre and O'Meally 7). For Fabre and O'Meally these tenuous yet articulate sites are themselves memory as a process, a dynamic location of collective and individual knowledge constantly refiguring, secreting and tearing.

These sites of memory are described as having corporeal qualities (for example, Nora's use of the word *embodiment*) and exhibit characteristics similar to Elizabeth Grosz's theorizations of the human body. In both *Volatile Bodies: Toward a Corporeal Feminism* and *Space, Time and Perversion* Grosz asserts that the body is not a material whole but, instead, exists as a series of surfaces that are not the erotogenic zones mapped and privileged by psychoanalytic imagination but, instead, are zones marked by levels of intensity and whose fluctuation disrupts the perceived hierarchy of a fully functional organic body. Grosz further argues that these surfaces are in fact bodies themselves, and as such they represent a multiplicity that irreverently contests the preeminent psychoanalytic notion of the body as (static and) subject to the psyche's manipulation. In making these claims, Grosz foregrounds particular attributes of these corporeal surfaces: they are "not inert; they function interactively and productively. They act and react. They generate what is new, surprising, unpredictable. . . . bodies . . . always extend the frameworks which attempt to contain them, [and] seep beyond their domains of control" (*Volatile* xi). These bodies, both as particle and collective, are volatile, which is the core of her thesis: "that human bodies have irreducible neurophysiological and psychological dimensions whose relations remain unknown and that human bodies have the wonderful ability, while striving for integration and cohesion, organic and psychic wholeness, to also provide for and indeed produce fragmentations, fracturings, dislocations that orient bodies and body parts toward other bodies and body parts" (13). Grosz's formulation of body volatility asserts that the body is not a whole but, instead, a series of surfaces or textures; therefore, corporealization is not attributed only to bodies in full but also to surfaces that manifest and "act" like bodies. Further, she asserts that bodies act in accordance to and in response to something other than order, even as they are, in some ways, highly ordered.[3]

Grosz's arguments not only provide a doorway through which I can assert memory's corporeality—its (em)bodiedness that is both surfeit and deficit, sly, seductive, and charismatic—but also its feminine character especially in her engagement of the Cartesian dichotomization and hierarchization of body and mind, a paradigm that leaves the body separate from and inferior to the mind as the female is to the male. The scope of the Cartesian slight to the body even extends to the binary of memory and history, the former being of inferior rank and therefore a subject of corporeality.[4] In a less academic sense memory in Black cultural lore is at least androgynous and often is the domain of the female. My intent here is not to invigorate further this gendered binary that my early chapters have sought to disturb; instead, I want to explore and wonder on what the representation of memory as a (feminine) corporeality means to Black culture and specifically to questions of subjectivity. If Black memory, then, is a Groszian volatility—an attribute of a body that can also inhabit and act upon a body and which is also potentially a fleshy entity of its own—what is its impact on the consideration of Black selfhood?

The narrativization of Black corporeal memory is nowhere else more evident than in Toni Morrison's novel *Beloved*. The character Beloved is a literal manifestation of memory as body, and her fleshly makeup is sprawling, inconsistent, and indelible. Beloved's body is her own but also is a collective of memories and dead bodies that emerge from the Middle Passage; she is specific and global, full bodied and lim(b)inal, alive but also deadened and awaiting engagement. Beloved's corporeal volatility manifests in two contradictory qualities: on one hand, she lives and imposes her excessive body upon the world, an insatiable and indominatable surface that has and exhibits a center (her excess is her center); on another, she feels centerless and fears her own disintegration as she clamors for Sethe against self-dissolution. For me the key question of *Beloved*/Beloved is of possession; that is, who possesses, or can possess, Beloved or who possesses, can possess, the body memory. With this question is the shifting denotation of the word *possess* and its varying degrees of totality (as well as its impossibility): Beloved has been possessed (or owned) as a slave; possesses (haunts) the characters of the novel; and is possessed by (haunted but also claimed) other characters in the novel. Beloved's movement between being possessed and possessing represents different states of (un)free, and she is literally self-possessed, overwhelmed by her own unforgiving collectivity, which often interferes with her desire to be singularly Sethe's daughter.[5] She is, as a text, ultimately unmarkable, for, though she sometimes imitates singularity and self-containedness, her constitution and character are inflected by the other bodies she interacts with and/or inhabits.

Beloved is an unflappable presence (even in absence), a palpable flesh to be/held and behold. She is undeniable. But as much as she exhibits memory's precision and irrepressibility, she also enunciates its ambiguity and fluency. She is without clear referent, and, like the opening story of this chapter, she fades and evaporates as much as she crystallizes and endures. These competing characteristics constitute Beloved's identity, her Black and female *body*, and the indelibility and vagary of her flesh is the essential identity that can only be articulated through memory. Morrison's novel theorizes memory not only as an embodiment but as a *Black* and *female* body with sisterly impulses. And, even in its unreliability, this body, memory, is the closest thing Black people have to an essence—the site that may concede a livable and possible subjecthood.

What Morrison's narrative architecture offers is a vast and contradictory set of characteristics that define and exceptionalize memory, that prove and unsettle its essentiality, that help to flesh out the nature of memory's corporeality as well as its subjectivity. For example, well before Beloved arrives in flesh, Sethe's caution to Denver about the past identifies memory as a live and rootless/ruthless body:

I was talking about time. It's so hard for me to believe in it. Some things go. Pass on. Some things just stay. I used to think it was my rememory. You know. Some things you forget. Other things you never do. But it's not. Place, places are still there. If a house burns down, it's gone, but the place—the picture of it—stays, and not just in my rememory, but out there, in the world. What I remember is a picture floating around out there outside my head. I mean, even if I don't think it, even if I die, the picture of what I did, or knew, or saw is still out there. Right in the place where it happened. (35)

Sethe's floating "thought picture" is a surface that embodies past places and experiences, and her use of *still* is not intended to suggest a passive body; instead, the presence of the memory, its stillness (as in *always*),[6] is its volatility. Rather than fading away and becoming mute, Sethe's thought picture is dangerous because it has a will and life of its own. This danger intrigues the young Denver, who asks "Can other people see it?": "Oh, yes. Oh, yes, yes, yes. Someday you be walking down the road and you hear something or see something going on. So clear. And you think it's you thinking it up. A thought picture. But no. It's when you bump into a rememory that belongs to somebody else" (36). The rememory is palpable and living and in fact can "belong" to someone else. Memory is not restricted to a particular place, person, or history; as an embodied surface, memory is someone else's, yours, not yours, not theirs—it is irreverent, willful, and without referent; colloquially, it has a mind of its own.[7]

Evident in Sethe's admonition to Denver is the suggestion that memory is not merely an attribute or character of her self but also exists as independently as a wicked body. In an earlier conversation both Sethe and Baby Suggs affirm memory's self-sustenance:

"We could move," she [Sethe] suggested once to her mother-in-law.

"What'd be the point?" asked Baby Suggs. "Not a house in the country ain't packed to its rafters with some dead Negro's grief. We lucky this ghost is a baby. My husband's spirits was to come back in here? or yours? Don't talk to me. You lucky. You got three left. Three pulling at your skirts and just one raising hell from the other side. Be thankful, why don't you? I had eight. Every one of them gone away from me. Four taken, four chased, and all, I expect, worry somebody's house into evil." Baby Suggs rubbed her eyebrows. "My first-born. All I can remember of her is how she loved the burned bottom of bread. Can you beat that? Eight children and that's all I remember."

"That's all you let yourself remember," Sethe had told her. (5)

The conversation shifts from the presence of a ghost body, to the loss of bodies, to the absence of memories, such that all three subjects become conflated and the very body of memory is christened as the body of the dead. But memory is itself not dead, nor merely representative of the dead and missing; in fact, memory's volatility is in its ability to destabilize death's certainty with its own (un)certainty, as is the case when Paul D arrives, and Sethe tells him that she thinks Halle is dead: "It's not being sure that keeps him alive," she says (8). Her expression exacts a congruent, if not equal, relationship between Halle's body and memory's bodiness.

Memory's corporeality is full-bodied for sure, but it is also piecemeal, multiple, like a scar—a literal body part, or part of a body; immaterial even, acting as a sensation or psychic sensibility. Morrison offers an evocative example of memory's varying corporealizations when Sethe, sitting in the Clearing, desperately calls out to a now dead Baby Suggs for peace and guidance: "Just the fingers, she thought. Just let me feel your fingers again on the back of my neck and I will lay it all down, make a way out of this no way. Sethe bowed her head and sure enough—they were there. Lighter now, no more than strokes of bird feather, but unmistakably caressing fingers. She had to relax a bit to let them do their work, so light was the touch, childlike almost, more finger kiss than kneading. . . . Baby Suggs' long distance love" (95). In this moment two memories are embodied in the fingers that Sethe feels: there is Sethe's own (invoked) memory of Baby Suggs's loving massage; and there is Beloved, whose fingers caress Sethe's neck and who possesses an intent different from Sethe's will. These two bodies of memory intersect and (e)merge as one palpable memory experience, and in this case memory is and generates ambiguity but also defies and characterizes possession.

In the theorization of corporeality afforded by Morrison's novel, memory is a keen and complicated mediation of chaos and unpredictability, a denial of singular reference. Memory here has many qualities. For example, it possesses and exhibits energy, evidenced in the heat and boisterousness that serenade Beloved's arrival at the carnival: abundant laughter and flirtation and pungent, dead roses that cause dizziness and thirst—a literal system of thermodynamics.[8] Memory also appears as a vibration or tremor, like Paul D's memory that both makes his body tremble and is a body that trembles: "Out of . . . Mister's sight . . . Paul D began to tremble. Not all at once and not so anyone could tell. . . . It began inside. A flutter of a kind, in the chest, then the shoulder blades. It felt like rippling—gentle at first and then wild. . . . Sometimes . . . in his leg. Then again it moved to the base of his spine. By the time they unhitched him from the wagon and he saw nothing but dogs and two shacks in a world of sizzling grass, the roiling blood was shaking him to and fro" (106–107). And, still, memory is a rumbling system of sound, like the click Sethe hears when she recognizes the song that Beloved is singing, which is the one she, Sethe, invented, or the roaring of the voices Stamp hears in 124 (175, 181). But, more than a system of movement, sound, or heat, memory is a sense, a mode of perception, like the hearing Denver temporarily loses in her attempt to ignore Nelson Lord's questions about what has happened and how much Denver can, or will, remember.

Memory, this thrilling Black female body: it impairs and is susceptible to impairment. Is past and present and even future. Dead and alive and ailing. Material, partial and immaterial. Elusive and allusive.[9] Is stable and collapses; hard to trust and impossible to ignore. Fully alive but not always engaged and hence can be, or appear, deadened. Improvisational. Essential.

Morrison's novel highlights the individual and collective tension of memory within the context of colonization. As the body memory, Beloved is possession and dispossession; she is the need for claim, the experience of its opposite, and the impossibility of desiring or making claim. She is a contradiction, an abyss of sorts, because who she is, and the value she bears, is both infinite and finite.[10] Her body is a Black female symbolic text(uality), and her contradictions, memory's contradictions, are the living (in)consistencies of Black subjectivity.

THESE CONTRADICTIONS *embody* memory, at once characterizing how memory works and also imbuing and endowing memory with a dynamic lifelikeness. The corporeality of memory evident in Morrison's novel echoes Paule Marshall's *Praisesong for the Widow,* a novel whose protagonist, Avatara, in name and in behavior, is an incarnation of what has passed before her.[11] On a leisure-filled Caribbean cruise, Avey is compelled to reencounter herself and her past through two dreams, the first of which is of her Aunt Cuney, who had helped to raise her in South Carolina. In the dream Aunt Cuney and Avey fight each other as the former tries to nudge Avey out of her forgetfulness. The fight is so real that "all during the [next] day, in the dim rear of her mind, she [Avey] had sensed her great-aunt still struggling to haul her off up the road. Even now her left wrist retained something of the pressure of the old woman's iron grip" (47). Avey's memory of Aunt Cuney manifests as a (dream) body, feisty and combative, articulate and self-contained. But it is also noteworthy that Avey's memory imprints her own body, another manifestation of memory as corporeality. Challenged by this encounter, Avey's leisure gives way to sustained states of disorientation—motion sickness, psychic unsettling, emotional confusion—states that mimic the eruptive volatility of memory's body. She eventually settles into being both unsettled and unsettling as she locates subjectivity not as a modern-day Black woman but as a shifting composite of a Blackness past. This, then, is Avey's and Black memory's changing same—the essence that is hardly an institution, the reliable that is barely accountable.

As is the case in Avey's tussle with Aunt Cuney, memory's body materializes as the sisterly an/other to be negotiated and embraced, a significant texture in the consideration of subjectivity. As a girlfriend an/other, memory is unreliable and selfish and cannot be possessed; still, memory has to be claimed, embraced as mine, not-mine. When Denver recognizes Beloved as her sister, she makes an attempt to own Beloved for herself, to cuddle Beloved as the body that would field her fear of Sethe. But Beloved is neither Denver nor *Denver's*, and, when the two are in the shed looking for cider, Beloved disappears from Denver's attempt to hold onto her. Denver, who herself is made up of memory,[12] experiences the loss of memory (Beloved) as a dissolution of her own body: "[Denver] can feel her thickness thinning, dissolving into nothing. She grabs the hair at her temples to get enough to uproot it and halt the melting for a while" (123). Her unrequited desire and coveting reveals that memory cannot be placed or held at command. Memory cannot provide certainty, and, though Denver has to claim Beloved, she also has to become her own (un)certain.

The process of engaging memory as a body is an oscillation between a coupling with memory ("us") and a recognition of the "me" that Sethe's last words in the novel echo; that is, a subject has to engage memory toward finding the me-ness of her own relationship to memory, the *memory* of her own body. "She mine, she mine," these women of 124 Bluestone sing, each clinging to and claiming a she, a lost sister, a memoried body that will overwhelm their own body but will not, cannot, satisfy the need for this "she." Sethe, Denver, and Beloved each must recognize her own body memory, must be content to grapple with her own unclaimed volatilities.

Memory is a Black woman's an/other, the bodied subject whose presence is an indispensable and uneasy girlfriend.[13] This uneasiness is developed in Marshall's *Praisesong,* in which a nameless character becomes a symbol of all the hard-living Black women of Halsey Street, an urban area where Avey and Jay lived before becoming more economically solvent. This woman is Avey's other in the most literal sense—she is the one who Avey sometimes made fun of and always wanted *not* to be like. Avey and Jay would listen to this woman arguing with her husband across the way, her despair and hopelessness palpable yet distant. But the distance was not nearly as great as Avey imagined, and the relationship between her and this other woman was much closer than she wanted to accept:

> Some Saturdays the woman . . . made the five-story leap to the
> hallway bedroom to stand over Avey—or so she [Avey] felt at times.

Lying there next to Jay, listening to the voices from below, she would sense the woman's enraged presence on her side of the bed; would feel her accusing eyes in the darkness. Yeah, they saw, the eyes said, the way she always quickened her step when passing the house. . . . She didn't want anything to do with her kind.

Standing over her, the woman also envied her . . .

Then abruptly, . . . her anger would vanish and, bending close to Avey, tears in her eyes, she would quietly beg her not to turn her back on them, not to forget [them]. (108–109)

This woman, who would "plead with her to be remembered" (141), is Avey's sister-memory: she is Avey, Avey's fears, Avey's liberation; her past, her possible future, and—in the ways that Avey herself is trapped by imperatives of economic success—her present, for both characters are Black and female and are subject to the pulses of marriage. Although they are both others in the greater social narrative, they are not (yet) others for each other. This woman is memory, and she wants to be engaged, to be held, to be danced with; she, like Beloved, is raging, petulant, haunting.

In the context of girlfriend subjecthood, memory is an exploration of the other body toward self-revelation. The relevance of Avey's relationship with memory (the Halsey Street woman) becomes apparent as she is on a boat toward Carriacou and experiences seasickness and a body awakening: "as her mind came unburdened she began to float down through the gaping hole, floating, looking, searching for whatever memories were to be found there. While her body remained anchored between the old women who were one and the same with the presiding mothers of Mount Olivet in their pews up front, her other self floated down" (197). This other self of Avey's who floats down is arguably the woman from Halsey Street, and it is toward a relationship with this woman (memory) that Avey moves. Avey's journey is also a journey toward memory, toward having a self-defined relationship with memory.

Considering memory's unreliability and especially its political urgency, achieving self-determinedness is challenging. In the novel's closing sequence Avey is watching the Out-Islanders perform the "Beg Pardon," a dance that is (a) memory in motion, for, as their bodies "memory" the dance, the dance itself becomes a corporealized memory, an entity of its own that can be remembered, encountered, engaged.[14] Movement, memories, and bodies all convene and converge, creating "the *essence* of something rather than the thing itself. . . . All that was left were a few names of what they called nations which they could no longer even pronounce properly, the fragments of a dozen or so songs, the shadowy forms of long-ago dances and rum kegs for drums. The bare bones. The burnt-out ends" (240). The description here of fragments,

bones, and burned-out things points attention to the piecemeal and irreverent nature of memory as well as its undeniable presence. Like the memory of
the chant, place, and time in the opening of this chapter, memory scraps are
powerful and prayerful bodies that command attention, bodies that, because
they are both volatile *and* representative, evoke a definiteness that is not so definite, an essential quality that is not quite essentialist. This dance is reflective of
the political urgency and necessity of memory in self-decolonization.[15] Lebert
Joseph, who becomes Avey's spirit guide while she is in Grenada and Carriacou,
voices this imperative in his exuberance as he explains that the dance is about
the "Long-time People. Each year this time they does look for us to come and
give them remembrance." He warns, "You best remember them! . . . If not
they'll get vex and cause you nothing but trouble" (165). Memory here embodies the ancestors, and the warning is for those "people who can't call their
nation," a warning against forgetting (175).

But the idea of forgetting is yet another contradiction in theorizing
memory precisely because forgetting *is* an act of memory as well as memory's
opposite. Forgetting is a memory body and anti-body and reveals memory as
a quintessential girlfriend whose perpetuity permits its being sustained by that
which it is not, by that which seeks its undoing. The imperative is voiced but
is not a mandate; the urgency is not execution. All forgetting is not the same:
Avey's attempt to forget the Halsey Street woman is appraised differently than
the Out-Islanders' disregard of Avey's clothes and luggage as markers of her
foreignness and well-to-do status (176). This contradiction, in which the latter forgetting counters colonization and the former articulates its pinnacle,
crystallizes memory's ambiguity, and suggests that the valence memory carries
is determined by a subject's agenda, by her own personal relationship to the
project of memory. More clearly, the corpo*realization* of memory demands that
memory's body be realized, or put into a practice of selfhood. And this practice of selfhood is inevitably in tension with the communal determination of
just what is appropriate for self.

Memory as individually imagined or collectively engaged is not exclusively
liberating and in fact can colonize, as Beloved does to Sethe and Denver as
well as herself.[16] Although colonization interferes with memory, it does not
as much prevent memory as it uses memory to reinvent narratives (memories) that colonized subjects accept, revise, remember, and pass on. That
memory sometimes works against itself is one of the ways that it can colonize
a subject, can interfere with a subject's process of selfhood. This clash between
memory and its counter (which is also *named* memory) is evoked in a short
vignette that Ama Ata Aidoo presents at the opening of the third chapter of
Our Sister Killjoy:

Said an anxious Afro-American student to a visiting African professor, "Sir, please tell me: is Egypt in Africa?"

"Certainly," replied the professor.

"I mean Sir, I don't mean to kind of harass you or anything," pressed the student, "but did the Egyptians who built the pyramids, you know, the Pharaohs and all, were they African?"

"My dear young man," said the visiting professor, "to give you the decent answer your anxiety demands, I would have to tell you a detailed history of the African continent. And to do that, I shall have to speak every day, for at least three thousand years. And I don't mean to be rude to you or anything, but who has that kind of time?" (111)

The student's anxiety is informed by narratives of African inferiority; the professor's curtness by the daunting task of using memory to undo memory. The professor recognizes that the false memories the young student has been raised on represent both the absence and presence of information, memories that are both unmemory and master memory; he cannot possibly correct either the student's memories or process of memory(ing). That is the student's own work to do.

Memory as a complication is a colonial legacy. For most Black people in the Diaspora, especially those living in the United States, colonialism and slavery have been so extensive and effective that memory is often a matter of convenience. That is, who remembers what, and for what purpose, shifts, becomes unreliable, and is often engaged for the achievement of partialized agendas. Since much of what is our memory inheritance is the burned edges of things, the act of memory is a profound unsettling, as profound a transformation as anything human flesh experiences. And, faced with that prospect, most people choose memory-lite: oppressed subjects sighing about the "GOOD OLD DAYS / BEFORE INDEPENDENCE" (*Killjoy* 56), which affirms that the enslaved (recent) past was a better present and future; or thinking up pristine images of a life before colonization, images that enunciate stifling nostalgia: Sethe resolved to quiet acceptance of a ghost, Denver determined to stay inside, both convinced that the little that is there, the fragments and ashes, are not enough to make a full story, not enough a body with which to dance that awful, awesome dance of subjecthood. But, if a little crawling baby girl, or an across-the-street woman is any evidence, memory cannot be killed, eliminated, or even disregarded, and its body is always capable of engagement. Memory for Black people is an immortal dangerous body, a spirit that potentially passes from person to person.[17] The work of self-decolonization, which is also the work to articulate and define a relationship with memory, necessarily involves retelling and inventing stories to counter the oppressor but also presupposes a more intimate relationship to memory, one that acknowledges a communal agenda but remains entangled in memory as a selffull enterprise of one's subjectivity.

Theorizing memory as a body makes possible an essentialism that opens up to multiplicity and selffullness: everyone has memory, has a memory practice; and memory crystallizes what is core, essential, with an untempered instability. Corporealized memory both reveals the living inconsistencies of Blackness as well as the indelibility of the Black corpus.

Memory as a Black and female body is essential, is muse, artist and art, and must be engaged toward the achievement of a self-defined voice, toward the encounter of the memory of one's own body—the girlfriend memory.[18]

Chapter 5	The Practice of a Memory Body

IF MEMORY IS corporealized, then the process of coming to (a relationship with) memory is an ontological process, a process of becoming and being, a practice. As an ontology, the practice of memory gives name and texture to a subjectivity that is ultimately unnameable and many-textured; that is, memory is the performance of a selfness that cannot possibly exist but which must exist, a yield that generates from and folds in on itself. In this chapter I want to consider how memory's ontology is represented in two permutations of self: voice as the representation of an individual achievement of memory, the accumulation of self-stories that compete, contend, and coalesce with other stories and which help to pronounce the selfhood of a one; and home as the collective voice, the expression of a group's stories of selfness. Of course, the division between individuality and collectivity is somewhat fallacious though, I think, still useful in establishing a relationship between corporealized memory, voice, and home as well as in asserting, as I am, a Black female–centered nationalism: not the superficial celebratory odes to the "motherland" or the masculinist pedestalizing of women that so often populates nation-discourse; instead, a conceptualization of collectivity that locates the agency of the nation through its feminine principles (voice, home), that considers nation as an unbecoming parallel to girlfriend subjecthood. This is a collectivity that is overwhelmed by the aesthetics of the one. My arch argument here is that, if memory is an esteemed conceit in Black identity, then its corporeal femininity determinedly transforms how nation is articulated and what nation means . . . or whose body becomes nation and how.

It is story that propels memory, voice, home; stories, these bits of memories corporealized—narrative of, as well as that is held by, an arm's strength, a back's break, a smile's deviousness; the invention of a reason for the bounty of a season. This is memory: the making and telling of stories that contend and compete with other stories, each clinging to and resisting the body of its other, striving for supremacy when, in fact, supremacy is impossible. A fanciful dance as each story's existence depends upon its other, its refutation; its vitality is its frailty, a tenuous interdependency that reassures us that "all stories are true."[1] The tension of storytelling, then, is a girlfriend tension, one somewhat imprecise and unreliable and yet potentially transformative. The value of the story, or even of its act of telling, is never more than its potential to hurt, to cause disarray. The necessary ambivalence.[2]

Both Warner-Vieyra's *Juletane* and Walker's *Color Purple* enunciate a relationship between a narrative body (story), memory, and voice, evidenced in Juletane's diary and Celie's letters. Similarly, in Morrison's *Beloved* the title character is a memory body, but she is also the narrative of and a voice for the disremembered and dead of the Middle Passage. She, Beloved, is a story composite, and the multiple and unfounded stories *about* her as well as those that *constitute* her slip and shift as they materialize. After the women have rescued Sethe, Paul D is trying to

> make sense out of the stories he had been hearing: whiteman came to
> take Denver to work and Sethe cut him. Baby ghost came back evil
> and sent Sethe out to get the man who kept her from hanging. One
> point of agreement is: first they saw it and then they didn't. When they
> got Sethe down on the ground and the ice pick out of her hands and
> looked back to the house, it was gone. Later, a little boy put it out how
> he had been looking for bait back of 124, down by the stream, and
> saw, cutting through the woods, a naked woman with fish for hair. (267)

It is not verity but simply engagement that makes story transformative, and, as each character struggles to remember, her sense of self is strengthened, clarified, and complicated. The story is a potent repeating body, a remnant that fortifies like the small piecemealed narrative about a time, a chant, a place and a people.

Contesting and engaging memory's body confuses the boundary between individual and collective, for memory is simultaneously private and public.[3] In the epigraph of *Beloved,* taken from the Bible's Book of Romans, the power of individual memory collectively to re-body a group is announced:

> I will call them my people,
> Which were not my people;

And her beloved,
Which was not beloved.

The corrective memorying signaled here is both an attempt at reclamation and redefinition: to call "her beloved, / Which was not beloved" is an act of renaming as the memory body that is claimed as the beloved is rescripted, reimagined, and reexperienced as a body constitutionally different than it was some time before. This difference characterized by the "not-beloved" becoming the "beloved"—by the conflation of the pronouns *I, them, her*—is the complication and whimsy of memory and story, their unpredictability. Even if one appraises the revision positively, the power of story to counter story as well as literally to change the essence of an/other (story), is unsettling, disconcerting, especially if verity and stability are expected. At the novel's end, when the women come to save Sethe, they do so because their meanness toward her has eased and because, in remembering, they *become* different people, something other (or more) than victims of Sethe's arrogance and bounty. The exorcism that happens is as much of their bodies as it is an assault on Sethe's psyche. The evidence is in how they re-member Sethe and in turn themselves: "All of them knew her [Denver's] grandmother and some had even danced with her in the Clearing. Others remembered the days when 124 was a way station, the place they assembled to catch news, taste oxtail soup, leave their children, cut out a skirt. One remembered tonic. . . . One showed . . . the border of a pillowslip . . . French-knotted in Baby Suggs' kitchen. . . . They remembered the party. . . . One said she wrapped Denver" (249). Their collective memorying consists of small intimate stories, bodies they had dismissed and discarded that they now gather in their Sethe-mosaic. It is a revision full of competing narratives, all of which are true.

Achieved through the invention and reclamation of stories and bodies, memory's voice always points attention to the self to be/hold. It is an intricate voice, one that is part process and part product, one that is but also has a voice, that becomes a subject's voice as well as is the subject of voice. A narrative example might help clarify the multiplicity I am trying to represent here: the character Beloved is a body that reminds Sethe and others of a particular past and, as such, is literally a corporeal voice, an aural script. But Beloved also has a voice of her own, one scratchy and new and hardly used. Further, Sethe's engagement of Beloved is also Sethe's practice of her voice, her self-expression against eighteen years of silence about the shed and its haunting. Sethe's relationship to her own voice—which she makes an initial step toward when she says at the story's end, "Me?" and then, as if to hear her own voice again, as if in surprise at its presence and its ability to mouth the word she has long given up on, she repeats, "Me?"—coincides with her ability to talk about Beloved as subject; her ability to move from "I don't have to explain none of it" (to Beloved but especially to Paul D or Mr. Sawyer, who wants to chastise her when she is late for work) to admitting that she has been colonized and decentered by her (absence of) voice. Sethe is unable to speak Beloved's name because she would also have to recognize who Beloved is (not) as well as recognize her own subjecthood, a corpo-realization that would send Beloved away. Sethe cannot even call Beloved "beloved" because she has given up her own body to (the) Beloved and has nowhere to call from. Hence, her ultimate utterance is both an act of coming to voice that realizes her body and an articulation of voice that uses her newly realized body.

Morrison's profound irony—that voice colonizes and silences—is a commentary on the complicated business of memory that is too often altogether simplified in nationalist agendas; further, Morrison is disturbing the easy use of voice as a feminine trope. The linguistic malleability of the word *beloved* is similar to the shifting character of memory's voice: *beloved* can be an adjective (relational, object status), a noun (subject), or, when split into *be loved*, as it appears in the novel's coda, an imperative (radical verb). Each part of speech that B/beloved can become bears a different relationship to subjectivity, agency, and voice, and yet all three forms are different and necessary narrative bodies of memory. Voice, like memory, is a practice, a thing to be always achieving, as represented in the phrase "I hear where you are coming from, as if the voice itself were a traveler, arriving from a distant place. Which it would be, which it is."[4] This voice, like (its) memory, is a roaming textuality, existing within and beyond time and place, uncommitted.

The essential action of this memory practice is repetition, the reengagement of the memory body that yields a notable difference between that body and the one that precedes or succeeds it. Memory is ritual, and, though the difference between one body and its repetition is the essential disposition of memory, the space between the two bodies often appears unremarkable, if it exists at all. This false sameness perpetrates a sense of stability and facilitates the intimation that memory is either dead and finished or that the practice of memorying is facile, one body undynamically exchanged for its exact other. This deadness is evident in Sethe's struggle with embracing her subjectivity as she cautions Denver about the power of rememory, opening her comments with a sad and almost acquiescent tone: "It's so hard for me to believe in it," she says of time, yet Sethe does not want to give up on time. She wants to be able to move forth, to help her brain find other things to fix on. But her experience tells her that this will not happen, that nothing, especially as related to her, passes on. Instead, the memories of her world are unchanged and terror-ful, no different than when they first occurred; it is this unchanging presence (the perceived absence of difference) that makes necessary her admonition to Denver: "You can't never go there" (36). Sethe is trying to find some freedom from memory, for she has long given up on the freedom that might be found *in* memory.[5]

Memory can close down time and space, enacting a stillness that creates claustrophobia, cuts off breath, and sets bodies to atrophy. Memory can be a small place, to echo the title of Jamaica Kincaid's essay on the colonization of tourism in Antigua, a work that is useful to my thinking about this particular aspect of memory: "In a small place," Kincaid writes,

> people cultivate small events. The small event is isolated, blown up, turned over and over, and then absorbed into the everyday, so that at any moment it can and will roll off the inhabitants of the small place's tongue. For the people in a small place, every event is a domestic event; the people in a small place cannot see themselves in a larger picture, they cannot see that they might be part of a chain of something, anything. The people in a small place see the event in the distance heading directly towards them and they say "I see the thing and it is heading towards me." The people in a small place then experience the event as if it were sitting on top of their heads, their shoulders, and it weighs them down, this enormous burden that is the event, so that they cannot breathe properly and they cannot think properly and they say, "This thing that was only coming towards me is now on top of me," and they live like that, until eventually they absorb the event and it becomes a part of them, a part of who and what they really are, and they are complete in that way until another event comes along and the process begins again. (*Small Place* 52–53)

In places under colonization people cultivate a quiescent relationship to their world. Events are "turned over and over," corporealized as fixed memories that are fabric and fiber of communal identity. These people cannot escape the events, not only because the events themselves reoccur but also because the events are engaged as calcified, unchanging memory bodies. There is no difference between one event and an/other, whether that other event is literally a new event, or a reinvention of the previous one; there is no difference and, hence, no way to live the event except to surrender to it. The event is a body with an imminent and single-minded will to colonize, a body that is not only omnipotent and omnipresent but also a monopoly: the only event. The intensity of this obsessive characterization matches Sethe's experiences described in *Beloved*.

The memory that Kincaid describes is tireless and tiring; it is sprawling and inexact yet precise in its impact. It overwhelms and colonizes, leaving a

body unable to experience anything else. "The people in a small place cannot give an exact account, a complete account, of themselves," Kincaid says,
because they have lost (the ability to sense) themselves in relation to anything other than the event (53). Kincaid's insight here further elucidates Sethe's
evocative *me* at the end of *Beloved*, for Sethe has been thoroughly possessed
by a memory body (Beloved) that gets angry "when Sethe did or thought anything that excluded herself" (100). Under the weight of Beloved's self-mono-
mania, Sethe gives up on memory, refusing to live outside of it and also refusing
to struggle with it. "Whatever is going on outside my door ain't for me" (183),
she proclaims upon recognizing Beloved as her dead daughter, adding later
that her work with memory is done ("I don't need to remember it" [184]).
Sethe works hard to unremember, a resounding choice that partially shuts
down her own agency (via memory) and also interferes with Beloved's. That
is, Beloved becomes haunted and impaired by Sethe's act of unmemory, an
act that limits the space Beloved has to roam and recreates the claustrophobic voyage of the Middle Passage. Sethe's unmemory, her colonizing and colonized memory, effectively condemns both her and Beloved to a small space.

Under colonization memory is a small place, a ritual of stifling. It takes
the form of a dark-skinned, shining eighteen-year-old Black girl; or a dream,
with inviting and dangerous gaps and lush colors; or a picture and its action
at a full stop; or nostalgia. It is a spell, a holding cell of the past and its bodies,
like a museum or a prison. It hungers and lingers like a ghost, laps and limns
breath. Memory subjects.

GAYL JONES'S second novel, *Eva's Man*, is a study that explores how the
achievement and engagement of memory becomes voice for a violated Black
woman.[6] The novel tells the story of Eva Medina, a forty-three-year-old Black
woman who drugs Davis Carter, a man she is living with, and dismembers his
penis with her mouth. To get to this climax, the story travels through a haunting and convoluted history of Eva's subjectivity determined and delimited by
sexual violence—her body reduced to its eroticized parts, renamed and usurped
by men. This is the small place Eva lives in, a world of dazzling stifle. When
Davis picks her up in a diner and sequesters her in his small apartment, refusing to let her leave or to comb her hair, she escapes in a way that is violent
but which hardly has the fanfare and arrogance often associated with violence.
It is not Eva's rage that is palpable in the novel; instead, it is a sense of claustrophobia, a closing down and in, that monopolizes the reader as the novel
re-stories the various attacks upon her body. These stories become strains of
Eva's blues song, her volatile, sad, and powerful first-person narration that is
an exquisite example of the relationship between memory and storytelling.

The story is about Eva, but it also *is* and is not Eva; the story is her sister, her other, the body with which Eva has to become intimate. Eva uses the story literally to re-corporealize her body, shielding herself from violation and inventing a self that is something other than partialized and trapped. The entire narrative is Eva's engagement of memory, told in past tense and written mostly as dialogue; hence, everything is a memory, a repetition, a precise and unreliable version of what has happened. No other truth is allowed prominence in the novel's donnée other than the indisputable truth of one Black woman's struggle with memory, a memory that is sometimes Eva's own therapy and salvation but which also mimics and fulfills the voyeuristic impulses of a society fascinated by her dismemberment of Davis and by her own suspended Black female body.

As the novel shifts between various stories of sex, girlhood, violence, and vulnerability, the variance between the stories is a source of unreliability but also empowerment. They articulate Eva as well as help her to develop a sense of how articulation works (and fails); they are Eva's voice as well as her consideration and achievement of voice. Eva learns early on that very few people (would) believe a woman about her experience of sexual violence. "I tell the psychiatrist what I remember. He tells me I do not know how to separate the imagined memories from the real ones," she tells us (10), one of many instances in which her memory has been rejected and reshaped by someone else's ideology: the psychiatrist's neat binary of real and imagined memories; her ex-husband James's elaborate fears and fantasies; her prison mate's desire to bed her down. So, Eva begins to lie outright, or at least to stop exerting effort against deception, and, instead, tells the story in the way that it comes to her: in mixed pieces with frequent revisions and retractions. The intensity of any one particular memory changes via its relationship to another memory, as evidenced in her brief relationship with James, who attacked her because she reminded him of a woman who refused his control. James describes this other woman as one who "didn't care one way or another. She never loved no man. Never did. Not one single day in her life. A woman that'll just fuck because it's there—cause he's got something down between his legs—a woman like that can't love a man" (162). Or, more precisely, a man cannot love that woman because he has on her no locus of control. James beats and rapes Eva because he resents this woman, wants to ensure the stability of Eva, but also because he imagines Eva to be this reckless woman. Eva remembers his violence imprecisely and with quick revisions: "He slapped me. . . . Naw, he didn't slap me, he pulled my dress up and got between my legs. . . . Naw, I'm lying. . . . *Naw I'm not lying*" (163). As a person in a small place, Eva, like Kincaid's Antiguans, is unable to make a singular and reliable account of herself, which makes sense because her selfhood is not singular or reliable. Furthermore, Eva's fluctuating verity is situated within a social context of Black people as liars and is especially informed by the archetypes of Black women's sexuality as whore, as Jezebel, as loose and lascivious, as sturdy and passionlessly passionate. These two master narratives about Black women mythologically interrupt the validity of Eva's experience and the integrity of her body; their mythology disturbs her girlhood and partializes her, offering her no access to legitimate sexual curiosity without inviting sexual violence.

But Eva's response to and within these mastering fictions also impedes the integrity of her (experiencing her) body, whatever integrity there is to be encountered: faced with so few viable options, Eva invents her own corporealized mythology to counterintuit the body she has and has socially inherited, composing herself as the Queen Bee and a host of other powerful women.[7] That Eva's self-fashioning is a corpus, at once about the body and a body itself, is evidenced in the legend of the Queen Bee, a real woman whose life is mythicized because she had sex with men without commitment, causing a heartbreak that led to her suitors' suicides. As the story goes, when the Queen Bee found a man that she really cared about, she killed herself to keep him from dying. It is clear that the Queen Bee is a prototypical rebellious woman, trying to control her own sexuality in a world where Black women's sexualities mostly possess violent currency, where their bodies are public domain, their pubic hair is "public hair," and there is no "first time" for a sexual experience but only an infinity of sexual violation.[8] The myth exploits and alternates the central role sex plays in women's subjectivities, but not to be missed is its sense of tragedy and, more important to me, its withholding: that the myth is less about reckless surrender than control, less about being possessed than possessing. Without disregarding the social politics that make such choices necessary—that, for example, make terms such as *being possessed* nearly impossible for Eva's character—I want also to highlight the complicated, tenuous, and flaw-full quality of the freedom that Eva is investing in.

Eva fantasizes herself as a cadre of powerful, defiant, and *sexually self-centered* first women, including Eve, Medusa, and the gypsy Medina, her grandmother; women who were without precedent in their communities. In the context of repeated violent imposition, Eva's identification with these women is an act of agency. More so, she does not merely identify as the Queen Bee but literally becomes the Queen Bee, with a significant difference: Eva does not kill herself for the man she loves but, instead, kills the man for the self she loves, or is trying to love.[9] She reinvents the Queen Bee but also reinvents herself as the Queen Bee, both of which are acts of narrative corporeal memory.

This revision is an attempt to disrupt the piecemeal violated body she was to inherit socially.

Eva's grand act of memory is mythmaking, the creation of a body via repetitious narration of herself as other mythical female bodies. Yet myth as a function of memory is also unreliable, and potentially colonizing to Eva, especially because memories compete with one another for validity and accuracy and because the violations Eva experiences are overwhelming, even triumphant. Eva's engagement of memory is complicated, for she is literally trying to unmemory violence and memory agency, with neither process being exclusive of the other. Her act of memory is multivalent and does not offer unfettered freedom. In one key example a young Eva is assaulted by Tyrone, her mother's youthful boyfriend. After placing her hand on his penis, he invokes memory through his questions, like an incantation:

> "You remember how it feel, don't you?"
> I said nothing. He said it real soft, almost in a whisper. Mama was in the kitchen and had the radio on.
> "You remember how it feel your hand down there, don't you? I know you remember it, cause I remember it." (33)

Tyrone uses memory for the purpose of advancing his assault and sears the image of this violation onto Eva's memory (body), exploiting and contributing to the myth that women like to be violated. Years later, when the psychiatrist comes to visit Eva in jail, his discursive subjectivity resonates with Eva's memory of (past) violence, evidenced in the language he uses in his line of questioning: "I want to help you, Eva. . . . You're going to have to open up some time, woman, to somebody. . . . How did it feel, Eva?" (76–77). This question is a continuation of Tyrone's "you remember how it feel," an invocation of memory against Eva and in the name of violence. The question also rings familiar to questions Davis, Elvira,[10] and news reporters impose on her—How did it feel? You're going to have to open up to someone, woman. Or, "You know you frustrate a man" (80), which are the exact words of the psychiatrist, Davis, *and* Moose (a man whose hand Eva stabs during an assault).

Eva's memory of the Queen Bee is not sufficient against the breadth of these archaeologies that legitimize sexual violence, structures that are imbedded in language, consciousness, and social culture. In fact, her own bluesy mythology is in an insoluble tussle with these narratives of violation, a corpus of stories that all run together: "Davis squeezed my ankles. I squeezed the boy's dick. It was like squeezing a soft milkweed. I reached down and squeezed the back of his neck. The musician made me put my hands down between his legs" (49). Memory bleeds into memory, and Eva's own attempt at a restorative story—her self-mythologizing and voice—is propelled against and around the interwoven narratives of her experiences. At the end of the novel Eva is the Queen Bee sitting on her throne, but she is also constipated, full of violences that she cannot flush from her body; she gives into Elvira's request for sex, a request that both brings two women together but which is also tainted by the language of coercion and compulsion that Eva (and probably Elvira) had experienced all her life from men. At the end Eva is still left withholding and giving in but hardly able to have faith enough to let her body go.

Eva's acquiescence to Elvira's overtures has been the site of much scholarly discussion about the quality and nature of her liberation. Most notably, Melvin Dixon, in "Singing a Deep Song: Language as Evidence in the Novels of Gayl Jones," makes a powerful case that "Eva never gains control over her voice, her past, or her identity" (245).[11] Dixon indicts Eva as a "femme fatale" and as a replicator of violence in her silence and confusion; that is, because Eva does not (choose to) master voice in a public way, especially in a novel that is so aware of the relationship between speech and power, she becomes a part of the violence that is done to her. He achieves this argument by pointing to the accomplished way in which Jones uses voice and expression (as opposed to silence) in *Corregidora* and by arguing that there is no orgasmic pleasure in the sex between Eva and Elvira. What I think Dixon misses, however, is that voice for a woman, especially a Black woman in the context that Jones is writing about, is not always about mastery in public ways. If we are to think of the novel as a blues text, then its silences and its low murmurs are as powerful and evocative as more conventional (read: masculine) articulations.[12] My argument here is not intended to assert that Eva has a fully realized voice; that is simply not the case. Still, Jones's novel is about the *development* of a woman's subjecthood under profound violence and colonization, a development that seems less about mastery and more about practice. I am hard-pressed to ignore the nuances of Eva's subjectivity, the ways that Jones's use of blues enunciates a vocal proficiency that is not entirely about normative, straightforward self-expression and which is also not ever fully resolved. Eva's voice is like those blues women Angela Davis talks of in her study, those women whose songs are, among other things, complicated (and sometimes unsatisfying or even unsatisfied) expressions of female subjectivity. Such sometimes has to be enough, for it is sometimes all there is or can be.[13]

Whatever compromise becomes of Eva's voice by the novel's end, the bluesy myth of the Queen Bee is, nonetheless, a momentarily powerful enactment of memory in that it allows her liberally to invent, collapse, and revise stories in her mythology as a means of self-protection: a new bedazzling corpus. One day Eva meets a man on a bus while traveling to West Virginia. As it is with all men, he eventually reveals that he wants her sexually, and his proposition is violent, especially considering the story he tells just prior to his overture:

> "My father used to carry a jackknife around in his pocket all the time. Guess what it had printed on it?" he asked.
> "What?"
> "In big gold letters," the man said. "'Trust in God.'"

There is in this telling, especially within earshot of his sexual overture, a threat, a device meant to further coerce Eva to think, and rethink, about his offer. Years later Eva remembers and revises this story in a moment with Davis, claiming it as her own and placing the knifepoint of the threat at Davis: "'My father used to carry a jackknife around in his pocket all the time,' I told Davis. 'Guess what it had printed on it?' I asked" (117). We never get the rest of the exchange or the potent punch line, but surely Eva has made this memory hers, a lie made as her own story and one that helps (even temporarily) to protect her from Davis's violence. Eva's relationship with this body (the lie) revitalizes her own body even as the reprieve is only momentary and must have later on further incited Davis, especially if he felt its threat. So, Dixon's arguments are not dismissed from my consideration of this scene: they remind me that Eva's story is not easily confined to neat summaries that the discourses of sexism and racism often make possible. In many ways what Eva needs is to be opened up, is to open up, yet, in the history of her experience, the idea and its language are already threat and assault. Therein the impossibility, maybe even the failure: when the peril of being open is both excessive and exact.

Eva's only protection is her revised memory body, her mythology, which has to compete against the mythologies of the world and which itself is not ever her reliable. It is insular, somewhat false, and unopen. It is a heavy weight to be under, a particularly imbalanced struggle, and a small small place from which to spring for freedom, especially since memory is neither exclusively on her side nor ever on her side at all.

Time and Place, Nation and Home: Collectivities of Memory

Memory eludes specificity by distorting time and space, seeming bigger than the outlines of any one human body, manifesting as an uncontainable embrace, which it is and is not. This enormity is memory's appeal to communities, for whom it is a necessary metaphor for the collectivities of their lives.

Think how Beloved's character is intended to represent the unspeakable losses of the Middle Passage and the institution of slavery: it is her formlessness, her body that is not a body, that cements her typology. She is out of time and without literal place, as she belongs nowhere and is everywhere. This disturbed relationship to time and place affords memory, and those who form a relationship with it, the latitude to juxtapose events and to invent home places. For example, Eva's construction of a myth must work within and against the idea of time, of what is past and forgettable and what is a present haunt. Jones herself says: "In Eva's mind, time and people become fluid. Time has little chronological sequence, and the characters seem to coalesce into one personality" (qtd. in Tate 96). When Eva remembers Davis's touch—"Davis squeezed my ankles"—she also remembers a litany of gropings: "I squeezed the boy's dick. It was like squeezing a soft milkweed. I reached down and squeezed the back of his neck. The musician made me put my hands down between his legs" (49). This memory occurs across time, appearing as both multi-timed and timeless, as myths tend to be. That memory makes its own time, but also funnels and torsions the time of the social body, further enhances its volatile corporeality. The time of memory is magical, eluding familiar constructs and posing an agility that is somewhat freeing; like a dream or hallucination, memory is timeless and time specific. Sometimes a precise time, strict in beat and measure; sometimes a fluid temporality.[14]

In *Praisesong for the Widow* Marshall uses dreams and hallucinations to reflect memory's overlay of past, present, and future as a multi-timed sensibility. Marshall makes clever narrative use of film and picture technology, presenting her novel as a double (or multiple) exposure, a shifting and unsettling that parallels the time of memory.[15] The dreams Avey has of Aunt Cuney and Jay/Jerome create unfocused but hauntable images, like the cloudy haze of blurred pictures taken while the subject is still in movement. Via these dreams, Avey begins to reencounter past racial violence and is less able to leave an old life behind. "Her dreams were a rerun" of the nightmares of Black life in the United States, especially "the bomb that exploded in the Sunday School quiet of Birmingham in '63 went off a second time in her sleep several nights later. And searching frantically amid the debris of small limbs strewn around the church basement she had come across those of Sis, Annawilda, and Marion" (31). Avey's memory materializes as a violence that threatens her daughters, a memory timeless and bodyless, belonging to no one and making claim on everyone.[16] Years later, on a cruise with her friends, Avey has another experience of timeless memory; while standing on the ship's deck and watching the passengers shoot at clay pigeons, Avey revitalizes a scene from Halsey Street:

She and Jay had watched the pale meaty hand repeatedly bring the night
stick down on the man's shoulders and back, and on the head he sought to
shield with his raised arms . . .

For a long minute she stood gripping the railing, trying to steady
herself and clear her head. Where had that night surfaced from? How
could she, after all these years, *hear* the thud and crack of the belly
and the man's screams *so clearly*? Her ears, her memory seemed to be
playing the same frightening tricks as her eyes. (56; emph. hers)

This memory is so unusual that Avey considers it a hallucination, having no
other reference for this image that seems so out of time and place.

Marshall's narrative aesthetic repeatedly conflates time as a metaphor of
memory. The Out-Islanders, for example, whom Avey names as a hallucination, are literally memory bodies that exist outside of (their) time and place
and who live with/in the past through their acts of memory. Marshall evokes
a similar anachronism with the Ibos, the mythical Africans who were brought
to South Carolina and their "future memory":[17] the Ibos, who could see in(to)
the future, had an insight that was both hindsight and foresight, which Aunt
Cuney passes on in her telling Avey how the Ibos just up and walked across
the water, back home to Africa: "Those Ibos didn't miss a thing. Even seen
you and me standing here talking about 'em. And when the got through siz-
ing up the place real good and seen what was to come, they turned, my gran'
said, and looked at the white folks what brought 'em here. . . . And when they
got through studying 'em, when they *knew* just from looking at 'em how those
folks was gonna do, do you know what the Ibos did?" (38). This told-every-
summer story always ends with the question that Avey, by now, knows the
answer to—they turned around and left the (slave) Landing, laughing and
smiling in their purposefulness. The story of the Ibos, which Avey hears on
her visits to Tatem, displays memory as a temporal simultaneity of past, present,
and future—like Beloved, a memory pregnant and poised to give birth to what
is to come as much as it reflects what has happened and what haunts the now.
This timelessness is what allows the Ibos' bodies to transcend the limits of
corporeality, so that they not only could walk across water but could also exist in the present (literally as the subject of story). Marshall further articulates placelessness in the description of Carriacou and Ibo Landing, places that
literally do not appear marked on maps. These two sites of Black salvation
are memories; they only exist so long as people remember where they are and
what exactly has happened there—an imperative that is tenuous and unreliable at best.

Marshall's examples capture the appeal of memory as a narrative aesthetic
in Black culture. Memory is at once so elusive and possible that it allows for

wild invention. Whatever historical records cannot provide, whatever colonization has destroyed, memory can and will restore. Memory is our grandest metaphor, and its hyperbole, imprecision, and subtlety capture the varied and almost inconceivable life of Black populations. Memory is not only the source of Black nationalism; it is itself nationalism embodied. For people in the Disapora the grand idea "home" is (a) memory as well as the inverse: memory is (a) home. These two interchangeable textualities evoke a similar volatility, an uncapturability, yet both live and rise in consciousness, cultivating strong feelings and inspiring staunch loyalties. They are imagined bodies whose very corpus depends upon an agreed-on imagination, a communal acquiescence that seems to presume that either home or memory can be controlled and determined.

As such, the consideration of memory is a consideration of nationalism, of the corporealization of nation. Ernest Renan usefully describes a nation as "a soul, a spiritual principle," based on "the possession in common of a rich legacy of memories" (19). Frantz Fanon goes even farther in his famous thesis on nationalism, arguing that a "national culture is the whole body of efforts made by a people in the sphere of thought to describe, justify, and praise the action through which that people has created itself and keeps itself in existence" (*Wretched* 233). Later he describes the storyteller, who is the one who speaks this nation into being: "Every time the storyteller relates a fresh episode to his public, he presides over a real invocation. . . . The storyteller once more gives free rein to his imagination; he makes innovations and he creates a work of art" (241). As Homi Bhabha has famously suggested, the relationship between nation and narration is almost tautological, and Fanon's valorization of the storyteller's nationalism evidences the corporeal trinity of memory, body, and home.

So memory feeds and facilitates this powerful locality, home. But memory's body is unreliable and ultimately cannot be determined. That is, the collective dependence on memory to sustain the idea of home is a suspicious prospect, for memory cannot evidence a liberating national consciousness. For one, its propensity toward nostalgia works against the agency that nationalism is intended to foster. Consider the case of the people in Antigua that Kincaid describes in *A Small Place*. "To the people in a small place," she writes, "the division of Time into the Past, the Present, and the Future does not exist. An event that occurred one hundred years ago might be as vivid to them as if it were happening at this very moment. And then, an event that is occurring at this very moment might pass before them with such dimness that it is as if it had happened one hundred years ago. No action in the present is an action planned with a view of its effect on the future" (54). This small-place time construct, by virtue of it being a "small" place, is compromising; the spatial dimensions are limited and claustrophobic. These people are overwhelmed by their memory of what had happened and are unable to develop and facilitate a relationship with remembering. What they have is myth, and they are trapped by the apparent staticness of mythos.

Memory's placelessness is also a burden, for it bequeaths an ethereal invulnerability to a people's cherished spaces, inventing a sometimes false safety in which violence was before. Memory is too broad and big and vague: consider that often the concepts of Black collectivity are feminized—the idea of home, the term *motherland*, the impulse to "protect our women." Yet such examples of femininity are surface and immaterial and hardly change for the better the place and position of women in the collective unit. The idea of woman as a correlative of collectivity, while inspiring, loses its usefulness because it becomes a type, a construct, an unachieved relationship with a collective corpus. Nationalism often sacrifices women, which is precisely the danger of memory as nationalism's heartbeat—it can undercut the spirit of the very agency it is supposed to embolden. Further still, nations themselves are not meditative or thoughtful but, instead, anxious corpuses all the while determined to protect their impossibility.

But the idea of home might also hold a key to understanding how memory can work in the achievement of a national consciousness. Consider again Eva's mythmaking, her grappling with cultural and social narratives in her passionate and often-failing encounter with memory. Eva's process is local, though it has grand implications; it does not produce an easy home—in fact, the place that Eva creates for herself and her salvation is tentative. Still, it is a place that is her own and which offers some of the refuge that the idea of home is supposed to offer. Eva's process is a process of nationalism, a local matter that is less concerned with outlining and defining the characteristics and terms of the nation and more concerned with what creates and sustains the *agency* of the nation: what will inspire and motivate her body to action, what will funnel its energies toward her greater good. Hers is an intimate and intense relationship to "nationalism," to the invention of her home space and the achievement of self-determination. Eva's example, as well as the examples of the women in *Beloved* and Avey in *Praisesong*, suggests that there is, really, no collectivity; instead, there is only one's wild relationship with memory, a tussle between roaming bodies. This tussle *is* the nation, a thing that cannot be named, held, analyzed, cajoled, a body that is happening as we live and which cannot be fashioned. Not a normative nationalism but a ritual of movement and struggle—a Black and female–centered nationalism.

A Ritual of Movement

Memory is inherently a repetition, always in movement, always shifting; it operates via placement and position whereby one memory body gains meaning through its relationship to another memory body, a relationship that is never static. In this way movement is at once a characteristic of memory's body as well as what embodies (corporealizes) memory. This mobility and volatility reveals the ontological disposition of memory: that memory is a practice or the opportunity to put one's body into practice. Therein lies its agency.

Movement is a key quality of memory, evidenced when Sethe finally tells Paul D the story of the shed scene; here the memory puts Sethe's body in motion:

> She was spinning. Round and round the room. Past the jelly cupboard, past the window, past the front door, another window, the sideboard, the keeping-room door, the dry sink, the stove—back to the jelly cupboard. Paul D sat at the table watching her drift into view and then disappear behind his back, turning like a slow but steady wheel. Sometimes she crossed her hands behind her back. Other times she held her ears, covered her mouth or folded her arms across her breasts. Once in a while she rubbed her hips as she turned, but the wheel never stopped. (159)

Sethe's circular story and motion "made him dizzy. At first he thought it was her spinning. Circling him the way she was circling the subject. Round and round. . . . Then he thought, No, it's the sound of her voice; it's too near" (161). Sethe's memory body is literally in motion, traveling closer as if coming from a far-off place. Memory and voice here are (a)live roaming textualities, a groundswell of motion, "[a] flutter of a kind. . . . like a rippling—gentle at first and wild" (106). These descriptions of memory are characteristic of girlfriend subjectivity in which movement and mobility are of a premium.

As a series of motions, memory embodies both conscious and involuntary movement. The conscious movement is the willingness to make a claim on the memory body, the reaching out toward the other body that is not other, not yours, also yours; the unconscious movement is the scope and impact the memory body causes on the self, how a dance comes over the body and causes it to move as if involuntarily, how a group of memory bodies bump into one another and make myths, stories, nations. Memory's incarnation is a willed and will-less movement, like a call and its response, and, though memory is not ours to control, "humans, / not places, / *make* memories" (Aidoo 81; emph. added).

This emphasis on human potential, on a subject's will, is crucial because the achievement of memory is not a given. In fact, the dangers of nostalgic memory that yields an arrested consciousness are effectively noted in Kincaid's dissertation on colonialism in Antigua. She is critical of a people who surrender to time and inactivity, such that events happen to them against their will: "When the future, bearing its own events, arrives, its ancestry is then traced in a trancelike retrospect, at the end of which, their mouths and eyes wide with their astonishment, the people in a small place reveal themselves to be like children being shown the secrets of a magic trick" (54). Kincaid's harshness is one of frustration and compels me to extend her question by asking: what if, as things (events) happen to people, people also happen to things?[18] What if the human body can interact with time and space as much as time and space impact the body? This dialectic between body and time/space/history is the potential agency that the articulation of memory as a corporeality makes evident.

And, still, the difficulty of possession: on one hand, memory has to be claimed as well as allowed to make claim on a subject; on the other, such claims will not, cannot, hold—they do not sustain and are certainly not within the control of any one subject. Hence, the practice of memory is part will and part surrender. Such is the liberating practice exhibited in Avey's movement into the dance in *Praisesong*: she takes a willful step forward, followed by the unconscious slipping "into a step that was something more than just walking" (248). As she steps in and claims the community of dancers, they step out and claim her; she claims and is claimed. Her (memory) body possesses and is possessed by and in a movement: "Just as her feet of their own accord had discovered the old steps, her hips under the linen shirtdress slowly began to weave from side to side on their own, stiffly at first and then in a smooth wide arc as her body responded more deeply to music" (249). This movement is freeing because it puts agency back in the Black body: the body is an agent in the practice of naming itself and claiming its love, and the faith in this love (of self and other) is grand enough to permit surrender without fear of risk. That claim on self, that faith in self, is unreliable, but it is an indelible, sustaining thing. The practice of memory is a re-membering of that particular faith.

The faith of the undeniable body: Baby Suggs tells the people in the Clearing that "freeing yourself was one thing; claiming ownership of that freed self was another" (95). So begins her instructive prayer of the body, naming the arms and organs and private parts that need re-membering, which form the only body we can have faith in. Her prayer is for me a nationalism of the flesh, and her command to claim one's freed self (which is exactly where the freedom is—in the claiming) echoes Patricia Williams's suggestions that Black people have moved from being owned to being disowned, without really being permitted to be owners (of) themselves (156).

Memory is a practice of freedom, literally an act of breathing life into unclaimed body parts. When Avey falls sick during the Carriacou excursion, Lebert and some women from the community take care of her. While one of them bathes and massages her body, Avey remembers other times her body was handled like that, and it is in the memory that her body comes back to life:

> She [Rosalie Parvay] was oblivious to everything but the sluggish flesh she was working between her hands as if it were the dough of the bread she had baked that morning or clay that had yet to be shaped and fired.
>
> Until finally under the vigorous kneading and pummeling Avey Johnson became aware of a faint stinging as happens in a limb that's fallen asleep once it's roused, and a warmth could be felt as if the blood there had been at a standstill, but was now tentatively getting under way again. (223)

This massage, this embrace and claim, is a movement against unrecoverable fragmentation, for, though the diasporic memory body is fragmented, there is still an undeniable something there, an "essence of something rather then the thing itself," which can be recovered "bone by bone" (*Praisesong* 240).[19] Memory is, or can be, a breathing of life (into), a reflection and enactment of self-generosity—an active meditation. Memory as a body re(-)minds us of who we are, which is literally a re-formation of the communal body via a re-recognition of its members. It is the claim that Beloved seeks and what the woman hovering over Avey says: Do not forget, struggle to remember, tussle and tangle with memory. Memory as a body is an essential subjectivity that is not fixable, that shifts between the self and the not-self; a body and a practice whose motion produces breath. Memory, a study in faith, a nationalism, a practice of freedom, a "daily, prose-bound, routine" (Rich, "For Memory" 22).

Memory: "a potentially kinetic quality [that] must impel us to action," this essential Black female subjectivity (Nourbese Philip 20).

Chapter 6

Toward a
Language Aesthetic

T HERE IS A house that is really a room; truth walks in and does not ask to be welcomed. This truth *is*, such that the verb *is* exists as its infinitive meaning: to be. This truth, in this house, is.

Imagine that the house in this aphorism is a metaphor of nation; that truth is an individual's articulate(d) self; and that the barely expressed tension is of the struggle between the Black female subject and the confines of nationhood, a struggle whose integrity depends on this word *truth* and its relationship to a discourse on language. In contemporary critical thought language plays a primary role in the formation of the subject or, more precisely, the subject's sense of being—her subjectivity. Generically, much (post)modern ideology concludes that language is altogether and irrevocably unreliable, hyper-ludic, and fragmentary, descriptions that also characterize the subjectivity it abides. Many Black women who are artists, essayists, theorists, exhibit a similar ambivalence about language (what Monique Savage has quotably called "a healthy disregard"), though such is coupled with a strong faith in and affinity for the power of the word. Theirs is a profound contradiction evidenced in two textual examples: on one hand is Celie's necessary struggle for language and against the silence of coercion, white supremacy, and patriarchy; on the other is Sethe's determination that none of the words in that newspaper article could possibly capture her very Black and female experience. Celie's relationship to language signifies on a larger Black cultural equivalence between language use and freedom. But this esteemed appraisal is sobered against Sethe's awareness that language itself has been deployed against Black selfhood, that language itself is a colonization. At this impasse language manifests, like memory, as an irresolute credential of Black subjecthood.

If there is a notable difference between Black women's language ambivalence and that articulated in contemporary theory, it might center on the appreciation of wholeness. For most postmodern theorists wholeness is largely a maligned, even outdated, concept, disproved and disavowed by the vagaries of multiplicity; for Black women, however, the promise of wholeness is neither impossible nor superficial. In fact, the utility and viability of language turns on its proposition of wholeness, its potential to restore and repair—an always failing promise for sure but one that is nonetheless instructive as a subject moves toward that which is her integrity. This, then, is a girlfriend language practice, a Black woman's facility with and failings within language; it is a pragmatic aesthetic that grapples with the politics of colonization, enunciates itself as difference, and gives the word back to the body. Such an engagement of language is neither futile exercise nor frivolous exhibition; instead, it is linked to a complicated and undeniable commitment to self-centeredness. Remember: it is not language (play) that is a premium but the self, the corpus that language practice disturbs but also makes clearer. In contrast to some contemporary theory, this inflection of girlfriend selfhood proposes that language does not (un)make the subject; instead, a subject's repeated encounter with her capacity to love is her constitution as well as her undoing.

This, then, is the work: to engage language as a girlfriend, imagining the subject as an artist and her stumblings as an aesthetic.[1]

The Politics of (Black) Language

"What is the political / position of stars," Dionne Brand asks in "Canto II" in her 1982 collection *Primitive Offense*. Hers is the right invocation for my consideration of language, which necessarily puts aesthetics in direct relationship with politics and, more specifically, ethics, creating a triangular relationship between what is political, spiritual, and theoretical. Such triangulation is an intimacy that rejects the apolitical face of academic production, the "objective" stance that is often an implicit requirement to be considered a serious writer and scholar. Instead, here, intellectual work gets no broad immunity from real life.[2]

This commitment to political relevance is the framework within which Marlene Nourbese Philip theorizes Black language. In her prize-winning *She Tries Her Tongue, Her Silence Softly Breaks* Nourbese Philip combines poetry and prose in gorgeous exploration of "the anguish that is english in colonial societies." The book opens with the essay "The Absence of Writing or How I

Almost Became a Spy," a lucid deposition on the role writing plays in the Caribbean and the uses to which English has been put. Hers is a bare and incisive declaration of writing as an enterprise of the project of subjecthood: "Only when we understand language and its role in a colonial society can we understand the role of writing and the *writer* in such a society" (11; emph. added). She claims that the function of the writer's "be-ing" is to be a prophet, one who "translate[s] the i-mage into meaningful language for her audience" (12). This i-mage, which has a European counterpart in the artist's image, is Nourbese Philip's term that privileges the "I," that devilish and modern at-tribute of selfhood. Using and expanding on the dialectic between sign (word) and signifier (i-mage) that is well discussed in critical theory and language studies, Nourbese Philip writes of the pull and thrust between i-mage and word, each creating and inflecting the other. The role of the "i-mage maker," then, especially unrestrained, is to "continually [enrich] the language by enlarging the source of the i-mages" (14). Nourbese Philip's argument that word pro-duction, via the i-mages such production creates, has a direct implication on the lives that people live is especially attractive to me not only because it gives emphasis to a Black and female "I" that challenges and defends its integrity but also because it borrows from and augments poststructuralist and decon-structionist thought. I engage her primarily for her keen appreciation of Black experience with language but also because she does not create a divide be-tween the theoretical and the artistic. For her, as for many Black writers, voice is metaphorical but also literal power, and what is at stake in the writing pro-cess is not only knowledge but also human livelihood.

It is no accident or mere flourish, then, that Nourbese Philip argues dra-matically that colonialism is the demise of the African, destroying the pro-ductive and progressive relationship between word and i-mage. Such is the denial of voice and vocal power, an operation she conceptualizes not only as the death of the i-mage but also as the death of "the capacity to create in one's own i-mage" (15). However declamatory this claim may be, it is certain that the introduction of Africans into a New World landscape did disrupt the dialectic between word and i-mage, on one hand, and i-mage and articula-tion, freedom even, on another. It does not matter if this disruption was tem-porary, passing, for the thing still had impact: the introduction of "alien and negative European languages" meant that, when "the word/i-mage equation was attempted again, this process would take place through a language that was not only experientially foreign, but also etymologically hostile and ex-pressive of the non-being of the African. *To speak another language is to enter another consciousness*" (15; emph. added). That last phrasing is the profundity of Black language politics, the acquiescence that is alterity, this nonbeing capacity of the European tongue—and here she means English—that complicates both the Caribbean writer's relationship to language as well as to her people. The trust is severed and language is untrustworthy, a vehicle of erasure, violence and separation. Whether it is definitively true that all nonnative languages constitute a different consciousness and that such consciousness is necessarily harmful to dominated populations, it is surely true in the specific case of African people and English, for the African did not exist as human in English word concepts. To use English was to use a language that could not name/affirm one's existence, an ontological dilemma or, perhaps even more profoundly, the absence of such a dilemma; Nourbese Philip later writes, "Once the i-mage making power of the African had been removed or damaged by denial of language and speech, the African was then forced back upon the raw experience without the linguistic resources to integrate and eventually transcend it" (15). For the New World African, language is an almost-impossible and a violation, for, "over and above her primary function as chattel and unit of production, the English language merely served to articulate the non-being of the African" (16). Language, then, is an initial site of colonization, making and marking difference, sanctioning value to a difference made up.[3]

Nourbese Philip's dissertation sometimes takes too broad sweeps and over-idealizes African languages; still, she succinctly articulates the imposition that English acquisition and use is for a Black subject. In this context writing is something "hard against the soul," which is how Dionne Brand, an acclaimed poet of Trinidadian descent, describes it in her collection *No Language Is Neutral:*

> this is you girl, this is the poem no woman
> ever write for a woman because she 'fraid to touch
> this river boiling like a woman in she sleep
> that smell of fresh thighs and warm sweat
> sheets of her like the mitan rolling into the Atlantic
>
> this is you girl, something never waning or forgetting
> something hard against the soul.
> (4)

She continues the rhythm a few pages later, citing

> the faces, masked in sweat and sweetness, still the eyes
> watery, ancient, still the hard, distinct, brittle smell of
> slavery.
> (7)

Brand's narrative voice describes the unspeakable horrors that poetry's intimacy makes unbearable—those faces and communities left in shambles by colonial disruption. Depending upon the quality of the prepositional *against*, the poem's title can be positioned in two ways: this "something" is damaging to the soul or is the soul's steadfast, sturdy, committed—as in soul-hard. Brand's narrator leaves bare the character of language—never quite neutral not only because of the burden of history but especially because all language is the quality of its use—its put-into-practice-ness by an agent. A subject is no more trapped by it than she is trapping of it, which is language's defiant place in the (un)becoming of the subject.

Aware of the fallacy of neutrality, Brand's narrator determines to put language to intimate use—to reveal bonds of human embrace, to re-corporealize losable bodies, to try—however flawfully or failingly—to use voice to give voice. This in chronicling two women whose lives of resistance punctuate the phrasal "hard against the soul": Phyllis Coard, an imprisoned revolutionary, and Mammy Prater, a Black woman who had her first picture taken when she was 115 years old. Neither women speaks in the text because language is unyielding to their speech (not only in the text but also in their actual lives) but both are present either by photograph, or a note "not even from [her] own hand [. . .] / but from some stranger who dragged it / from a prison wall" (8). The responsibility, then, is the narrator's to do them justice in language, to almost become them, an act of girlfriendliness that she believes is impossible because she is only (and barely) capable of seeing the bleeding sea, of seeing a woman tearless in the face of youthful death, of seeing a girl's look full and unrealized. The narrator reaches an impasse:

> I have tried to write this thing calmly
> even as its lines burn to a close. I have come to know
> something simple. Each sentence realised or
> dreamed jumps like a pulse with history and takes a
> side.
> (31)

It is inevitable that the elegance of difficult living, a subject ripe for poetic expression, collides with the impossibility of language—its unresolved history, its demanding corners, its pretension of objectivity. In the clash between ethics and aesthetics, the narrator quickly aligns herself with the former. Although she has not condemned language, she is certainly suspicious of language's ability to colonize and separate:

> What I say in any language is told in faultless
> knowledge of skin, in drunkenness and weeping,
> told as a woman without matches and tinder, not in
> words and in words and in words learned by heart,

told in secret and not in secret, and listen, does not
burn out or waste and is plenty and pitiless and loves.
(31)

The words she uses are not only the words of a master tongue, those learned
in proper English schoolhouses and absent of creole thickness; she, the narrator, also speaks in words that are *not* words, words learned from nonverbal expressions, words that are the living language of her mother and her grandmother
and her uncle, who narrates (to her) his version of the story of her mother;
words that are capable and disappointing, like a lover's body.

She is adamant about her position, not as an outsider to the community
she speaks of (for example, an anthropologist) but as a Black woman in contention with language as much as she is in use with it:

> listen, just because I've spent these
> few verses fingering this register of the heart,
> clapping life, as a woman on a noisy beach,
> calling blood into veins dry as sand,
> do not think that things escape me,
> this drawn skin of hunger twanging as a bow,
> this shiver whistling into the white face of capital, a shadow traipsing,
>   icy veined and bloodless through
> city alleys or wet light, the police bullet glistening
> through a black woman's spine in November, against
> red pools of democracy bursting the hemisphere's
> seams, the heart sinks, and sinks like a moon.
> (41)

This writing is not an escape of the hard against the soul, but in fact is an
entrance into the hard, because words not only form but *are* a sentence: they
sanction and convict. They are precise and literal violence, like the description of the newspaper story in Brand's follow-up collection *Land to Light On*:

> One gleeful headline drives me to the floor, kneeling,
> and all paint turns to gazette paper and all memory
> collides into photographs we could not say happened,
> that is us, that's what we did.
> (16)

The words are wrong and the pictures too, and their wrongness is an affront
and something more: a violation, a stomach-wrenching physicality that leaves
the would-be subject sickened, reeling.

It is in the ultimate section of *Land to Light On* that Brand makes her most searing comment on language's violence, a section appropriately titled "Every Chapter of the World":

> she knows that every chapter of the world describes
>
> a woman draped in black and blood, in white
> and powder, a woman crippled in dancing and
>
> draped in dictators' dreams, in derelicts' hearts,
> in miners' lights, in singers' shoes, in statues,
>
> in all nouns' masculinities [. . .]
>
> [. . .] a woman gutted
> and hung in prayer, run on with fingers, sacredly
>
> stitched, called history and victory and government
> halls.
> (95–96)

In every chapter of the world, this woman (and other women) are abused by language and its use at the hands of others, "hacked [. . .] in paper classifieds" and left for dead (96). Brand's critique is a fiery sermon of unrhymed but rhythmic couplets, her version of the heroic, epic form. She is literally rewriting every chapter of the *word* to give voice to the women trapped under words' weight, because she, this woman

> cannot speak of this or that massacre, this
> or that war like a poet. Someone else will do that. She
>
> sees who dies. Someone with not a hope but a photograph
> of someone they loved.
> (98)

Brand's narrator indicts the governing bodies and the recording institutions for their collusion in this chapter of the world, paralleling Toni Morrison's accusation in her "Nobel Lecture" against heads of state and their vicious power merchants. The language these abusers use and their presumption of neutrality—that theirs is the articulation that says it "once and for all," theirs says it accurately and summarily—is erasing; it is: "diplomatic language [used] to countenance rape, torture, assassination. . . . seductive, mutant language designed to throttle women . . . the language of surveillance disguised as research; of politics and history calculated to render the suffering of millions mute; language glamorized to thrill the dissatisfied and bereft into assaulting their neighbors; arrogant pseudo-empirical language crafted to lock creative people into cages of inferiority and hopelessness" (Morrison, *Nobel* 17–18). A language that is more disease than not and which disarrays the cling of girlfriend subjectivity.

Mastering English

That was the indictment, and a formidable one it is; this, then, is the writer's defense: to bear the unencumbered weight of her attraction to and facility with language, including especially the impact this makes on her relationship to her home community. Under the legacies of colonization, in which her people have varying levels of access to the master(ing) tongue, she stands before an intricate calculus that imagines and institutionalizes intellectual and artistic traditions in ways that put the marginalized at a serious disadvantage, if they are in consideration at all. Outside of her home, she, the writer, is largely perceived as both an exception (one of the few) and one who is exceptional (having overcome extraordinary conditions)—these being not only her subject position but also intended to be her subjectivity. At home she is potentially afforded something more celebrated, something that looks, at first glance, like claim and embrace. As S. S. Lewin argues, the Black artist is for her community "an interpreter, a voice that makes intelligible the deepest, most meaningful aspirations of the people . . . a channel through which their resentments, hopes, fears, ambitions, and all the other unconscious drives that condition behavior are expressed and become explicit" (cited in Gladstone Yearwood 138). This requires, as Gladstone Yearwood notes, "art that is aesthetic, functional, situationally relevant and politically meaningful" but which also makes her job precisely impossible, destined and designed for failure (138). What, then, seems like the status of celebrity is also an imposition of demand and a suspension of artistic license.

The tapestry between artist and her community—how each encounters itself as a subject, which is also how it encounters the other's subjectivity—is inflected by the "anguish of English": that mastering English is at once a cultural necessity and a colonization. Mastery gives a subject access to (some of) the cultural currency that non-Black English dialects possess, the reality that the closer one's English is to accepted standards, the more intrinsic value it has. This valuation is a seduction for those who have the means to learn the master tongue, and English acquisition is a way out and up, individually and communally. But it also initiates resentment and distrust as learning and using English becomes both marker and keeper of neocolonial social hierarchy. The mastering of English creates and then widens disparities, attenuated by the titillating reality that the matter is one of degree and quality—that most subjects involved have some familiarity with English but not all are fluid thinkers and speakers of the right kind of English. This perhaps only facilitates more resentment, as the possibility (but only a possibility) of access often does. Further still, because language is a cultural imposition, the quality of English's value is decidedly ambivalent, and its use often means metaphorically if not literally leaving home. Writing: this privileged conundrum, one that disturbs rather than generates community, hardly seeming to serve the immediate political, social, or economic needs of home. And, where writing is valuable to the national project, it is more often a man who is the authorized narrator of the political experiences and desires of the people. In these contexts Black female writers are deemed insignificant or frivolous, their writings are wrongly political, if political at all. Even the fraught status of "voice of the people" is not hers to have.[4]

This reflection on language must also consider how essential English is in the attainment of a wide readership—that being a solvent and viable artist often means commanding support of a majority that is not your own people and who often trivialize, exoticize, or appropriate native aesthetics. Being a writer, then, is a stuttering and unsettled subjectivity, a meditation on exile, a restlessness of affinity and abandonment, or urging and disavowal, at once on the inside and the outside.[5]

These are the principal players: a language of anguish and unyield; an artist's practice apprehended; the broad melee of nation, colony, gender; the tender struggle to subject forgotten, surpassed. She the writer acknowledges "that having adapted herself to a vehicle of communication for historical and cultural moments between a dominant culture and a dominated one, language is becoming one more tool of subordination, replacement, pressure and distortion" (Cecelia Busamente, qtd. in Nourbese Philip 17). There is then a need for a different kind of practice, a minor reconstruction to interrupt the murk of language politics. For sure, already, there are the re-lexified languages of dominated peoples: the creoles and dialects and patois that invigorate the master tongue.[6] This notion of repair, of making language *be* or *do* something else, is an attractive and common starting place for some artists, because, "in the absence of any other language by which the past may be repossessed, reclaimed and its most painful aspects transcended, English in its broadest spectrum must be made to do the job" (Nourbese Philip 18). This English is the language we have, with all of its "impurities" and its histories, and the artist's work is to massage and stretch it into something that evidences her, to "heal the word wounded by the dislocation and imbalance of the word/i-mage equation" (21).

Perhaps the work of language triage is really as simple as making language do what it ought to do: give close approximation of human vagary. It is this that the young children in Morrison's "Nobel Lecture" yearn for. Although scolded by the old woman and neglected by the adult world, the children are faithful about what language can be, even as they are cognizant of its limitations. When the old woman refuses to answer their question and, instead, leaves them with her invocation of their responsibility for the dead(?) bird, they become angered by her silence and offer a litany for language: "Don't you remember being young, when language was magic without meaning? When what you could say, could not mean? When the invisible was what imagination strove to see?" They want a language, or at least a promise of a language, "full of vitamins" (27), for they are already familiar with one populated with "cruelty and mediocrity" (26):

> You are an adult. The old one, the wise one. Stop thinking about saving your face. Think of our lives and tell us your particularized world. Make up a story. Narrative is radical, creating us at the very moment it is created. We will not blame you if your reach exceeds your grasp; if love so ignites your words that they go down in flames and nothing is left but their scald. Or if, with the reticence of a surgeon's hands, your words suture only the places where blood might flow. . . . *Language alone protects us from the scariness of things with no names. Language alone is meditation.* (27–28; emph. added)

The children respond to the old woman's scolding with their own powerful comment, asking and imploring her to remember what language can do: how it shimmers and dazzles, invents and makes possible; how it can touch the edges of slavery, turning far away ships into nearby warmth. They clamor for a language of possibility, a language that is once again magical.

The young children caution against becoming hopeless in the face of failed and misused language, language that is surely assailed but whose arc ought not be surrendered to the abusers and misusers. There is a similarly poignant moment in Brand's *Land to Light On* when the narrator reminds the reader, and herself, that even slight poems are a break from the weight of the world, "even if they / only wave and even if I only look up late to see / your shadow rushing by" (*Land* 81). Brand, perhaps more than any of these writers, is painfully aware of the anthropological current that lights the colonial language apparatus, a thing that bestows objectivity on the artist while potentially objectifying her subjects. Many of Brand's narrative poems meditate on the responsibility of being an artist and to whom the final genuflect belongs. Her aesthetic is unrelenting in its attention to the artist's position as a communal outsider and the search for an "inside place" from which to write. In *No Language* Brand's narrator is uneasy both with her own position outside of the prison, while Phyllis, her revolutionary sister, sits inside (an interesting inversion of the binary of inside/outside); and with the interference this distance creates. Softly, and with a tender girlfriend salutation, the narrator asks: "Girl, how come is quite here I hear from you, / sitting in these rooms, resenting this messenger"

(10). These slim lines use the torque of patois as embrace: the aural synonyms *quite*, that which is certain, and *quiet*, that which is hushed; the visual illusion that makes *resenting* that which is sent back, as in *re-senting*, which is more what the word sounds like in dialect. The narrator's anxiety of distance is, for the moment and under the cover of incarceration, calmed by this exchange, this sly sisterliness that twirls language, this example of one body and another in encounter and repel; this shapes what the narrator (un)becomes, her conscientiousness sitting right beside the rigor of her craft. This narrator, who earlier reminded us that "each sentence [. . .] takes a side," is acutely aware that she could become, might be expected to be, a decoder, prophet, and representative both to her community and those without; as such, her body takes the impossible place of another, whether self or other desire the transposition. Seemingly, she speaks *for* them and *to* a dominant outside group, even for the writer who resents this easy opposition. The writer's movement is always away from and toward, each motion an unsatisfying imperative: the necessity of leaving home, the foreign of her body in new and unforgiving terrain, the words she writes that can hardly be heard.[7]

In the section of *Land* titled "Dialectics" Brand gives these concerns their fullest articulation, exploring "this understanding we are caught in" (64), which is the understanding between the writer and her people back home; between the writer, the one with language, and the women written about. The narrator sarcastically remembers her aunt's diseased foot as good poetic detail:

> I had thought my life wider, had counted on my cleverness
> at noticing not just her sweet hand but her sore leg and
> congratulated myself even then on analysing the dialectic,
> the turned cornmeal, the amber pain hanging at my Aunt
> Phyllis' foot. I liked detail.
> (*Land* 52)

In this moment the artist is a native anthropologist looking in on her people and recording them, an observer but not a participant. She aims to manage a clear distance between seer and seen, writer and subject. On this visit she keeps to herself, "brewing ways to sit and close the door / and not touch anything that may fall and *left you to living* (65; emph. added). This is a girlfriend tension, a struggle to become that is also about being undone, and soon enough the me/not-me ambivalence breaks into the artist's measured p(r)ose:

> No I didn't want their life and I wanted their life
> because they didn't know that they were living it and I envied
> them that. (65)

I love the word *envied* there because it is so honest and unsoiled: a deep pas-sion that is part admiration and part malice. Something irreconcilable and unreasonable. The revelation to be had is in the slippery "left you to living," how the word in its gerund form is unencumbered, how the directional *left* seems to assert what is not hers to leave. The narrator becomes the poem's subject, her aunt ultimately unrepresentable by language of any, but especially this, kind.[8]

The resuscitation of language all along asks whom does art serve and how. For this artist it is never merely sufficient to memorialize her foremothers in language, capturing images of them in prose and poetry, since often they nei-ther care to nor can read what she writes. Such memorialization of home, past, and people is further insufficient because the artist cannot find herself there amid the wasteland that colonialism has engendered. The artist needs, instead, an intimacy with and through language, a language that will tease and corral her subjectivity.

This struggle between artist and community not only parallels the binary of self and other but suggests more particularly the impact of modernity. Sim-ply, the relationship between artist and art has changed dramatically in the onslaught of modernity and its relatives—capitalism, globalization, individu-alism. For one, if she wishes to be an artist of some repute, she must interface with the forces of the First World and its aesthetic prejudices. She does not have to succumb, but she must engage the possibilities of grants, of writing in English, of patrons and patronization—all the result of the professionalization, individualization, and specialization of art, all an anxiety of audience. Truth-fully, even absent of a desire for reputation, the nature of what it is to be an artist (and therefore of art) has changed, a revised subjectivity that is part coro-nation, part license, part entrapment. The artist in the modern miasma faces an uneasy subjecthood, a trajectory of encounter and rejection and possibil-ity, a triple bind that is nicely summarized by Trinh T. Minh-ha: "She who 'happens to be' a (non-white) Third World member, a woman, and a writer is bound to go through the ordeal of exposing her work to the abuse of praises and criticisms that either ignore, dispense with, or overemphasize her racial and sexual attributes" (6).[9]

Difference, Narrative, Anxiety: Story's Body

All is not loss or losing: the negotiation of the politics of mastery requires a language practice that can slip, one that is self-aware and self-conscious; an artfulness that is predisposed to a sense of putting disparate parts together, of fusing irreconcilables, of making congress out of discord; a language art that is a capable sister for unease. For a while, I had been thinking that *hybridity* might be the term to encapsulate the narrative aesthetics of Black women, but now I think it misses the mark. No, not hybridity but better *difference*, which evokes deconstructionist principles and retains a sense of what is irresolute. "Difference," which Trinh T. Minh-ha claims as a particular contribution that Third World Women have made to postcolonial discourse, is the right metaphorical vehicle for it articulates hybridity's play and transgression but also sustains an awareness of power and a critical suspicion of theory. Not hybridity, its radar trained too speciously on that which dominates, its body framed too extensively by modernity's imperfections—but difference: a critical and discerning posture of alliance and dissipation.[10]

As an aesthetic practice, difference embodies (in)congruities and tensions and sustains the anxiety hybridity would erase. Literally, the text marked by difference emerges as metatextual, self-aware, unsettled, all coalesced and propelled by a vibrant and anxious narrator, one who is almost disruptive and counterproductive—an unreliable subjectivity intending to confuse and confound but also one whose own (un)becoming is the text's central dilemma, its realization. Let's assume that this narrator is a woman and is Black: she is surely playful but is also determined to disturb the unreliability of the language she must use. She works not against truth per se but against its violence. She is at once the percussive and melodic narrator of Brand's poetry, whose own body is like a stone tossed about and shaped by language; as well as the narrator of Aidoo's *Our Sister Killjoy*, a voice whose journey is sister to Sissie's. She is rageful and poetic, and her volatilities are an aesthetic. She is a girlfriend, a subject engaged in the practice of girlfriend selfhood.

There is a useful example in Morrison's "Nobel Lecture" in which the narrator manifests as an interruptive corpus. At the beginning of the essay the old woman says a few words that are punctuated by the stark "it is in your hands." The rhetorical trick of Morrison's treatise is in the narrator's ventriloquism, her populating the old woman's brevity with eloquence, elegance, and biting abundance. The narrator, the determined "I" of the essay, positions herself as the old woman's executor, and it is as much to her interpretation as it is to the old woman's silence that the children respond; a response whose polish and flair seems again like another manifestation of the narrator's fluency. Whatever the case, it is clear that the narrator meddles in the text, an evocative interference that not only puts her anxiety front stage but also and especially Morrison's own fitful body, she too a narrator squarely arrived in the story's frame. Morrison is, truthfully, not the narrator: she marks a space between her salutation and the story she is telling with the repetition of the oral sign "once upon a time"; and then again between the story's end and her closing appreciation. No, the narrator is a volatile body announcing and shaping the text, hiding and flaunting her own worried heart, and flashing the light on Morrison's own contemplativeness. After all, Morrison's Nobel moment is a meditation on self-authorization, a consideration of language, agency, and power; the award invites her, as it does to the world at large, to think about the arc of creative agency, the pitfalls of modernity, the profound differences that constitute her artist's subjectivity. Notice how the lecture's meta-story reflects her confrontation of such differences: she a Black woman, "the daughter of slaves," whose wisdom is without question, speaking to the "calcified" academy. Surely she thought about what they wanted to hear, this pantheon that, despite its best intentions, is more staid than daring. Her moment is one of an honor long and well deserved and an impossibility to speak for herself and her people in ways that resist objectification (her of her people, they of her and her people, language of her and her people). It evokes well the politics of mastery and the dilemma of authorization for a Black woman artist, this grappling dalliance with what authority means, how it is mobilized, and what agency is afforded by the name (artist) and the practice (art).[11]

Honestly, Morrison's traversal of this dilemma is stunning: she begins with a quiet salutation to the uses of narrative and announces her story, particularly fairy tale, as her method of choice for this momentous and esteemed occasion. This opening points attention to and aligns with the very visible difference, between her Black female body and the academy's largely white masculinity, as well as the less visible one, the marriage of folk story and modern treatise. Hers is a theoretical adventure in language, one that eschews the hierarchy implied by lecture (as a genre) in favor of storytelling, an aesthetic that depends on materiality, on the power of language practice to uncover (the artist's) body and to invite, inspire, initiate, contact between flesh and other flesh. Story, which, like a girlfriend, emerges as a body with which the artist can engage but also reveals to the artist her own body.

The characteristics of story, especially fairy tale, highlight the way its form is not only corporeal but even parental: it is familiar and folk, is in our company from a young age, soothes and cautions. Stories are often old and legendary, offering wisdom like a community's elder, but they can also be new; stories are like memories: they change, reinventing themselves to fit a person's need, narrating myth and heroines, giving life to those who they are about, those who tell them, and those who hear them. They are playful, secretive even, but not irrevocably deceptive; complicated but not impossible. They materialize as fragments, without the need to be written, like the ghost bodies of the African folk tale about faith in chapter 4. They are their own ontology; they make human living possible. Trinh T. Minh-ha offers a theory of story in *Woman, Native, Other*, which itself takes narrative form: "Let me tell you a story. For all I have is a story. Story passed on from generation to generation, named Joy. *Told for the joy it gives the storyteller and the listener.* Joy inherent in the process of storytelling. Whoever understands it also understands that a story, as distressing as it can be in its joy, never takes anything away from anybody. Its name, remember, is Joy" (119; emph. added). As she suggests, story is generous and mutual, a joy-giving member of the community. This body, story, "circulates like a gift; an empty gift which anybody can lay claim to by filling it to taste, yet can never truly possess. A gift built on multiplicity. One that stays inexhaustible within its own limits. Its departures and arrivals. Its quietness" (2). It circulates among those who touch it, is boundless: "The story never really begins nor ends, even though there is a beginning and an end to every story, just as there is a beginning and an end to every teller" (1). It is communal: "The story depends upon every one of us to come into being. It needs us all, needs our remembering, understanding and creating what we have heard together to keep on coming into being" (119).

Story is "counsel," as Walter Benjamin argues; it takes on a corporeal quality, a body to be filled and refilled, circulated and exchanged among people, bringing them closer to one another and closer to that fullness of themselves; it negotiates rather than prevents community. And this: that story merges form and content so seamlessly that its form seems nonexistent, which it is—story's form is its content; its content is its guise. I speak of story here in contradistinction to the novel, which Michael Wood deems to be in crisis. Wood's definition of this crisis is instructive and so elegantly written that it bears quoting: "There is the sense that the lonely novel, the work predicated on the isolation of the reader, had shut too many things down. . . . The story is less fussy than the novel . . . more welcoming to variety. . . . *A story is not necessarily radical; can be liberal too; or even more conservative than the novel, because often more traditional, less wedded to the modernizing world*" (3; emph. added). It is his claim to resuscitation as well as his catalog of story's vagaries that I covet the most. Story is not inherently radical; its quality is its use. Story is not easy but a body to encounter, a choiced selection and arrangement that appears artless, but which is crafty and form-ful. It demands engagement and is likely to yield both agency and disappointment of girlfriend subjectivity.[12]

These qualities are unmistakably evident in Morrison's "Nobel Lecture," in which, in the exchanges (stories) that pass between children and an old woman, it is the children who point to the radical adhesive corpus that story is: "Make up a story," they say. "Narrative is radical, creating us at the very moment it is being created" (27). They want to hear a story of ships turned away from shorelines at Easter, placenta in a field. Tell us about a wagonload of slaves, how they sang so softly their breath was indistinguishable from the falling snow. How they knew from the hunch of the nearest shoulder that the next stop would be their last. How, with hands prayered in their sex, they thought of heat, then sun. Lifting their faces as though it were there for the taking. Turning as though there for the taking. They stop at an inn. The driver and his mate go in with the lamp, leaving them humming in the dark. The horse's void steams into the snow beneath its hooves and the hiss and melt are the envy of the freezing slaves.

The inn door opens: a girl and a boy step away from its light. They climb into the wagon bed. The boy will have a gun in three years, but now he carries a lamp and a jug of warm cider. They pass it from mouth to mouth. The girl offers bread, pieces of meat and something more: a glance into the eyes of the one she serves. One helping for each man, two for each woman. And a look. They look back. The next stop will be their last. But not this one. This one is warmed. (29–30)

This story that the children tell the old woman, the one they themselves want to hear, is quiet and tense. The vocabulary of their story evokes a sense of touch, a tactileness that is articulated and actualized in the words but especially in the *gestures* the words make between the characters of the story, the old woman and the children, as well as between the narrator, Morrison, and the listener/reader. The children's longed-for story is a communication that hardly uses language but which speaks, instead, through touch, through warmth that aims to re-cognize the *flesh* of those whose presence is often denied in the very language they are supposed to use. Their story is embracing, and an embrace is exactly what the children wanted when they asked the old woman the question about the bird. They confess this desire to be touched near the end of the lecture: "Why didn't you *reach out, touch us with your soft fingers,* delay the sound bite, the lesson, until you knew who we were?" they ask her (27; emph. added).

At the end of their pleading, their chastising, and their story, there is silence again. Then, the old woman speaks to them but also to herself: "'Finally,' she says. 'I trust you now. I trust you with the bird that is not in your hands because you have truly caught it. Look. How lovely it is, this thing we have done—together'" (30). This thing that can be *looked* at, this thing they have done together, is story. They have enraptured each other, old and young, artist and not, and broken the back of language's penchant for disconnection and dissonance. Both the old woman and the children are reminded of the magic of story, of how warm it feels, how rigorous and responsible it can be . . .

how sweet. These children travel to her on-the-outskirts-of-town home not to bother her, not even to enact a childish ruse; they travel there to be touched by her (language). Perhaps she also knew that she wanted to be touched by them; maybe that was also her longing, for the cleverness of their question (that they understood the politics of language as well as knew whom she was and what she was capable of as an artist) reveals the cunning of her response: that curt "it is in your hands," repeated so as to punctuate the urgency, is the real ruse, a performative trick intended to shift the agency to them—instead of giving them the story, she gives them the responsibility for its creation and propels them to become artists, not consumers. These young new storytellers facilitate touching language as they receive and pass on story's generosity. This the beauty of Morrison's lecture: a dynamic story in form and content as well as a model for language practice, it envisions an authorization of a Black women's artist subjectivity through the negotiation of the politics of mastery.

The aesthetic of story is its materiality, its ability and responsibility to touch, to corporealize the interface between flesh and flesh. In *Sisters of the Yam* bell hooks narrates a moment that expressively captures story as the exchange of touch. To soothe the fears of young ones in her life who are afraid of the dark, hooks invents for them this story:

> In a space before time and words, the world was covered in a thick blanket of darkness. It was a warm and loving covering. Since it was hard for the spirits who inhabited this space to see one another, they learned to live by and through touch. So if you were running around lost you knew you were found when arms reached out in that loving darkness to hold you. And those arms that held the spirits in that beautiful dark space before time are holding us still.
>
> This is a little origin story I made up. I thought of it one day when I was trying to explain to a little brown girl where the babies lived before they were born—so I told her they lived in this world of loving darkness. I made up this story because I wanted this little brown girl to grow up dreaming the dark and its powerful blackness as a magic space she need never fear or dread. I made it up because I thought one day this little brown girl will hear all sorts of bad things about the darkness, about the powerful blackness, and I wanted to give her another way to look at it. *I held her hand.* (80; emph. added)

This story eases fear and wards off self-hatred in two ways: first with a suggestion that warmth and touch, as acts of love, override the need to see, the need for light, which is what the blind woman knows and what the children come to know; and then with a story that is itself an example of that touch, right down to the act of holding that is its conclusion.

Like Morrison's, hooks's story *does what it is* (or is what it does), merging form, content, and function and putting the body back into the process of making and doing language: instead of bodies characterized as irrelevant or otherwise violated in the exchange of words and the making of social cur-rency—bodies that consume and are disconnected—these bodies are entangled and engaged through the politics of language, through encountering an/other's difficulty and disparateness. The language of story provides an (un)reliable body to lean on, a tension to fuel the self's (un)becoming. Literally, it is touch given to words, a reach across linguistic gaps that is "living by the word,"[13] not only an overhaul of the language but also a putting it into different prac-tice. Story is always urgent, even when it is quiet, and is elliptical, possessing noticeable gaps and ambiguities because understanding is not in the words and their tentative and fleeting connection but in the speaker and story making: when the children ask the old woman the question, she does not give them a long answer but, instead, reminds them of their responsibility to embrace her, and thereby, themselves. There was, of course, a risk that the children might only hear what she said ("it is in your *hands*") but would not *feel* it as a heft, would not recognize that what was really in their hands was their ability to touch. But, when the children demand of her (and of language) to hear of slaves and become the storytellers they covet, they acknowledge that they did *feel* what the old woman said: it is in *your* hands. So, they tell the story with love and generosity, capturing its warmth and its faith, outlining better than camera or poem the bodies of those slaves, remembering the prized moment of the girl's serving of glance—they tell this story with care. And the old woman's response, again, is short and suggests a connection that might not be readily evident in its words but is there for the one who has been listening and has been *touched* by the story: "Finally, I trust you now. I trust you with the bird that is not in your hands because you have truly caught it. Look. How lovely. This thing we have done. Together" (30). Her *finally* is a connective adverb, indicating time, logic, and a sequence of unarticulated interactions; her poise is this idea of trust that all the while was the real dancing impulse of the exchange between her and the children: how does the artist trust her-self as well as those who are (not) a part of her?

T HE OLD WOMAN'S comments are elliptical and summative, "epic" in their pro-fundity and breadth, like storied remnants of a people's legacy. Hers is an "epic speech," a hyperrepresentative and truncated language practice that takes full advantage of the gap between sign and signifier. Cognizant of language's fu-tility and its dissolution, this aesthetic is, instead, attendant to and depen-dent on the body-to-body interaction between users. The imperative of epic speech is to return flesh to relevance in language politics, to institute regard for the subject, however vagaried. Epic speech is the uneasy re-mattering of language, the re-materializing of bodies that is also what makes language matter.[14]

There is an attendant and irresolute danger in overemphasizing the corporeality of language, especially under the gaze of the Cartesian binary. But maybe Baby Suggs, whose own moment of epic speech in *Beloved* names the flesh as the thing to be loved, offers respite from this theoretical legacy: "Here in this place, we flesh" (89). I read Baby Suggs's comment as a reminder that the flesh to be loved is not what the flesh means in social ideology but what flesh means by virtue of its living—its capacity to soothe and love, the way it holds, its unencumbered subjecthood *and* its ability to exchange story with other flesh. When the old woman in the "Nobel Lecture" resists the children's question, Morrison points attention to their engagement of her (dis)ability as a normative discursive paradigm: she is blind and in some way unable(d). At the end of the lecture these children have a different way to understand just what her disability means, a flesh reconsidered.

The language of story, this epic speech, is a language of the body, or a language that moves toward and returns to the body. The gesture of touch is in and facilitated by the language and is ultimately necessary for the language to work. The speech is truncated but also thunderous and resonant: Nel's evocative "girl girl girl" when she feels Sula in the air; the exchange between the two revolutionary women and Clare Savage at the end of *No Telephone;* Sissie's simple and pronounced opening to the love letter "My Precious Something, First of all, there is this language"; Sethe's dual embrace in response to Paul D's touch: "Me? Me?" All are language utterances that speak beyond their moments and are also ultimately their moments literalized, materialized. Urgent and imperatived, epic speech moves toward language measured by agency and intentionality. It is purposeful, willful, requiring the strength to bear loss and heartbreak. The old woman had to be strong enough to bear what looked like the children's violence, to have enough her self to endure the possibility that they might either not hear her call to their own agency or that they might not be able to imagine embracing her. The practice of language is a matter of self-regard, ultimately irresolute and unreliable but possible nonetheless. It tumbles as a girlfriend subjectivity in need of an/other and open to failure. It is what it is to (un)do and (un)become.

Chapter 7　　　　　　　　My Own, Language

I HAVE BEEN THINKING of that lovely poem by Roland Flint "A Poem Called George, Sometimes," in which he remembers a poem his son made up before he died. Ethan, his son, gives the poem the name "George" but later claims that it is sometimes also called "Jack." What is most endearing to me is Ethan's vagary, that he has cultivated a relationship with his art, enough so that what he calls it can and does, in his own imagination, change. Perhaps the fluidity of the poem's name matches Ethan's perception of language work as a live, fleshy thing, something he can make but which also exists beyond the necessary narrow of his scope of claim; as an artist, Ethan's language art is a living body with which he has a relationship, a language of his own, tender and vagaried. The same is true for his father, who uses words to reveal connections and loss and whose retelling is itself an artistic moment that uncovers his own relationship to language, a relationship forged between his need for consolation and his son's deft articulation of the selffull properties of word-work. Ethan, Roland, and "George/Jack" suggest the role that language can play in matters of human living, the way that art can be (about) the intimacy of one's life.[1]

In her poem "School Note" Audre Lorde writes that

> for the embattled
> there is no place
> that cannot be
> home

nor is.
(*Black Unicorn* 55)

The sentiment of home—its expansive totality, its precious promise of a resting place, of a familiar embrace, of engagement and appreciation, of intimacy—is a precise metaphor for the intersections and impossibilities Black women face in their negotiations of language. Home is at once anywhere, necessary, impossible. At the axis of this particular consideration of language is a critique of the separating impulse of language work, the ways that the politics of modernity and mastery yield that which is severed and fragmentary, that which is without complement. Both Lorde's wisdom and Ethan's poem suggest a connective possibility, a sense that there is still a meaningful association to be had between art practice and human life. Let's call this sensibility a pragmatism—that Black women's language aesthetic grapples to enunciate a relationship between the artist's subjecthood and her art product, a liaison that must be more complicated than mere equivalency (art is life, life is art), more existent than disavowal (the converses). This pragmatism aims to produce an intimacy that counters the fractious potentialities of language play, to give room to a practice that is artful and useful, creative and political. This chapter, then, will examine Black women's engagement of this pragmatism, especially their refiguring of the rhetoric of the narrator in textual landscape. It will argue that, in attempting to make language more pliable, Black women writers disarm the narrator as a site of objectivity, instead introducing a narrator who manifests as a subject and whose agency is in peril and on display as one of the text's corporealities. The narratorial acquiescence to subjecthood constitutes a volatility that thrusts writer, narrator, and text into turmoil, revealing language as a girlfriend of the self, the an/other body that is tussle, surrender, and abandon and which demands and yields everything and nothing all at once.

Materializing toward Tender: The Narrator's Body

Part of the impulse of fracture generates from the role of the narrator as keeper of the word and teller of lives and events. Narrators are manifestations of authority, existing at the threshold and negotiating the compact between author and reader; are articulate bodies that signify what is imaginary and what may be real.[2] Although David Lodge rightly argues that the narrator in modern novels is largely suppressed and self-conscious, it is also true that such manifestation often reinvests the narrator's authority through the construction of complicated plot lines and narrative architecture.[3] Even narrators who are inept and unreliable are not neutered or neutralized as their follies and fallacies power the narrative forward or sideways or inward and reveal a shadow of the author's imagining of the power to make and unmake selves. The narrator as a construct of Western literary discourse announces and maintains a hierarchy of authority and entrance, a fluctuating and potent dalliance between writer, narrator, subjects, and audience. And, in absence of the vagary of oral storytelling, the potency of the narrator is hard, perhaps impossible, to disarm.[4]

The history of narratology is populated with a concern not so much about the rhetoric of the narrator—that the narrator exists as a trope of authority—but about the visibility of the narrator, about certainty and clarity of the narrator's appearance.[5] The discussion of free indirect discourse or unreliable narrators or implied author and reader reflect this, which is also, by extension, a concern about the presence of the author.[6] It is, in fact, a dynamic that reaffirms the author's integrity by re-presenting the author—or the author's permutation, the narrator—as lacking definitive integrity, a sleight of hand that all the while points attention to the mastery of the artist. For example, although the author seemingly experiences a demotion in New Criticism, the attention and argument given to the author in poststructuralist aesthetics (think of Foucault's "What Is an Author?" or its predecessor Barthes's "The Death of the Author") serve more to concede the integrity if not of the author then for sure of the authoring function and disposition. Such serves not to question the author (or his authority) but, instead, to complicate where his authority may lie. Hence, the imagining of narrative art as both a hierarchy and a conundrum of power is still operative, if not intact.[7]

But I am not ready yet to talk again about the author; I am interested still her twin, the narrator.

Narrators are never, hardly ever, tender. How could they be? Their role is to discern and delimit, to mark and exclude, to set up and out; their intent to elaborate and invite but to do so within the confines of a narrative trajectory that is, to them, more familiar than not. And, as relations, maybe even cousins, of the authorial persona, narrators guard carefully the text at hand even while maintaining a sense of distinctness from authors themselves. A narrator is a grand performance, a ruse: even when she is determined to be clean, clear, honest, the condition of the novel demands her to be otherwise to sustain and promulgate the rubric of fiction. Narrators are, therefore, untender—never really open, already committed to the integrity of the novel as a straight or a playful discursive tool. Even playfulness and unreliability are not synonyms of my word *tender* . . . tender is to manifest as flesh, to be subject and object of vagary and willfulness and their opposites; to unsettle the

arcs of narrative trajectory . . . to be vulnerable. A tender narrator is impossible. The urge, then, of Black women writers is to approach breaking, to get
near to pliability: not full upheaval of the narratorial disposition but to introduce fleshly uncertainty to the narrator; not a performative uncertainty but,
instead, an anxiety and abandon of a subject, a selfish and selffull tension, a
girlfriend subjectivity that is also the negotiation of the politics of language
mastery . . . to move the narrator closer and closer to her tenderness.

It is toward this kind of narrative corporeality that the narrator in Toni
Morrison's Jazz develops. Throughout the novel the interruptive and anxious
narrator keeps a close eye on Joe and Violet and has early on wishfully marked
their relationship for failure. Although genderless (and arguably raceless), the
narrator nonetheless embodies some particularly gendered practices, especially
the way she adopts and mobilizes the culture of city gossip as a female-centered
discursive practice. Whatever the case, the narrator is certainly unwilling to
surrender herself to the unfulfilling lovelessness that she experiences modern
Black life to be. She is guarded and willful, beyond the point of surrender and
without peer; her voice is the jazzful solo, aching and staccato, edgy and without peer, male in its abandon and armament. So, when the novel opens with
Violet's disfiguring of her husband's young lover, whom he has murdered, the
narrator assures the reader and herself that this too is another failed love practice, a story that is unachieved and complete.[8]

The function of the narrator throughout Morrison's novel is that of both
conductor and lead soloist: the narrator guides and propels the other narrative voices that flesh out the story but also records with a vocal acuity and
acerbity that commands, even seduces, the reader into attention. Here is the
stunning part—the narrator is wrong about Joe and Violet, and she boldly
claims her error at the end of the novel as she watches their loving and, more
important, as her narrative objectivity disintegrates: "When I see them now
they are not sepia, still, losing their edges to the light of a future afternoon.
Caught midway between was and must be. For me they are real. Sharply in
focus and clicking. I wonder, do they know they are the sound of snapping
fingers under sycamores lining the streets?" (226). The sigh of the narrator is
palpable, carried on that phrasal "when I see them now" and its acknowledgment of a past way of seeing, of a new way of seeing, of even a sense of longing to see these two lively bodies. The narrator literally materializes—develops
a body—within the artful, colorful, corporeal words she uses to talk about Joe
and Violet; that is, she is talking about her own body, anxious and formative,
no longer unaffected. The lost edges and the ambivalence of "was and must
be" are her own as is the realness. Morrison's art here is a deft transposition, a
reflection of one's self on another; her attentive introduction of sonorous and

musical words—clicking, snapping fingers—announces the narrator's moment
of girlfriend subjectivity, the becoming and the undoing. Even the syntax of
the sentences—full of hesitation and still bold, volatile and active and *still*—
the syntax itself is an (un)becoming.

This is the narrator's intimate meditation on Joe and Violet's bodies, on
her own body thrown into furious tussle with theirs; and where before her anxieties had (dis)quieted the text, now she herself is (dis)quieted, acquiescing to
the vulnerability of subjecthood that her arrogance was supposed to protect
her from. Listen to the quiet, appreciative, even despair-full tone of her dissolution:

> It's nice when grown people whisper to each other under the covers.
> Their ecstasy is more leaf-sigh than bray and the body is the vehicle,
> not the point. They reach, grown people, for something beyond, way
> beyond and way, way down underneath tissue. They are remembering
> while they whisper the carnival dolls they won and the Baltimore
> boats they never sailed on. The pears they let hang on the limb
> because if they plucked them, they would be gone and who else would
> see that ripeness if they took it away for themselves? . . . Breathing
> and murmuring under covers . . . because they don't have to look at
> themselves anymore. . . . They are inward toward the other. (228)

That phrase *leaf-sigh* is precisely what ecstasy is, a thing that is still and mobile, secret and coveted, her own coming to ripeness that is so precious, it is
metaphorized through the passage about journey, failure, and the surety of the
other that is never a loss of self.

The narrator is now fully a subject of the story, not a subject in guise in-
tending to control the arc of the narrative but a subject in full vulnerability.
When she pines over their settled self-regard and longs to be seen the way
Joe sees Violet, she is surrendering to her own exposure: "He [Joe] saw Violet's
dark girl-body limp on the bed. She looked frail to him, and penetrable
everyplace except at one foot, the left, where her man's work shoe remained.
Smiling, he took off his straw hat and sat down at the bottom of the bed.
One of her hands held her face. . . . He undid the laces of her shoe and eased
it off. It must have helped something in her dream for she laughed then, a
light happy laugh that he had never heard before, but which seemed to belong to her" (226). Joe is not seduced into violence or even aggression at the
sight of Violet's tender body in repose, and the narrator's care in looking at
the wordless exchange is her own surrendering to the story. Violet's body is
the narrator's, as is Joe's gentle affection; she yields to their image and proclaims them her an/other. She is not a voyeur but, instead, is a witness, is part
of the miracle that is happening.

No longer outside the story and its volatile tactility, she can afford to have her heart broken, can break herself under the weight of an interaction so difficult and cherished. She can admit that she has for a while and does now "envy them their public love":

> I myself have only known it in secret, shared it in secret and longed, aw longed to show it—to be able to say out loud what they have no need to say at all: *That I have loved only you, surrendered my whole self reckless to you and nobody else. That I want you to love me back and show it to me. That I love the way you hold me, how close you let me be to you. I like your fingers on and on, lifting, turning. I have watched your face for a long time now, and missed your eyes when you went away from me. Talking to you and hearing you answer—that's the kick.* (229)

What was obstinate is now also pliant, pliable, faithful; the narrator's testimony is grand evidence of her flesh, populated with a lovely litany of first- and second-person exclamations, verbal enunciations of the self and the other, the me and the not-me. The doubled-ness of her self-centered focus is characteristic of girlfriend subjectivity, and her reverie even performs speech to an/other body that might not even be there.

This is a remarkable transformation that she herself says she cannot admit out loud, in the presence of the other: "But I can't say that out loud; I can't tell anyone that I have been waiting for this all my life and that being chosen to wait is the reason I can. If I were able I'd say it. Say make me, remake me. You are free to do it and I am free to let you because look, look. Look where your hands are. Now" (229). The tense of this self-prayer switches to the subjunctive, to the thing of possibility, which is the most vulnerable place, for the subjunctive exists on that which is absent, has to make material what is not material at all. The subjunctive is a promise; there is, after all, no other body but the narrator's own, sufficient and capable. Her confession is a rhetorical masterpiece, embodying the creativity with its clever repetition (*make/remake, free, look*), announcing agency with its exclamations (especially the understated *Now*), gesturing and wishing and torquing. Hers is a language that does, a language that is literally flesh, that is an imperative and a question and a whisper all at once; the resonance of the image of hands here is with the image of the hands at the end of Morrison's "Nobel Lecture" and the trust and touch and labor implied in that loveliness between the old woman and the children is also between Violet and Joe, between the narrator and her an/other self.

This is language work, a narrator materialized as the subject of the novel, the story as a story in the fullest sense of the word, which is the point that

Philip Page gets to in his lovely essay about the narrator's coming to intimacy and her blurred corporeality: "Thus the narrator commits the same logocentric mistake that the characters commit. In her solitude, her privileged selfhood, she thinks that only she knows, that only her perceptions have truth, or at least that her view and her imagination are superior. She privileges self over other, present over past, her narration of events (the sjuzet or discourse) over the events themselves (the fabula or story)" (62). Page's comments send us back to the process of storytelling as well as project this as a matter of selfhood and otherness: what surrender means, what risk it is to love, the particular feel and flesh of story.

Morrison's use and revision of the unreliable narrator highlights the ways that authoritative knowledge is over-attributed to the narrator or even the author. This over-attributing is the basis of a kind of narrative certainty that often hides what is most uncertain in and about narratives, especially what the narrator knows about other people as well as about herself. The rhetorical constituency of the narrator—what a narrator knows and does not know, how she gains and parses such knowledge, how she herself develops—is crucial, I think, not only to the idea of the Black novel but especially to the larger historical trajectory of Black subjectivity. Consider, for example, the profound function first-person has assumed in the discursive conundrum of Black written expression, from slave narratives on. The communal imperative has often, if not always, been on truth—a kind of restorative, confrontational, authenticating responsibility to correct that which is wrong about the Black self and to do so in the master tongue. Although the writer, Black and female, cannot merely abandon this imperative, she must surely attenuate it, lest it stifle, coerce, co-opt her own body. And, still, she must also contend with the politics of writing as imposed against her from without; that is, it not only against the imagining of narrative (and its role) in her home community that the Black writer must struggle but also against the ways the world of letters participate in colonial arrogance—the ways that stories are less what we tell, authors are less real, narratives are more play than revelation. She wants intimacy, even if intimacy means surrendering the authority that is her authorship. She is strategic, aware of the imposition of representation but determined to also be abandon.

This struggle is evident in Morrison's *Jazz* as well as in her "Nobel Lecture." In fact, Michael Nowlin's essay "Toni Morrison's *Jazz* and the Racial Dreams of the American Writer" argues convincingly and elegantly that the novel is Morrison's contemplation and assertion of her place in the national literary landscape, her unsettled disposition as an American writer. Hers, he argues, is an ambivalence that matches the tenor of the novel's narrator, an autobiographical venture of self-authorization.[9] But more so, I think, and not only in regard to Morrison, this anxiety of self-authorization is inspired by the notion of the ideal that manifests as a part of the fabric of authorship; that, in the universe of the novel, writing is a crisis of four contentious principles, four roommates in the (prison) house of language: reader, narrator, subject, writer, all permutations of one another, all propelled by imagination, all ideal or at least subject to idealization. It is the process of idealization that potentially troubles the Black female writer's place, for she is never the ideal, can never be, in this imagination, ideal. Neither can her subjects. Instead, then, she, the writer, opts to create an intimacy that disturbs idealization and which gives into the unease that intimacy so often is. Maybe I am fooling myself here because intimacy too is idealized. And, still, it is useful, this idea, which by now should be familiar: her intimacy is a girlfriend subjectivity, an intimacy whose political disposition is to center the specificity and particularity of a Black woman's coming to subject. This intimacy may have no more integrity than any other, but its locality is important. Or, as Sula reminds us, a loneliness or fallacy that is one's own, not one that is secondhand. For sure, Morrison's construction of Jazz's narrator as a narrative corporeality is a comment on the authority of the author; that is, as the narrator mirrors the author's authority, so too is her undoing the author's introduction into the vagary of girlfriend subjecthood. The practice, then, is always metanarrative, always anxious and aware and posing, but something else: always determined to let go, to surrender.[10] Let me turn, then, more clearly to this question of authorial witness and talk more about the role of the artist.

To Be a Witness

What is tender and what is witness: throughout Dionne Brand's No Language Is Neutral the narrator has struggled to give poetic and narrative voice to many women from home, all the while questioning the feasibility of the representations. Her craft is not imperiled, but she moves cautiously, strategically, trying to surrender herself to her own subjects, to become a flesh with and in conjunction with their own. She wants their liveliness on the page, even if it is false, wants more than her own artfulness, and with the section titled "Blues Spiritual for Mammy Prater" the narrator achieves a poetic moment that parallels the vitality of Ethan's poem-as-friend and which elides the staticness of artistic representation. The evocation of Mammy Prater is many-dimensioned, a body that emerges as a subject but also as an/other to the narrator; the two as girlfriends in a process of (un)becoming. Representation yields to expression as the Mammy Prater who materializes remains just outside the scope of both Brand's vision and her narrator's voice and manifests as a changing volatility, a flesh that can be touched, embraced, but not owned.

The note just below the poem's title sets the context of the language moment: "On looking at 'the photograph of Mammy Prater an ex-slave, 115 years old when her photograph was taken'" (14). This subtitle points attention to the still-life that is photography and poetry, the distances between subject, object, and artist that are already in place—set off by quoted captions, framed by light and pose, rearticulated within the measured lines of poem; one person is looking at another person who cannot look back, which is how art usually works but is also why art usually does not work. But Brand's narrator is determined to give the poem a life, and she articulates Mammy Prater's fierceness such that it overlaps and subsumes, giving expression to her own, to itself:

> she waited for her century to turn
> she waited until she was one hundred and fifteen
> years old to take a photograph
> to take a photograph and to put those eyes in it
> she waited until the technique of photography was
> suitably developed
> to make sure the picture would be clear
> to make sure no crude daguerreotype would lose
> her image
> would lose her lines and most of all her eyes
> and her hands.
> (14)

The poetic voice is elegant and patient, and the first two lines perform their own waiting—the withholding of the subject through the repetition of *she waited*. Interestingly, the narrator assigns creative agency not to the photographer but to the photographed subject, who waited until she was sure that what would be taken and represented is as close to her own art-full life as possible. Mammy Prater's waiting is her own, an act of will that disrupts the normative relation between the subject (object) of art and the artist as well as an act that disturbs and asserts a useful mastery. Brand's writing is patterned to match this patience, as lines appear piecemeal and in mimic of photography's slow development as outlines manifest and image fades to clarity. In fact, Brand's poetic lines develop even more patiently than a photograph might, even more circuitously. The poem's rhythm is ambling and definitive, determined to not settle too quickly, if at all.

Brand's writing here is clean, unmarked by anything other than the most exact and noninterfering language:

she knew the patience of one hundred and fifteen years
she knew that if she had the patience,
to avoid killing a white man
that I would see this photograph
she waited until it suited her
to take this photograph and to put those eyes in it.
(14)

The second turn of the poem notes the rage that surely always follows patience of the sort Mammy Prater had to have, especially the patience of one hundred and fifteen years. But, rather then being stasis, waiting is a profound motion that shapes the poem but also the narrator's future; Mammy Prater's waiting is visionary and revolutionary, self-contained and selffull.

The poem continues to wait, to unfurl, its measured dexterity the exact rhythm for Mammy Prater's pose, which she perfected over those years:

she sculpted [the pose] over a shoulder of pain,
a thing like despair which she never called
this name for she would not have lasted
the fields.
(15)

Prophetically,

she waited, not always silently, not always patiently,
for this self portrait
by the time she sat in her black dress, white collar,
white handkerchief, her feet had turned to marble,
her heart burnished red,
and her eyes.
(15)

The reader's patience as well as the narrator's is rewarded with more details about the photograph and more imagery that is not elaborate or colorful but striking: black, white, feet, marble, red, eyes; her eyes and their subtle suggestion that she was not always patient and not always quiet. The rage that Mammy Prater must have lived is a model for the falling of the poem layer by layer with ease and care, aware that something other than her own perceived inferiority is at stake:

she waited one hundred and fifteen years
until the science of photography passed tin and
talbotype for a surface sensitive enough
to hold her eyes
she took care not to lose the signs

to write in those eyes what her fingers could not script
a pact of blood across a century, a decade and more
she knew then that it would be me who would find
her will, her meticulous account of her eyes,
her days when waiting for this photograph
was all that kept her sane
she planned it down to the day,
the light,
the superfluous photographer
her breasts,
her hands
this moment of
my turning the leaves of a book
noticing, her eyes.
(16)

The poem concludes with the narrator beginning at the beginning while fine-tuning our focus on what Mammy Prater knew—her in-sight and her will. Concerned and aware of the limits of photography and of writing, Mammy Prater put her whole will in that photograph, *will* here meaning both agency and last testament. Her agency is her story of patient artistry, a story that becomes an unending gift to the narrator and writer, a poem delivered with perfect photographic velocity. This spiritual of Mammy Prater does not aim to capture her voice but, instead, in its stillness, works to give flesh and movement to a woman whose patience, will, and determination for perfection transcended photography and writing (language) and yielded her connection to an/other woman yet to come. Her reach across yet-to-happen years to articulate (to) the poem's narrator is a profound and liberating example of language use, her body an elegant cartography of girlfriend subjecthood, blurring lines between author, narrator, and subject.[11]

Brand's poem does not image Mammy Prater as a servant, nor does her physicality evoke eroticization, absences that disavow the role of Black servitude in marking sexuality in early photography and in visual culture in the eighteenth and nineteenth centuries. Contrary to the impulse of nascent photography to juxtapose the cultured and civilized against the primitive and natural, a juxtaposition intended to chart the progress of human development, the aesthetic of portraiture in "Mammy Prater" is centered in the subject formation of a Black woman.[12] Brand deploys the nuance of photography's art with poetic success, rendering her subject as one human being whose substance is not her partiality but what is implied and what the reader—be it the narrator or a literal reader or even Brand herself—can feel by virtue of a chosen and potentially unsuccessful alliance with Mammy Prater. The bits of Mammy Prater's body we are given tell us nothing; really everything is subtle and suppressed and yet still evocative, provocative even. The poem is grand and daring, makes mockery and use of the term *mammy*, folds in on itself even as it promises a visual. And key to Brand's achievement is to exploit and confound the notion of the domestic at least three ways: as an identity of labor, as a synonym of what is private and public, and as a signifier of family membership. The art of the poem is well aware of the discipline of photography, an art that is somewhat invisible, contested even as art, quiet and powerful; an art of signs of arrested moments that are unarrested, set loose by the vagary of possibilities; an art that is sly, that promises flesh and yet never delivers. A ruse.[13] Brand makes and announces the photo (as) art, putting a capable klieg light on Prater's achievement, and, still, she maintains the idea that this is spiritual—not merely a narrative trick but a prayer reverent and reverend.

As artists, Prater, the poem's narrator, and Brand herself all choose a language practice of witnessing—that the identification of one woman with an/ other, of one woman (un)becoming her other, is the vehicle and structure of expression. Later in *No Language* the narrator explicitly reflects on her relationship to the subjects in her view and finds that she has not been excluded from her own possibility; she has, instead, been brought closer to her own artistry, her own body of light as her language practice yields girlfriend subjectivity:

> I have become myself. A woman who looks
> at a woman and says, here, I have found you,
> in this, I am blackening in my way. You ripped the
> world raw. It was as if another life exploded in my
> face, brightening, so easily the brow of a wing
> touching the surf, so easily *I saw my own body, that*
> *is, my eyes followed me to myself, touched myself*
> *as a place, another life, terra.* They say this place
> does not exist, then, my tongue is mythic. I was here
> before.
> (50; emph. added)

This is her poetry: the realization of another woman with whom she has to make a connection and negotiate an identity, the finding of herself again and anew, a revelation selffull and singular.

Brand's "Blues Spiritual for Mammy Prater" argues that the struggle is not only with the limits of language but also with the limits of the subjectivities that language and its intellectual traditions offer. This specificity is key for many Black women, who recognize that being an artist necessarily interferes with the accepted life roles afforded within and without her community. But she, the artist, also recognizes that being a writer is a serious assertion of self, that there is nothing more political, more significant, more her than being an artist. She wants to be an artist free within herself, an artist who is a witness, in the way that James Baldwin uses the term: not an observer of what has happened to her people but one to whom the happening also happens.[14] A witness: a subject position of agency and *spirituality*—like the witnessing of miraculous acts, which is also the creating of the miraculous, for she who witnesses and tells of miracle necessarily (re)creates it. Witnessing is the artist's subjectivity, as is the case with the conjuring language used in "Blues Spiritual," a language that not only records but also invents a girlfriend relationship. The artist as witness does not serve as a native informant, nor is she a representative of/for those back home. She is an artist for herself, a participant and creator, a subject and agent; her work is for her own selffullness, inspired by the intricate contradictions of selves she is full of.[15]

This work of witnessing is often heartbreak and requires a kind of bravery:[16] she has to be brave enough to imagine herself in a language not meant for her, in words that neither gesture nor touch; brave enough to fill the gaps of language with her desire for and willingness to be embraced and touched; brave enough to imagine an earnest proposition, as Brand's narrator does in *Land to Light On*, "what if we left the earth / ajar like this?" (94). This bravery is not a sense of being without fear but is, instead, the acknowledgment of fear as part of the self: she feels fear but is not afraid; she does not let fear become a state. This artist-witness, in her selffullness, is brave: amid all that there is to be afraid of, she speaks and lives (by) the caption of Carrie Mae Weems's photographic panel titled *Not Manet's Type:* "I knew, not from memory, but from hope, that there were other models by which to live." She, this artist-witness, is a diva.

On Diva Subjectivity

In a world where all the women are white, all the Blacks are men, all the world is west, all the west is U.S. American, and all language is English, there are some brave, brave people who are divas.[17] These people have no specific and acknowledged language, tradition, land, or place but are brave in their profound regard for themselves and those whom they love. They are willful, patient, and sometimes not-so-patient. They are divas not in the name itself but in the vigor that the word connotes . . . not the word but its character. Perhaps more accurately, these artists are not "divas" but possess diva subjectivities.

This term *diva* in a contemporary and Western sense is commonly attributed to aspects of cultural production that are readily influenced by Black women (for example, female singers or gay drag culture). Like any term generally accorded to women, and Black women specifically, *diva* is complicated in its permutations, always under a state of recovery, useful and altogether too easy. Still, I am captivated by the idea of a diva subjectivity, an undeniably self-righteous and self-regarded temperament that imposes itself on the world (rather than the opposite). This disposition is Sula's keen appreciation of the fragility and agency of her place in a system of social order, as a person Black and female. Lauren Berlant offers a workable construction in her description of "acts of Diva Citizenship":

> I call these moments acts of Diva Citizenship. Diva Citizenship does not change the world. It is a moment of emergence that marks unrealized potentials for subaltern political activity. Diva Citizenship occurs when a person stages a dramatic coup in a public sphere in which she does not have privilege. Flashing up and startling the public, she puts the dominant story into suspended animation; as though recording an estranging voice-over to a film we have all already seen, she renarrates the dominant history as one that the abjected people have once lived sotto voce, but no more; and she challenges her audience to identify with the enormity of the suffering she has narrated and the courage she has had to produce, calling on people to change the social and institutional practices of citizenship to which they currently consent. (223)[18]

I would not want my excerpting of Berlant to misrepresent the full body of her conceptualization: for her, as for myself, diva subjectivity is not always or only dramatic and fierce, though it is certainly urgent. Think of Mammy Prater, for example, whose subjectivity is expressed in her quiet astuteness, her understanding of the high political relevance of everyday living, her subtle photographic velocity that unfurls and falls and which renders the private public without much fanfare. The diva subject is not, ever, unassailable, not immune to the real-world costs of acts of human strength; in this way being a diva is playful, for sure, but not ever only play.

The artist's diva subjectivity is evidenced in her sincere struggle to be her own self, to be her own strong and not-strong. In her selffullness she becomes "free from attachment and aversion, but not indifferent."[19] These aversions are part of the almost unbearable costs of Black female selfness—the ones that say, like Albert in *The Color Purple*, "you're Black, you're poor, you're ugly"; you cannot be an artist. You "cannot speak of this or that massacre, this / or that war like a poet. Someone else will do that" (Brand, *Land* 98), for all the poets are things that you are not, speak and use language like you do not. You are a woman, are Black; you do not know the world. These aversions offer to a Black woman artist nothing to be or do, and out of that nothingness she must choose for herself something else. She the artist struggles to be connected and unconstrained, to be free, which means that there is no price that has to be paid for her, for she cannot be bought, but also that she has to pay no price for herself, for it has already been paid. She is, or at least can be through practice, her own.

After all, freedom is, as Baby Suggs discovers, a self-knowing: after Halle worked six years to buy her freedom, the already righteous Baby Suggs wonders:

> What for? What does a sixty-odd-year-old slavewoman who walks like a three-legged dog need freedom for? And when she stepped foot on free ground she could not believe that Halle, who had never drawn one free breath, knew that there was nothing like it in the world. It scared her.
>
> Something's the matter. What's the matter? What's the matter? she asked herself. She didn't know what she looked like and was not curious. But suddenly she saw her hands and thought with a clarity as simple as it was dazzling, "These hands belong to me. These are *my* hands." Next she felt a knocking in her chest and discovered something else new: her own heartbeat. Had it been there all along? This pounding thing? She felt like a fool and began to laugh out loud. (*Beloved* 141)

Baby Suggs's recognition of her spiritual freedom comes from the language of her body, from the re-mattering of her body. Her laughter is contagious, defiant, but also very private: she tells no one about the thing that has sweet her so. Her artistic moment suggests that claiming the freed self means accountability for one's language practice and rejecting the rhetoric of mastery.

Diva subjectivity is a meditation on vulnerability, a practice of radical (self-)compassion, the almost soundless articulation "I am free": not careless disregard or ignorance of the risk of the world but a realization that all you have is you, or, as stated earlier, "you are all you have," in which the adjective *all* is both finite and infinite, a warning and a call to celebration. This realization is a peace earned by the balancing of spirituality and materiality as the pliability of the word *all* affirms the need for agency even in the face of the unrelenting truth of the violence and madness of the world. The statement "you are all you have" is itself a moment of epic speech, a private and selffull moment that is neither without nor determined entirely by its social definition. In speaking about her son, Audre Lorde describes what she most wishes for him in life; she wants him to know "how to be himself. And this means how to move to that voice from within himself, rather than to those raucous, persuasive, or threatening voices from the outside, pressuring him to be what the world wants him to be" (*Sister Outsider* 77). What Lorde describes is a triumph, unmasculine, guided by an interior compass, a complicated architecture that is the best measure of artistic achievement, for, in the conundrum of language, gender, race, and colonial politics, it is only an artist herself who best understands and appreciates the spirit of her language work. Her success is gauged by more than prizes, even by more than the sweet appreciation of someone who is genuinely touched by her work. The truth of her work is its ability to move her.

She gaits through life with two opposing principles, each calming and sustaining the other: "First [is] . . . the acceptance, totally and without rancor, of life as it is, and men [sic] as they are: in the light of this idea, it goes without saying that injustice is commonplace. But this [does] not mean that one could be complacent, for the second idea [is] of equal power: that one must never, in one's own life, accept these injustices as commonplace, but must fight them with all one's strength" (Baldwin, *Notes of a Native Son* 102).[20] This keen balance between acceptance and resistance is the selffull artistic impulse. Think again of Mammy Prater's craft, which enunciated exactly this awareness—her waiting for the right moment, her patience and quiet as well as her vigor that had no room for patience. Her stillness is an activism or a blues ritual, a stillness that is also movement against and response to the impossible situation that Baldwin describes. This stillness is actually poise, the tranquillity that precedes movement. Mammy Prater is poise(d), "a balanced state between widely divergent impulses, . . . a state of readiness," both inaction and the moment before bounding action. Her photographic feat is (in) her poise . . . not triumph as defined by war and the imposition of might, but that which is more complicated, more heartful, that nonetheless encounters violence but that moves at a self-defined and self-contained rhythm . . . within as opposed to against the body. Her poise is her reckless mobility, her ambling with grace, passion, faith, love, and righteousness, her demanding, as she should, the very best of the world, of herself. This is what it is to be at, to make, home.

A Place to Belong

Home is the unforgiving and unbearable metaphor that nonetheless is perhaps the cleanest motivation for an artist: to find a place for herself, a place to belong, which is also finding herself. I do not mean this in an uncomplicated way: the act of belonging is concurrent with the undoing and unraveling of belonging (and its impositions on the self) such that belonging is tussle and fray and soothe. Home is tenuous at best, especially for the Black woman whose artistic legacy is to leave home, literally or figuratively. Further, the idea of home, of a land to belong to, remains a struggle for this Black woman artist, particularly because *home* and *land* and *nation* have been put to use in colonization, war, genocide, terms of nationalism that are irreconcilable to her sense of herself not only because they evoke and enunciate patriarchy and white supremacy but especially because they do not speak to the home she is longing for. She cannot give up on the idea of home, of a place to belong, but she cannot merely accept what other people have deemed home to be. Hence, home, like its distant relative language, is in need of repair.

Perhaps no writer here engages the conundrum of home as well or as thoroughly as Dionne Brand does in *Land to Light On*, which opens with the dangers of a heavy, cold, frozen Canadian road where language is untenable:

> I lift my head in the cold and I get confuse.
> It quiet here when is night, and is only me
> and the quiet. I try to say a word but it fall. Fall
> like the stony air. [. . .]
> [. . .] the air fresh, fresh
> and foreign and the sky so black and wide I did not
> know which way to turn except to try again, to find
> some word that could be heard by the something
> waiting. My mouth could not find a language.
> (5)

The landscape that Brand's narrator encounters is harsh and stark; her language ineffectively falls into a coldness that marks, exactly, homelessness. Her language is halting, stilted, breaking off, in the literally frigid atmosphere. She writes of "all these roads heading nowhere, all / these roads heading their own unknowing way" (8), pathways of migration that might, soon, offer a place to rest, if not belong, but which fail on both accounts, providing, instead, disconsolation:

> On a highway burrowing north don't waste your breath.
> This winter road cannot hear it and will swallow it
> whole.
> (14)

The line break places the emphasis on *whole*, separated from the action, *swallow* but also separated from the pronoun *it*, which represents the "breath." In her careful use of caesura the expression articulates that not only is the breath being swallowed whole, but the breath itself is separated from its wholeness.

These roads of loss and separation, of seeming hopelessness, are not only

Canadian: the narrator knows that while she is experiencing this winter road, somewhere else, on an island

> a woman
> sucks her teeth, walks into a shop on an island
> over there to stretch a few pennies across another
> day, brushes a hand over her forehead and leaves
> going into the street empty-handed. Her certainty
> frighten me. "Is so things is," she muse, reading
> the shopkeeper's guiltless eyes, this hot hope the skin
> tames to brooding, that particular advice, don't expect
> nothing good. Quite here you reach and you forget.
> (10)

All over, on each mass of land, people are coming up against the hard of life, the things that make living difficult and which make home not-home. Everywhere there is a "rough road ahead," even as some roads are more familiar than others.[21] In exploring migration, Brand is careful not to recreate home as a mythic paradise neatly juxtaposed against the hard, new, white place; still, she also acknowledges the sense of familiarity and comfort that an old place (the place of one's birth, for example) can generate and allows that this comfort makes walking the rough road different—a something that one can and should miss and long for. This ambivalence is captured in her language as this latter passage appears more fluid, less hesitant, less a thing of trace even as it is still breaking.

In these aesthetic moments migration is central to the artist's subjectivity. The lack of a homeland is both loss (an imposition) and refusal (a choice) and captivates the ways that language marks and denotes a land as well as the way that land determines a language that sanctions who belongs.[22] The title section of Brand's earlier work No Language evokes this compatibility between language and home, gliding easily from language to land and back again, never missing a beat, each term coupling and bolstering the other:

> No language is neutral. I used to haunt the beach at
> Guaya, two rivers sentinel the country sand . . .
> . . . one river dead
> . . . the other
> rumbling to the ocean in a tumult, the swift undertow
> blocking the crossing of little girls except on the tied
> up dress hips of big women, then, the taste of leaving
> was already on my tongue and cut deep into my
> skinny pigeon toed way, language here was strict

> description and teeth edging truth. Here was beauty
> and here was nowhere.
> (19)

There is an ambivalence in the last line, the beauty and the nowhere, that mocks the way tourist eyes perceive and tourist minds think of island places, a tone similar to Jamaica Kincaid's subtle signifying line "Antigua is beautiful, Antigua is too beautiful."[23] This ambivalence represents the complication Brand's narrator is pointing attention to: that the language that describes the land (the language *of* the land) fails when it becomes "strict description," a language that only knows beauty and nonbeauty and which facilitates the colonial assessment of the island's currency, the land's worth, its people's invisibility. This "neutral" binaried language is

> seared in the spine's unravelling.
> Here is history too. A backbone bending and
> unbending without a word, heat, bellowing these
> lungs spongy, exhaled in humming, the ocean, a
> way out and not anything of beauty, tipping turquoise
> and scandalous.
> (20)

The body and sand and sea trifle are all articulate histories, as is the creole that Brand writes about and in, bearing the mark of a territory's (un)becoming.[24] In these few pages Brand forces the politics and history of language to exist next to the everyday living of little girls on women's hips; of a sea that is beauty and promise, escape and maybe death; she makes the language lay down next to what it cannot describe and the violences it has made both in its flawed attempts at description and in its sanctioning of inferiority; she disavows neutrality and opts, instead, for the barefaced and shameful.

Both *No Language* and *Land* chronicle the lives and hearts broken and sutured by migration and especially the frailty of the connections between the migratory/exiled subject and her people. The land and the conundrum that land becomes for one who is migratory looms over this subject:

> In this country where islands vanish, bodies submerge,
> the heart of darkness is these white roads, snow
> at our throats, and at the windshield a thick white cop
> in a blue steel windbreaker peering into our car, suspiciously,
> even in the blow and freeze of a snowstorm, or perhaps
> not suspicion but as a man looking at aliens.
> Three Blacks in a car on a road.
> (*Land* 73)

The land is treacherous, like a heart of whiteness, a stretch of light and cold that offers no security.[25] The land is one of loss and longing, and not even the promise of an improved life makes the migration any less harsh. So, the subject is always in movement, a restless diasporic spirit. Movements from land to land are movements for political justice and equality, on one hand, but also for rest that is clean and simple and private. These movements across land and through language are repeatedly moments of alignment and disjuncture. Home, nation, land are all lies, myths that require undoing because they are a necessary part of subjecthood; remember that, for all its implication of collectivity, home is also a privacy, an intimacy, an emotional psychology, a sensibility that does not appear on maps, is borderless and altogether never truly reconciled; a yearning and an ambivalence.[26]

This ambivalence is evident throughout Brand's poetry as a hesitation to claim and cling steadfastly to any one place. In the title section of *Land to Light On* the narrator questions the validity of finding a land to light on: "Maybe this wide country just stretches your life to a thinness / just trying to take it in" (43). This realization comes after much rustling with the wide, white Canadian coldness, feeling isolated and feeling very much an unbelonging:

out here I am like someone without a sheet
without a branch but not even safe as the sea,
without the relief of the sky or good graces of a door.
(3)

This pining for traces of home, expressed brilliantly with an abundance of prepositions in adverbial dress, later runs up against the memory of land's own isolation:

But the sight of land has always baffled you,
there is dirt somewhere older than any exile
and try as you might, your eyes only compose
the muddy drain in front of the humid almond
tree, the unsettling concrete sprawl of the housing
scheme, the stone your uncle used to smash his name
into another uncle's face, your planet is in your hands.
(44)

The narrator offers a list-full contrast to the remembered beauty that the homesick might conjure, her statements assertively enunciated in tight subject clauses. Home is of her making, fit to the contours of her imagination and her needs, and, while exile may seem and may *be* intolerable, its distaste subsides when she, the exiled, realizes that her exile is, at least partially, herself, her earned subjectivity:

> I am giving up on land to light on, it's only true, it is only
> something someone tells you, someone you should not trust
> anyway.
> (45)

This giving up on land resituates and restores the narrator's agency: not a land ready-made and bounded, handed to her for consumption and uneasy fit, but a place of her own that will be nowhere but will be wherever she is, so long as she is healthy. Her own (self) something to land and light on.

This pronouncement of landlessness is freeing, so much so that it initiates a long critique of her longing for land:

> I am giving up on a land to light on, slowly, it isn't land,
> it is the same as fog and mist and figures and lines
> and erasable thoughts, it is buildings and governments
> and toilets and front door mats and typewriter shops,
>   [. . .] It's paper,
> paper, maps. Maps that get wet and rinse out, in my hand
> anyway. I'm giving up what was always shifting, mutable
> cities' flourescences [. . .]
>   [. . .] Look. What I know is this. I'm giving up.
> No offence. I was never committed. Not ever, to offices
> or islands, continents, graphs, whole cloth, these sequences
> or even footsteps
> (47)

The critique of land at once suggests that land is both too definite ("figures and lines") and too indefinite ("fog and mist"). Land is not sturdy enough, not a something to lean and rely on, like the warmth of a story or a girlfriend; when the desire to be land-ed couples with home, it becomes rigid and a violation: "bodies lie still across foolish borders" (48). It is both the unholding and the rigidity of land that repels the narrator, and she notes her dismissal in one definitive statement:

> I'm going my way, going my way gleaning shade, burnt
> meridians [. . .]
>   [. . .] I'm trying to put my tongue on dawns
> now [. . .]
>   [. . .] what I
> really want to say is, I don't want no fucking country, here
> or there and all the way back, I don't like it, none of it,
> easy as that.
> (48)

The beauty and clarity of the alternative she seeks is inspiring, and yet this territorial unbecoming is a practice, a thing to be repeated over and again, as she does later on in exploring the "dialectics" between herself and her aunt and in her fiery commentary on the violence done to women all the world over (in a section titled "Every Chapter of the World"). This practice, this acknowledgment of the repetition of (un)becoming, is especially crucial for this narrator, who in her migrations to Canada and to Trinidad will inevitably light on land—will see the land anew and afresh, will want to embrace the promise of return and the even more seductive promise of leaving, will want to covet either the place where she is or the place she was. There is no simple and undemanding truth to her relationship to land:

> The truth is, well, truth is not important at one end of a
> hemisphere where a bird dives close to you in an
> ocean for a mouth full of fish, an ocean you come to
> swim in every two years, you, a slave to your leaping
> retina, capture the look of it. [. . .]
> [. . .] This place so full of your absence [. . .]
> (*No Language* 30)

The truth is this beauty, this familiarity, attaches itself to the body, creating a desire to visit home, even when the desire is driven by identity politics and the fear of being marked out of home, to be too much from somewhere else and considered an outsider.

This struggle to be home, to visit the place of one's birth, is, for the narrator of *No Language* an almost unspeakable thing, one that does not gain full expression in language:

> In another place, not here, a woman might . . . Our
> nostalgia was a lie and the passage on that six hour
> flight to ourselves is wide and like another world, and
> then another one inside and is so separate and fast
> to the skin but voiceless, never born, or born and
> stilled . . . hush.
> (30)

The narrator interrupts her own reverie, her fantasizing about "another place, not here," and instead inserts a quiet and barely audible anxiety about home and loss in its place. In *No Language* the narrator's struggles are more youthful; there is a palpable desire to be home, a celebration of the things that make home familiar and strong and breath-full. In *Land to Light On* the narrator achieves a clearer (but no less complicated) sense of home and firmly rejects it as a myth; instead, she wants and lives a home that is work, an (un)belonging as the disposition of the girlfriend subject—a repeating textuality that informs and disturbs, that is reliable and imperfect, bereft and thorough. Through both

collections Brand argues that one of the challenges of living in migratory conditions: is to not let the leaving of home become a loss of self. The phrase
you are home is a quiet thing one woman says to herself, to her girlfriend; home
is wherever you are as well as wherever you are with your capacity to love.
There is no paradise or heaven to be sought for out there; instead, there is
the "complicated [and] demanding . . . view of heaven as life, not . . . post-life"
(Morrison, "Nobel Lecture" 19). This conceptualization of home does not deny
the need for material sustenance, for tolerable, fruitful, and/or familiar places
that generate good living; instead, this imagining of home as self is indispensable to and in conversation with what it means to make those material
achievements possible. Home is, after all, as welcoming and as nurturing as
one's own commitment to health is; home is only as possible as you are, as
demanding and vigorous as the vagaries of the girlfriend you.

Language as a Mate of One's Soul

Near the end of *No Language* Brand's narrator suggests that language is not
only a friend but also has helped her to make a friend of herself:

> I have become myself. A woman who looks
> at a woman and says, here, I have found you,
> in this, I am blackening my way. You ripped the
> world raw. It was as if another life exploded in my
> face, brightening [. . .]
>   [. . .] so easily I saw my own body, that
> is, my eyes followed me to myself, touched myself
> as a place, another life, terra. [. . .]
> (50)

In writing about complicated and sometimes unyielding connections with
other women and with her home, the narrator has found a new body that is
"a place, another life," land, literally restoring home(land) in herself and her
selffullness. The narrator's edges are solidified and rounded by the cushion of
her opening, "I have become myself," a phrase that is all confession and acquiescence and intimacy, an evocation that is quiet and patient and prayering,
reminiscent of the careful language used to speak of Mammy Prater. The
struggle of language has yielded this "beautiful, bright-faced" dancing other,
has literally brought the word home.

The work of the artist, then, is to make language a mate of one's soul—
to make manifest the relationship between language, self, and love. "Language," Morrison writes, "can be a device for expressing love" ("Nobel Lecture"

15), which is what Brand's narrator realizes. Both language and love are psychic and immaterial, things to be "done" more so than things that "are"; they exist only in process, only as unfoldings. But love, like language, is a conundrum especially because its predominant social narrative limits women's agency, demanding selflessness and thwarting self-achievement. The love then that is being spoken of here is one that is a profound self-regard, like that described by the love letter that Sissie writes to her other and herself in Aidoo's *Our Sister Killjoy*. I have written of that letter earlier, but it is again relevant because of the clear connection it makes between language and love. In this missive Sissie clamors for a language to love with, one that "does not have to be audible. It is beyond Akan or Ewe, English or French. . . . But there are some matters which must be discussed with words. Definitely. At least, by those of us who by the grace of God still have our tongues in our mouths" (113). She accepts the impossibility of language to articulate or manifest love accurately but also acknowledges its capacity to be partnered in love's project: "We have to have our secret language. We must create this language. It is high time we did. We are too old a people not to. We can. We must. So that we shall make love with words and not fear of being overheard" (116). This "secret language" is a home place, a place (or a someone) to belong to, which is Sissie's meditation as she returns to a home that is irresolute.

"Wherever one feels at home must be home," Sissie proclaims as she boldly interrogates why and how it is that any place at all even feels like home, this mesmerizing term. Even when her own yearnings for home remain centered in nation, her plea maintains a commitment to touch, to what those aggregate concepts can never capture: "So please come home, My Brother. Come to our people. They are the only ones who need to know how much we are worth. The rewards would not be much. Hardly anything. For every successful surgery, they will hail you as a miracle worker. Because their faith will not be in the knives you wield but in your hands; in your human touch" (130). The revelation of flesh to flesh, the beholding that is the gift of an/other.

Love is, after all, language-less, needing greater faculties and facilities than language can offer; love does not forgo language but perhaps works to create a language that is less crippled by mastery, something subtler, more intimate and precise, more clean. Like Joe and Violet's love near the end of Morrison's novel *Jazz*, which is represented as a clicking, a beat, a thing that manifests in the interaction between them. After two decades of difficult loving done mostly under a city's watchful (and dangerous) eye, Joe and Violet achieve a poise with each other that is almost wordless: his one-word call to her when he enters the apartment as if anyone else would be there; her hands dusting lint from his suit or his closing the neckline on her dress. Or the narrator's materialization under that phrase *leaf-sigh*, which is counterpart to the novel's final word, hers: *now*. Love is wordless work, our greatest intimacy, and where the thrill and tumble of subjectivity most readily resides.

This is what Black women who are artists do: they construct unfunctioning narrators who choose the vagary of subjecthood, materializing on the page and thrusting the author, herself, into disarray, a narrative anxiety that yields self-referentiality and agency and asserts that to be an artist is to forge a language of selffullness, to make one's own self the place to belong, to be(come) tender and to undo. Imperfect and without surety but home nonetheless.

Conclusion

...*What Is Undone*

MY CONSIDERATION in the previous chapter is necessarily truth and its relatives—certainty, verity, reliability—despite their dismissal as antimodernities, as concepts that have long lost their relevance. For sure, the concept of truth imagined here is not sister to the thirst that fueled the Enlightenment or invasions of Africa, producing along the way precise maps and Eurocentricity. That imperial and imperializing appetite for truth reproduces itself infinitely, dishonest and even unconscious of the searcher's motivations, yielding no satisfaction; it is a hungering mind, insatiable and believing that truth is out there, or at least that *if* truth is there it will be found, had, conquered. A quest that rarely looks at home, at self.

Not that truth. Instead, there is the commitment to truth expressed here in these final chapters but also evident through the whole body of the work, a loyalty that refuses the "out there" and which holds to one certainty: that truth simply is, as in "is possible" or "is necessary." Truth as ritual encountering, a continued practice of self-regard and clarity, a perception, a discernment, an analysis and response, a process that any human body can and must engage; truth as that which is located "at the end of a verifying process, though it remains contingent and revisable" (West, *American Evasion* 67). Not merely relative but informed by the vagary of human life . . . truth as an agency. Such truth is not (only) playful and not ever malicious; its multiplicity does not abdicate history and culpability, for they too are indispensable to discerning.

This book turns on an argument about essentialism, another relative of truth, a thesis that is, at the end, still hesitant: by revising and engaging principles

of poststructuralism, Black feminisms assert an essence that, whatever its vagaries, is nonetheless definitive and ascertainable. This essentiality is not a
mandate or a script, not a recipe for nation or behavior; instead, it is an indelible something, a trace, a varying body that is unreliable and undeniable.
Its corpus is announced and realized in the tension between "me" and "not
me," this phrasal assertion and denial of essence, a particularization that disavows anything other than wild fluidity and which still upholds the
centeredness and surety of this me, Black and female and selfish. "The essence
of something rather than the thing itself" (Marshall 240). Better concepts have
been made in our language for this ephemera: shadow or shade or glance; sigh,
whisper, or smirk; breath or smoke, grey and memory; story, wind, that which
lingers and is faint, that which is liminal. It really needs no more flesh than
these. It is what becomes and is undone, at once and again. As a subjectivity,
it yields "a center without walls," a sense of aggregation and dissolution, which
is the impulse that is at the heart of the Combahee River Collective's statement, Sula's girlhood dreams, and Janie's fantasy of shore and horizon.[1]

It is not a mandate or script, for these Black women cannot truly articulate or propagate nation; their self-centeredness is interfering, their bodies too
intersectional to be merely about this concept, nation, whose fluidity is no
match for their own. Their truth is never precise and clean and to be fascisti-
cally disseminated but is more a glimmer, an idea, a privacy, a small and us-
able something almost sure to fail or to be ineffable but whose utility is shored
up rather than compromised by its being tender, slight, volatile. This truth is
of and about the world, them . . . their poststructure, their love project.

"You may not be better than anyone in the world, but for sure no one in the
world is better than you." My grandmother, Esther Pemberton, died when I
was eight years old and remains the most vital and dynamic living compan-
ion I have. I am not sure that she ever really said these words to me. Maybe I
have made the memory up, maybe I heard this invocation told as a part of
someone else's story and claimed it as my own. Whatever the case, I identify
her with this articulation and find myself propelled through the world by this
little something I attribute to her: you may not be better than anyone in the
world, but for sure no one in the world is better than you.

There is a preciousness to these words, a sense of human commonness
("you *may* not . . . ") bolstered by a steady affirmation of specialness and worth
("but for sure . . . "). I remember coveting the boldness of the latter half of
this urging and using its trust as a quiet arrogance. It is only later in life that I
heard again the first half, the call to be generous, the suggestion that my gifts
were human gifts. As it was in her own living, my grandmother demanded

that my love and my self-righteousness not become tools of violence against other people. This woman, my mother's mother, understood that love was a fierce practice, one to be engaged attentively and patiently. She was not afraid that the complexities of loving were too much for my youth; in fact, she believed love to be the precise syllabus for my childhood.

This work is also, tacitly, about love as a Black feminist cultural idiom. Not love flattened and made superficial in widespread social discourse, expressed only in poorly considered and imagined romantic sentiments but love as a daring and complicated everyday life project, a philosophy of living. Love as a sister of the terrific arc of self, which is what Guyanese writer Beryl Gilroy terms it when she writes that identity is, for her, having "the strength of will to love deeply" (53).

And, truthfully, the study of love has long been and is my meditation, my most intimate engagement. I have and do love, have been and am loved, have failed in and coveted love. The seeming mine-ness of love is this book's most explicit motivation; I needed to lay down on paper these loveful struggles. I am aware that as the book moves on, I am on more of its pages, naked and explicit, my voice no longer pretending to hide but becoming a bold and playful and hesitant "I," desperate, longing to be captivated in my own telling. In my flourishes I slide into my own (un)becoming, am the materializing narrator falling into wonder. At the end I can see that love is this work's textual heartbeat and that I am wanting to find myself here—in chapter and verse. Me and my human yearning: to be loved, to be held, to remember.

And, even with that clarity, this as a conclusion still feels disingenuous, partly because the aim of closure seems impossible. Of necessity, then, I engage these finishing expressions, including first to acknowledge the massive body of contemporary Black women whose work fibrillates mine, people such as Carolyn Rodgers, Lucille Clifton, and Sonia Sanchez; Nikki Giovanni, Gloria Naylor and Rita Dove; Maryse Conde, Estella Majozo Conwill, Wanda Coleman, and Octavia Butler; Ntozake Shange, Tina McElroy Ansa, and Nawal el Saadawi; Edwidge Danticat, Mariama Ba, Harryette Mullen, Ruth Ellen Kocher, Andrea Lee, and Opal Palma Adisa. There are also women from earlier years, such as Zora Neale Hurston and Gwendolyn Brooks (her poetry but also the lovely *Maud Martha*) who are in my mind's heart as I think, write, delight, despair. And then other Black women who are not creative writers as well as other people who are not Black women . . . all amble through these pages, flawlessly, and where there is flaw it is my own.

This book is a beginning articulation of what I have learned from Black women's cultural production, the ways that some Black women think about and make sense of life, and the theoretical and epistemological paradigms that shape some of their thought. I wanted to try to put this into words, to have it appear as a thing, to look it in the face—the gift revealed. And so a final example, that of Sojourner Truth and her well-known "Ain't I a Woman" speech: I am especially attracted to a story from cultural lore about the controversy of Truth speaking at the 1851 Women's Rights convention in Akron. Accounts of the story vary, but the one I most appreciate is dramatic and invites examination: a white clergy man, in denouncing Truth's presence, claimed that she was not a woman and therefore had no right to speak at the meeting. In refuting his accusation, Truth bared her breast in a back room to prove that she was in fact a woman, astutely noting that the shame of the act was not hers but theirs.[2]

The politics of essentialism and corporeality here are interesting, but what most strikes me is Truth's articulation of shame as something foreign to her body, especially in a moment of her body's nakedness that is supposed to be most shameful. Truth resists the incorporation of a subjectivity that is not hers—that of fear, hatred, ridicule—and, instead, counters with words that inspire the titular question that determinedly centers Black female selfhood, "Ain't I a woman?" The question's interrogation is not of Truth or people like her but, instead, an inquisition of racism, sexism, and their human perpetrators. There is an interesting use of first-person both in the speech's title (as well as the implied "I am a woman") and later when Truth reportedly says, "I am a woman's rights." By employing first-person grandeur, both statements challenge the social order that pronounced but also simultaneously disregarded, disavowed even, Black women's gender. Here is a self-enunciation and self-composition (at least in "I am a woman's rights," since the title question is misattributed to Truth), a statement of immanence that literally gives birth to self out of faith, not out of degradation and humiliation. Her "I am" is a construct of essential arrogance, a self-righteousness that disturbs violence, highlights her agency, and celebrates the mindful vagaries of her human body.[3] What is more, Truth's body serves as a text that is specific and not—her body is representative, the sign that marks gender, race, and propriety, what is essential and not. And, considering the paucity of her own words that we have, she literally slips out of the room where she is still the center of (mis)consideration, a moment of becoming and undoing.

What I have learned from Black women's culture, what I think most represents their aesthetics, are two principles that arguably characterize Black culture as a whole: how to live an integrity that is change; and how to live a life that is relevantly lived.[4] The expression of the former is evident in the central argument of this book, that subjectivity is ultimately about change and fragmentation and unsettling. Such volatility is, in fact, a defining quality of human life, and, still, there is an integrity to it all—a politic or something less well defined, like a wish—that tempers and motivates change. A finer version of this is to ask what can it mean for a body, Black, to engage without having to be authenticity or its opposite; for this body to live in spaces between and betwixt that are ludic *and* political? What would it be for us to remember that for all the clarity in the world, for all the articulateness and determinedness, things are messy and chaotic and unclear and that this does not undermine the need to work toward having a relationship with understanding, does not eschew agency or liability? And then there is a "life relevantly lived"—three words that ought to be redundant, for each implies each other: *life* the noun, *living* the action, *relevantly* the condition. What else is there to do but to live this fiercely, flaw-fully; to get tired and to be depressed and to be angry, all of which are manifestations of living relevantly; to set the cosmos' rhythm to the drumming of your heart even in the face of sure disappointment? There is, really, nothing else worth doing. Our charge, then, is to be in a life that is itself an artful, useful, daring practice. This is not meant as frivolous superficiality, as if to suggest that there is an equivalency in every human being, that every (un)ease is the same. No, the commitment to a life lived relevantly gestures always toward recognizing one's place in and responsibility for human suffering.

THAT IS MY grandmother on the cover, her image fading into clarity. It was hard during the design process to watch her disappear—I had not seen a picture of her for years, but, more so, the realization of the book's completion and of her place in my heart was near unbearable. She has been dead since I was eight and still, always, is my heart. Quiet. So playing with the image and watching her slip and recede was too much, a literal test of my own arguments about subjectivity. There she was, even now, teaching me about the subject who is both sovereign and its opposite, the two being the same; about what it means to become a subject and then to surrender. There she was urging me to be mindful of the seduction of having a name, singular and stable and whole; of the intoxicating imperative for the marginalized to be and become that always disavows the necessary undoing that is human. There she was telling me that what it means, politically and spiritually, to matter is in debt to matter's contradiction. There she was teaching me that all fading was not loss and that all loss was not despair, that there is a wholeness that is and is not one.[5]

EVEN IN MY ending, still, over behind a cloud is a sliver, a faint impression of a thing. It is moonlike, quiet, patient, strong enough to shape the movement and meaning of water. Can you see it? No matter if it missed you: it is there, or was, and will be, again. It becomes and is undone.

Notes

Introduction   *What Becomes . . .*

1. I am inspired here by Denise Riley's lovely *The Words of Selves* and her explicit suggestion on page 11 for a need for such a politic.
2. The citation is from Bonner's essay "On Being Young—A Woman—And Colored" (5).
3. The phrase "when and where I enter" is from a famous passage in Anna Julia Cooper's collection *A Voice from the South* and is also the title of Paula Giddings's highly influential history of Black women.
4. For example, Anna Julia Cooper and Pauline Hopkins had both hinted at qualities of Black women's social position and cultural production in the 1890s, and certainly Mary Helen Washington has to be counted as one of the preeminent theorists of U.S. Black women's writings. Carole Boyce Davies, Elaine Savory Fido, Pamela Mordecai, Marjorie Thorpe, Makeda Silvera, and Slyvia Wynter were early theorists of Black women's literary approaches in the Caribbean; and Lloyd Brown, Abena Busia, Obiageli Nwodo, 'Molara Ogundipe-Leslie, Henrietta Otukunefor, Filomina Chioma Steady, and Efua Sutherland in relation to the Continent.
5. In her landmark essay "Black (W)holes" Hammonds argues that the conceptualization of Black female sexuality in relation to white feminity has left the full range of Black women's identities are largely unknown. Smith's argument, in this vein, seems useful in introducing another crucial aspect of Black female selfhood.
6. I am indebted to Karla F. C. Holloway's comments early in *Moorings and Metaphors*, in which she reclaims Smith as having made a successful argument about the category "Black woman" as a Foucauldian category, one of social relevance and specific currency, similar to the categories "Black" and "woman" individually (4). Joan Martin, in her essay "The Notion of Difference for Emerging Womanist Ethics," and Monique Savage, in personal conversations, have made similar assertions about the integrity of "Black woman" as a category, both suggesting that the two words be written as one. More recently, essays in critical race feminist discourse, particularly Adrien Katherine Wing's "Brief Reflections toward a Multiplicative Theory and Praxis of Being" and Angela P. Harris's "Race and Essentialism in Feminist Legal Theory," have contested the idea of "Black" without "woman." What all of this suggests is the room for mobility in these otherwise familiar and static categorizations.
7. I am being playful here, for surely Virginia Woolf's famous conceptualization of "a room of one's own" implies a selfhood to match.

8. I am referencing and engaging the version that is reproduced in *The Cultural Studies Reader* (ed. Simon During) because it is more useful and relevant than the expanded piece in *Signs*.

9. These are three signal examples in which Black identity arrives predetermined, even before the body that is Black itself has arrived: Frantz Fanon's famous recounting of a young girl's exclamation in *Black Skins, White Masks*; James Baldwin's arrival in a small Swiss village as the unknown but already familiar dark corpus in "A Stranger in the Village"; and Ann DuCille's smart description of Deborah McDowell (dis)appearing as both monster and mammy for Jane Gallop in "The Occult of True Black Womanhood."

10. In her article de Lauretis challenges the construction of cultural feminism as an impediment to the possibilities of poststructuralist feminism. I read her term cultural feminism to be interchangeable with Black feminism, a euphemism intended to soften the blow of her potentially damning appraisal of dominant feminist discourses. However de Lauretis does not aim to explain why there is this irreconcilability between the two feminisms—that poststructuralist feminism, raced white and liberated from the trapping of the body in racial terms, only needs to find a way to give up the body of its femaleness. That is, in a Cartesian binary system whiteness and maleness are freer terms, less tied to the body, locations of agency; the opposite is true for Blackness and femaleness. This characterization also defines how theoretical schools of thought are imagined, such that being female and/or Black—or at least being concerned intellectually with either of these locations of identity—is a trap, a perceived limit on one's capacity and vagary, a thing that is less sophisticated because of its necessary relationship to essentialism. The impulse, then, is to move away from the body, or, more precisely, from race and gender as sites that highlight and retain the body.

    Part of what de Lauretis is trying to do is merge poststructuralist feminism with cultural feminism, the latter being commonly seen as essentialist and the former as anti-essentialist. She is trying to be savvy and sensible about not replicating the inelegant and inaccurate charge that is often made against Black feminisms: that they are unsophisticated, uncomplicated, too reliant on an essential body; that they are disruptive. A well-noted example is Susan Gubar's sleight in "What Ails Feminist Criticism?" which more clearly says what perhaps many others want to say but hardly ever directly do—that Black women and other women of color are largely a troubling site of feminism. See Rachel Lee's smart "Notes from the (non)Field: Teaching and Theorizing Women of Color"; and Robyn Weigman's thoughtful "What Ails Feminist Criticism? A Second Opinion," which Lee's article pointed me to.

    The dilemma of the Black female body haunting white women's best discursive efforts is, in Ann DuCille's imagination, a replay of the maternalization of the Black mammy. See her essay "The Occult of True Black Womanhood," in *Skin Trade*. For an earlier discussion of this haunting and a savvy challenge to feminisms, see Elizabeth V. Spelman's *Inessential Woman*.

11. I am referencing the late Barbara Christian's arguments in "A Race for Theory" as well as "The Highs and Lows of Black Feminist Criticism."

12. I am borrowing the language here from Elizabeth Alexander's thoughtful essay "'Can You Be BLACK and Look at This?'" It is also worth noting bell hooks's early formulation of a constructive and evocative relationship between theory and Black identity (especially "Postmodern Blackness," in *Yearning*) and Patricia Hill Collins's feisty and useful chapter "What's Going On? Black Feminist Thought and the Politics of Postmodernism," for they are noted and noticeable parts of my intellectual atmosphere.

At the heart of the discussion here is the realization of identity's perimeters and theory's unbound. Jackie Goldsby, in her smart essay "Queen for 307 Days: Looking B[l]ack at Vanessa Williams and the Sex Wars," gives what I think is an effective comment on the matter; she writes that, "though other 'post' theories (namely structuralism and, now, feminism) are on the politically correct tip since they propose a new rationality based on pluralism, fragmentation, and nonlinear/narrative worldviews, they nevertheless manage to leave race less conceptualized than either gender or sexuality because theorists misconstrue what 'race' can mean" (182). Goldsby goes on to suggest that such oversight reflects the confusion between the meaning of race and the exploration of racism. I am with her here: this work is decidedly interested in the impact that race (and its oppressive manifestation, racism) and gender (and sexism)—to name two staticized localities—have on Black women's cultural idioms, but neither an anesthetized consideration of race nor a too easy citation of racism will do here. There must be something more.

13. *The Norton Anthology of African-American Literature* cites 1970 as a crucial marker in U.S. Black literary studies; Renee Larrier concurs in terms of Francophone writers in the Caribbean and the Continent; as do Carole Boyce Davies and Elaine Savory in respect to sub-Saharan African women. See Larrier, *Francophone Women Writers of Africa and the Caribbean* (esp. p. 4); and Davies and Fido's "African Women Writers: Toward a Literary History," in *A History of Twentieth Century African Literatures* (esp. p. 317). In studies of African literatures, especially sub-Saharan African literature, it is widely accepted that Black women did not become a major force of the literary landscape until 1970; the same is true for African-American literature. That time marker also bears significance for Caribbean literatures: Selwyn Cudjoe states that "the publication of Merle Hodge's *Crick Crack Monkey* (1970) ushered in a new era in the writings of women in the English-speaking Caribbean" (43); he also argues that "the rise of women's writing in the Caribbean cannot be viewed in isolation. It is a part of a much larger cultural expression of women's realities that is taking place in the postcolonial worlds and post–civil rights era in the U.S." (6); see his introduction to *Caribbean Women Writing*. Laura Niesen de Abruna expands this point with a larger claim: "Until the late 1970s, very little was written about these authors (women) because the critics' attention was focused on the male writers Wilson Harris, George Lamming, Edgar Mittelholzer, V. S. Naipaul and Edward Braithwaite" ("Twentieth-Century Women Writers from the English-Speaking Caribbean," 86). For sure, all three areas exhibit enormous increases in Black women writers in the 1980s and 1990s.

I am well aware of various criticisms of marking history in such ways (for example, many African scholars resist the idea, and its implications, that the publication of Amos Tutuola's *Palm-Wine Drinkard* in 1952 and Chinua Achebe's *Things Fall Apart* two years later constitute the beginnings of the modern African novel). And well one should contest such points. Still, I believe that markers can indicate points of relevance or even shifts in discourses, especially when such markers are subject to question and change. I find the use of a late–1960s/early–1970s referent useful and accurate for my purposes of grouping writers and their sensibilities.

14. I am using the term *postmodern blackness* from bell hooks's arguments in *Yearning*. I also readily acknowledge the Western slant of this project, an issue that I address near the end of this introduction.

15. Washington's American Studies Presidential address, delivered on 29 October 1997, was reprinted with the signal question in its title, "Disturbing the Peace: What Happens to American Studies if You Put African American Studies at the Center?"

16. See Christian, "Race for Theory."

17. There is, of course, a longer conversation that could be produced here. I am forgoing

that for the sake of elegance, though by the book's end I find and acknowledge the more and more of myself that manifest on its pages. My debt is clear, as is, I hope, my agency, and certainly my sense of freedom to not say more about my subject position is a beneficiary of the presence of scholarship such as Michael Awkward's oft-reprinted essay "A Black Man's Place in Black Feminist Criticism." I am grateful for the anonymous reader who nudged me toward a clearer expression of this positionality.

Chapter 1   The Other Dancer as Self

1. The citation is from *Their Eyes Were Watching God* (6).
2. This term *disidentification* is most readily found in contemporary cultural psychology; see Claude Steele. Another key referent is Jose Munoz's *Disidentifictions: Queers of Color and the Performance of Politics*, in which the term means the recycling of mainstream and heteronormative images and ideologies as a form of resistance. My use of the term here is intended to evoke more the classical psychoanalytic paradigm of a disturbance of the self's familiar identifications. As such, it is a process less willful than Munoz's, less determined to resist but perhaps no less effective as a resistant and creative praxis. More a spirituality.
3. The citation is from Trinh T. Minh-ha's *Woman, Native, Other* (40).
4. The phrase is the title of chapter 1 of bell hooks's *Feminist Theory: From Margin to Center.*
5. I am grateful to Brenda Allen, whose feedback made this insight succinct and clear.
6. The idea of a constructed or constructing selfhood has various origins in modern Western critical thought, notably Freud or Fanon or Foucault, and is the antithesis of Kantian and Cartesian ideology. Similarly, there is a large body of thinkers who suggest, explicitly or less so, that identity is achieved in relation to some other subject, body, discourse, metaphor, etc. (for example, Hegel, Marx, Lacan, as well as the aforementioned trilogy). And the particular representation of relational identity among women is not exclusive to Black women, though the context of assumed and totalizing selflessness that is a key thread of the aesthetic of girlfriend selfhood is particular to Black women's cultural work.
7. Reading Robin Kelley's *Yo Mama's Disfunktional* (esp. p. 23) helped me crystallize the intracommunal obsession, while reading Black women's critique of Black men's overengagement with white men in their masculine power affirmed my understanding of the intercommunal obsession. Frantz Fanon's argument in *White Skins, Black Masks* perhaps most clearly evidences both binaries.
8. It bears noting that readers of various versions of this work have resisted the suggestion that the discussion of identity necessarily engages psychoanalytic concepts, while other readers have found such a designation to be crucial. My own position is that the critical discourse of psychoanalysis permeates much academic scholarship in the United States, and, while I want to engage concepts that are perhaps psychoanalytic in their name, I also want to be unencumbered by its reach.
9. The inquisition of psychoanalysis's limits has yielded discursive strains of psychoanalysis that take greater note of that which is explicitly political: for example, the revisions of Lacan that many French feminist thinkers have been undertaking, revisions that arguably extend from Melanie Klein's object relations theory, compel the discipline to consider gender as a distinctly social and political category, as one often parallel to but not synonymous with sex. In fact, Klein's work highlights the real corporeal other (the mother, for example) who is unarticulated in the Freudian dialectic between self and fantasy/memory and, in this way, is useful to me here. It is also important to suggest that the relational identity I am arguing

for is not in opposition to a positional one (identity defined by position of power within social structures), as is the case with most interpretations of object relations theory (see Stephen Mitchell and Margaret Black's *Freud and Beyond: A History of Modern Psychoanalytic Thought*). In fact, the imperative for the coalition *is* an understanding of positionality. Mitchell and Black also cite Alfred Adler as a psychoanalyst who considers social and political influences upon a patient's experience of psyche and subjectivity. This is also the case with Erik Erikson's *Childhood and Society*, in which he considers the individual in a historical moment and cultural context.

10. The reconsideration of psychoanalysis in cultural studies has greatly influenced my own thinking about its possibilities in my work. See especially Claudia Tate (*Psychoanalysis and Black Novels*), Hortense Spillers ("Mama's Baby" and "All the Things You Could Be by Now"), Evelyn Hammonds ("Black [W]holes and the Geometry of Black Female Sexuality"), as well as Kaja Silverman (*Threshold of the Visible World*), and Anne McClintock (*Imperial Leather*).

11. See Patricia Hill Collins's encyclopedic *Black Feminist Thought* for a thorough discussion of terms.

12. The examples of scholars who argue for the prominence and importance of Black women's relationships with one another are too many to name. See especially Collins, *Black Feminist Thought*, 178–183. I will, instead, concentrate here on Barbara Smith's classic essay "Toward a Black Feminist Criticism," which suggests that Black women's narrative aesthetics highlight the relationship between and among women. In her essay Smith sets out to make "some connections between the politics of black women's lives, what we write about and our situation as artists. In order to do this I will look at how black women have been viewed critically by outsiders, demonstrate the necessity for black feminist criticism, and try to understand what the existence or nonexistence of black lesbian writing reveals about the state of black women's culture and the intensity of *all* black women's oppression" (158). My own work, especially in its use of Morrison's *Sula* as signal text, parallels Smith's in the attention to homosocial Black female connection as a location of a cultural aesthetic. But I am differently interested in the way this homosociality is a trope of selfhood and, therefore, how it reflects and challenges other manifestations of selfhood in critical theory. (The latter interest is further evident in the two succeeding chapters.) Smith's essay, on the other hand, is interested in explicitly justifying the need for a particular Black woman approach to reading literature. In some ways mine is a part of the larger project to which Smith was pointing attention.

13. I am playing off of the opening distinction that Hurston makes in *Their Eyes* between how men and women dream differently: men live on the horizon, and women are the shore. Janie in the novel represents an attempt to bring these two desires together in one Black woman's process of selfhood.

14. An early example of this disidentification is their deadly and dangerous play with Chicken Little, after which "there [is] a space, a separateness, between them" (63). Other moments include the argument about Sula's placing Eva in a nursing home (101) and the conversation they have at Sula's deathbed (142).

15. I am drawing here on Homi K. Bhabha's work on the third space, which I will discuss more explicitly later in this chapter. See his essay "Cultural Diversity and Cultural Differences," in *The Post-Colonial Studies Reader* (an excerpt of his longer work "The Commitment to Theory" from *New Formations*, 5). A similar mediated position is discernible from Hélène Cixous's representation of bisexuality in *The Newly Born Woman*. The problematizing of binaries is also the general thrust of deconstructionist critical thought.

16. I am borrowing the term *uncanny dissonance* from Coco Fusco's narrative for an exhibition catalog of Simpson's work.

17. When Nel asks Jude how his day went, he proceeds to tell her and Sula "a whiney tale that peaked somewhere between anger and a lapping desire for comfort. He ended it with the observation that a Negro man had a hard row to hoe in this world" (103). But Sula does not offer commiseration. Instead, she smiles and says:

    I mean, I don't know what the fuss is about. I mean, everything in the world loves you. White men love you. They spend so much time worrying about your penis they forget their own. The only thing they want to do is cut off a nigger's privates. And if that ain't love and respect I don't know what is. And white women? They chase you all to every corner of the earth, feel for you under every bed. I knew a white woman wouldn't leave the house after 6 o'clock for fear one of you would snatch her. Now ain't that love? They think rape soon's they see you, and if they don't get the rape they looking for, they scream it anyway just so the search won't be in vain. Colored women worry themselves into bad health just trying to hang on to your cuffs. Even little children—white and black, boys and girls—spend all their childhood eating their hearts out 'cause they think you don't love them. And if that ain't enough, you love yourselves. Nothing in this world loves a black man more than another black man. You hear of solitary white men, but niggers? Can't stay away from one another a whole day. So it looks to me like you the envy of the world. (103–104)

    Sula's comment notes the violence that surrounds Black men but also identifies the high visibility and centrality (itself violent) that Black men occupy in the American imagination and fascination (which is, she notes, a form of masculine privilege).

18. The relevance is widely evident: consider that in the last thirty years narrative representations of Black women loving each other have spurred various attacks by Black men on the works of Black women writers—for example, Robert Staples's well-cited criticism of Michelle Wallace and others and the general response by some Black men to Walker's *The Color Purple*. See Calvin Hernton, *The Sexual Mountain and Black Women Writers*, which nicely elaborates on the disdainful and demeaning reception that the contemporary explosion of Black women's literature has received from established Black male writers and critics (esp. pp. 42–48). And, while these have not been the only attacks made against Black women's literary production, they do reveal a level of disrespect for Black female selffullness. But perhaps these comments also affirm that Black women self-focus is revolutionary in the same manner that Joseph Beam proclaimed Black men's mutual love to be revolutionary—as a practice that is counter to the intentions of social oppression. Beam's comment is not a narcissistic conceptualization of same-gender love nor an elevation of Blackness as the essential body but, instead, echoes the commonly held idea that a Black person who, under colonization, chooses to love any other Black person is potentially evidencing a love of self. For sure, Beam's proclamation worried some people, including Issac Julien, who wondered about the essentialist nature of the argument. I understand Beam's statement in a larger context of decolonization, and interpret it liberally, even as I am conscious of the potential narcissism that is implied. This chapter will make a further comment on narcissism later. See Don Belton's "Where We Live" for the conversation with Julien (219).

19. Of all of Lacan's work that I am familiar with, it is "The Mirror Stage" that is most key to his revision of Freud and which is most often cited.

20. Such only holds for male children; for female children there is no subjectivity, be-

cause theirs is to bear and nurture male children toward subjectivity unfulfilled. This is a widely held conclusion of some feminist psychoanalytic thought; see especially Teresa de Lauretis, *The Practice of Love;* and Kaja Silverman, *Threshold of the Visible World;* as well as the general arc of Catherine Clément's, Luce Irigaray's and Hélène Cixous's works. Also see Elizabeth Grosz, who, in *Jacques Lacan: A Feminist Introduction,* writes that the phallus in Lacanian cosmology "signifies what men (think they) have and what women (are considered to) lack" (125).

21. It is worth noting that, even as Weems's work is less exclusively about women, this anxiety of the mirror manifests nonetheless. For the most lucid explication of modernity and the visual sign, see Sander Gilman's "Black Bodies, White Bodies."

22. The normalization of capitalizations is mine, as Weems's caption is entirely capitalized.

23. Various critics exploit the idea of otherness, including bell hooks (especially "Choosing the Margin," in *Yearning*), Valerie Smith ("Black Feminist Theory and the Representation of the 'Other'"), Michele Wallace ("Variations on Negation"), Bhabha, Cixous, Irigaray, and Kristeva. Trinh argues that woman (and woman of color) is other (in *Woman, Native, Other*) and writes, "Otherness becomes empowerment, critical difference when it is not given but recreated" (in "Not You / Like You" 418). Interestingly, the inspiration to reclaim and redefine otherness seems to come from its ubiquity as a site of oppression. The fascination with and deployment of otherness is clearly postmodern, yet it is not postmodernity I am most readily citing here, especially because so much of that discourse lacks the political sensibility that I think is indispensable. In fact, I would echo hooks's sentiment in "Postmodern Blackness" that the engagement of otherness is a decidedly Black cultural idiom.

24. Clearly, I have anxieties about using Lacan but am also thrilled by the possibilities of psychoanalysis, which I think can be quite relevant to thinking about Black subjectivity. For example, Hortense Spillers astutely argues in "All the Things You Could Be by Now" that substitutive identity is parallel to negation and negation is constitutive of Blackness; it seems, then, that Blackness and psychoanalysis have much in common. Yet it is also her work, especially "Mama's Baby," that assured me that I was to be uneasy about a too-easy use of psychoanalysis. Whatever the case, another notable disagreement and dissonance with Lacan generates from his representation of wholeness as contextualized by the mirror: since the mirror's offerings are illusory, then wholeness and agency are also illusory. Although Lacan's work to disrupt the idea of an idealized and whole self is important, the playful character and endless unfulfilling of his framework is less useful and less accurate. Mitchell and Black write: "At times Lacan seems to reify language, granting it a kind of transpersonal agency. The patient as presented becomes a puzzle, to be disassembled, so that the real meanings are revealed" (199), an assessment that corroborates with Clement's arguments and my misgivings about Lacan's work.

25. The quotation is from Anna Deveare Smith's introduction to *Fires in the Mirror.*

26. I think that this presence of psychic travel is a critique of the masculine trajectory of coming-of-age stories in Western literary culture, a trajectory that also looms large in much literature by Black men in the Diaspora. For a clear summative argument about interiority in African-American women's culture, see my essay "Black Feminisms and *The Autobiography of Malcolm X.*"

Homi Bhabha, Gloria Anzaldúa (*Borderlands*), and bell hooks (*Yearning*), to name a few, have variously argued for the transgressive possibilities that lay in mobility. Bhabha's notion of third space is especially crucial in this respect. Also see Carole Boyce Davies's very smart study of migration in Black women's subjectivity in *Black Women, Writing and Identity: Migrations of Subject.*

27. I am using the phrase from bell hooks, *Sisters of the Yam* (6).
28. I also think it is helpful to remember that Black women's specific cultural practices have widespread impact on individuals and communities who/that are not Black women, which is a logical extension of Walker's argument in her essay "In Search of Our Mothers' Gardens." Without recklessly appropriating Black women's cultures, I am committed to exploring the ways that such cultures, and the aesthetic, epistemological, literary, and philosophical principles that these cultures evidence, are decisive and necessary foundations of cultural production as a whole. Against the invisibility and erasure to which Black women's contributions are often subjected, I am trying sensibly to elucidate and highlight their widespread impact.

    Further, this mix of specificity and inclusivity is evident in key Black feminist texts; see, for example, the Combahee River Collective's Statement; Patricia Hill Collins, *Black Feminist Thought;* Michele Wallace, "A Black Feminist Search for Sisterhood," or Audre Lorde's "Uses of the Erotic." And, as Adrienne Rich evidences in her discussion of compulsory heterosexuality, *lesbian* is both a referent for specific sexual acts as well as a descriptor of a less-specific social, cultural, aesthetic, political expression or context (including the caveat against and risk of depoliticization); see *Of Woman Born* and *On Lies, Secrets, and Silence.* The matter of sexuality reappears in later chapters, though it is worth saying here that I am not precluding a lesbian possibility that is, after all, so at the heart of Barbara Smith's essay and other works that are to me counsel.
29. This is quoted from the Stanley Love Group description of the dance piece "Callico," taken from the program for the Tribeca Performing Arts Center's Work and Show Festival: Artists in Residence 2001–2002.
30. I am using the terms *differentiation* and *integration* from Arthur Chickering's model of college student development; Chickering borrows them from psychological discourse. See *Education and Identity.*
31. In *Sula* we are told that "the Peace women simply loved maleness," (41) which is both that they loved men and also that they loved manly characteristics (such as freedom and triumph). These comments on gender echo what Angela Davis argues in "The Legacy of Slavery: Standards for a New Womanhood" about the conflict between Black women's expected social roles and larger notions of (white women) femininity. It is exactly these contradictions that Sojourner Truth is elucidating when she notes that she can work as much as a man, which, in fact, makes her a woman. Such is the intersection of gender and race in a U.S. context—that gender for Black women is not based on notions of fragility, domesticity, piety. So, it makes sense that, as Sula lays on her deathbed, she revises Truth's statement, reminding Nel that being a woman and being Black is the same as being a man.
32. This reconsideration of Black men is also evident in Morrison's *Beloved,* in which Paul D's sweetness allows him to be the kind of man whom the women would tell all their secrets to, a disposition that I think facilitates his coupling with Sethe. Walker even represents Harpo and Albert coupled in girlfriend selfhood: Harpo holds his father's hand as Albert comes into old age, an act of kindness and gentility that the two men have learned by living in the company of women.

    In reading Evelyn Hammonds's "Black (W)holes," I am struck by this passage she must have written about the same time I was writing the original version of this chapter: "Rather than assuming that black female sexualities are structured along an axis of normal and perverse paralleling that of white women, we might find that for black women a different geometry operates. For example, acknowledging this difference I could read the relationship between Shug and Celie in Alice Walker's *The Color Purple* as one which depicts desire between women and desire between women and men simultaneously, in dynamic relationship rather than in opposition" (492–493). I am grateful for Hammonds's implied affirmation of my attempt to articulate part of that geometry here.

33. See Vashti Crutcher Lewis, "African Tradition in Toni Morrison's *Sula*," which unfortunately imposes a heteronormalized frame (of African priest and priestess) on an otherwise important exploration of the relationship between Sula and Shadrack.

34. One interesting comment on the political inflection of Black women's selfhood manifests in Donna Haraway's idea of a "cyborg," which she aligns with the political and politicized identity of women of color that "marks out a self-consciously constructed space that cannot affirm the capacity to act on the basis of natural identification, but only on the basis of conscious coalition, of affinity, of political kinship" (156). In spite of my hesitation to use Haraway, I do find her articulation of a politicized coalitional identity for women of color to be useful.

35. This idea is widely acknowledged as being central to deconstructionist theories and postmodern thought, yet Black feminist critics such as bell hooks have questioned the widespread centering of otherness in theoretical models that largely ignore the political reality of those who are othered (see *Yearning* and *Outlaw Culture*). This sense of otherness that I am discussing here is not merely fashionable otherness but otherness as an identity of agency.

36. I am borrowing from Morrison's comment in relation to her character Jadine in *Tar Baby*, made in her interview with Gloria Naylor (194).

37. In talking about the erotogenic surfaces of the body (a body that she has refigured to extend beyond the limits of corporeality), Grosz writes that "the relationship between these regions or zones cannot be understood in terms of domination, penetration, control or mastery, but in terms of *jealousy*, as one organ jealous of another, as the desire of organs and zones for the intensity and excitations, the agitations and tumultuousness of others. In order that one bodily part (whether an orifice, a hollow, a protuberance, a swollen region, a smooth surface) intensify its energetic expenditure, it must drain intensity from surrounding regions. . . . Each organ envies the intensity of its surrounding bodily context, craves enervation, seeks incandescence, wants itself to be charged with excitations" ("Animal Sex," in *Time, Space and Perversions* 197). The idea of narcissism as a construct of (pathologized) gay sexuality is obviously problematic and limited. As Michael Warner suggests, the homosexual is only narcissistic in normative heterosexuality; see "Homo-Narcissism; or Heterosexuality." But, even more so, this idea of girlfriend selfhood disavows narcissism as a frame because such selfhood proposes self-centeredness against the expectation of Black women's other-focus.

38. The phrase is from Cliff, *No Telephone*, 50. Cliff is echoing the Rastafarian colloquial exclamation "I and I." This idea of radical self-possession is one that I will discuss more completely in a later chapter in regards to Cliff's use of the term *ruinate* in her novel *No Telephone to Heaven*.

39. There is a moment early in *The Color Purple* when Harpo is wondering what to do about Sofia's wild spirit. Celie bluntly tells him to beat her and does not recognize until later that she has "sin[ned] against Sofia['s] spirit" (37). The re(-)pair of Celie and Sofia is concerned not only with this violation but also with Celie's need to claim Sofia as her sister now that Nettie has left. The actions of re(-)pair are small, but they occur largely through one act of sisterhood—the making of a quilt (53).

When Sofia lands in jail and is horribly beaten, it is Celie who visits her, a visit that re(-)pairs Sofia's body and their relationship and mirrors Celie and Shug's careful attention to each other's physical details:

> When I see Sofia I don't know why she still alive. They crack her skull, they
> crack her ribs. They tear her nose loose on one side. They blind her in one eye.
> She swole from head to foot. Her tongue the size of my arm, it stick out tween
> her teef like a piece of rubber. She can't talk. And she just about the color of a
> eggplant.
>   Scare me so bad I near bout drop my grip. But I don't. I put it on the floor
> of the cell, take out a comb and brush, nightgown, witch hazel and alcohol and
> I start to work on her. The colored tendant boy bring me water to wash her
> with, and I start at her two little slits for eyes. (77)

Celie literally rubs life back into Sofia's almost-dead body, an act of sisterly re(-)pair.

Chapter 2   Self(full)ness and the Politics of Community

1. Audre Lorde, *Sister Outsider*, 57.
2. These examples of outsiderness metaphorically characterize the tension between self and community, a tension that Valerie Smith explains as "the interplay between self-knowledge and social role" (*Self Discovery*, 123).
3. Various critics have noted alienation as a key characteristic of the novel, but it is Elzibeth Wilson's oft-cited "'Le voyage et espace close'—Island and Journey as Metaphor" that best theorizes the abjection aesthetic of Francophone Caribbean women novelists. The novel is also often read as a narrative of diaspora, though it is the place—not the movement—of Juletane that most interests me here.
4. For an efficient discussion of the binds of migration, see Carole Boyce Davies, *Black Women, Writing and Identity.*
5. It is noteworthy that, unlike other madwomen in literary convention, Juletane is not confined to a room with a mirror but, instead, is in a room that has an expansive window. The window here functions as a revised mirror, as a construct that seemingly frames and reflects the limits of space. But, still, the window undercuts its own ability to frame and limit space: the very border of the window points attention to things that are outside of the border, that do not fit within the frame. In this way the window articulates abundance and possibility, more so than the mirror, either metaphorically or in a Lacanian reading, which sets limits and produces the image that (over)determines subsequent images and knowledge. For a discussion of madness and the window in Juletane, see especially Evelyn O'Callaghan, "Interior Schisms Dramatised: The Treatment of the 'Mad' Woman in the Work of Some Female Caribbean Novelists"; and Anne-Lanscaster Badders, "Les plis dans les puits: Identity and Narrative in Myriam Warner-Vieyra's *Juletane.*" Also see Jonathan Ngate, "Reading *Juletane*," Elisabeth Mudimbe-Boyi, "Narrative 'je(ux)' in *Kamouraska* by Anne Herbert and *Juletane* by Myriam Warner-Vieyra"; and Shoshana Felman, *Writing and Madness* (esp. 252).
6. It is interesting in the scope of this claim to think of diaries and letters, employed in *Juletane*, *The Color Purple*, and later in *Our Sister Killjoy* and *No Telephone to Heaven*, as forms of the "female" self. In this context Wendy Wall's reading of letters in *The Color Purple* is significant.
7. The ambiguity about the deaths is reflective, I think, of Warner-Vieyra's construction of the slim novel as an arch-metaphor. For example, the places in the novel appear more representative than specific, and largely are defined through Juletane's experiences and interactions. In fact, it is arguable that Juletane's dream consciousness makes the names of towns and countries less relevant to the world of the novel.
8. Here I am engaging the way that Kaja Silverman talks about "identity-at-a-distance" (14), an identification model that she constructs to explore the possibilities for love in psychoanalysis. Silverman, using the work of psychoanalysts Paul

Schilder and Henri Wallon, makes a distinction between visual image as one location of subjectivity (exteroceptive ego) and the sensational body as another (proprioceptive ego) (10–17). She argues that, in a model of otherness, identification with the visual image of another, idiopathic identification, can be detrimental to the other, resulting in the "absorption of another self by one's own." She does, however, argue for heteropathic identification, the identification between a subject and the object of his or her desire that generates not from the image but from the sensational body (23). What is most useful to me in Silverman's work are the ideas that otherness is an appropriate model for identification and that embracing otherness is potentially dangerous. I am also motivated by her attempt to negotiate otherness outside of traditional hierarchies that often exist in binary models.

9. In "Eating the Other" bell hooks tells us that "contemporary working-class British slang playfully converges the discourse of desire, sexuality and the Other, evoking the phrase getting 'a bit of the Other' as a way to speak about sexual encounter" (22).

10. For a general reference, see Catherine MacKinnon, *Toward a Feminist Theory of the State*.

11. "Nobody knew the rose of my world but me. / I had too much glory. / They don't like glory like that / in nobody's heart."

12. Although Sula and Nel never have sex with each other in the space of the narrative, their coupling exists under a definitive subtext of sexual union. In fact, some critics cite this as a failure of Morrison's, even as others proclaim it to be the achievement of her subtlety and craft. As young girls, digging the hole together, their bodies are their own, as is their choice to merge together (see 58). This custody of one's own body is crucial for young Black girls, whose bodies and sexualities are often being possessed by the willful violence of others not themselves. Even after Nel is married, her laughter with Sula is ecstatic and orgasmic: "Nel lowered her head onto crossed arms while tears of laughter dripped into the warm diapers. Laughter that weakened her knees and pressed her bladder into action. Her *rapid* soprano and Sula's dark sleeply chuckle made a *duet* that frightened the cat and made the children run in from the back yard, puzzled at first by the *wild free* sounds, then delighted to see their mother stumbling merrily toward the bathroom, holding on to her stomach, fairly singing through the laughter: 'Aw. Aw. Lord. Sula. Stop'" (97; emph. added). Sula and Nel work each other to a frenzy that exudes from Nel the orgasmic cries, and, despite her claim in her postcoital meditation that she had only known "matchless harmony," Sula's relationship with Nel had moments of sweet and exact love—a love nurtured and returned.

13. As Gay Wilentz accurately notes, a key aspect of Sissie's self-struggle is her pursuance of such an education against her disdain for countrymen so educated who are then seduced into remaining in the West. Aidoo revises and feminizes the paradigm of exile to corroborate Sissie's coming-of-age. Most critics read Aidoo's own experience of exile as parallel to Sissie's being away from her country (see, for example, Gay Wilentz, "The Politics of Exile: Ama Ata Aidoo's *Our Sister Killjoy*"; and Mary E. Modupe Kolawole, *Womanism and African Consciousness*, esp. 134–136). Also see Sara Chetin's excellent article "Reading from a Distance: Ama Ata Aidoo's *Our Sister Killjoy*," which uses outsider status as a frame for exploring not just issues of exile but other manifestations of colonial condition. Also see Myriam J. A. Chancy's redefinition of exile in "Productive Contradictions: Afro-Caribbean Diasporic Feminism and the Question of Exile," in *Searching* (1–30).

14. José Rabasa's essay "Allegories of Atlas" (as titled and excerpted in *The Post-Colonial Studies Reader*, from his book *Inventing America: Spanish Historiography and the*

Formation of Eurocentricism) reveals how cartography uses the body of white women as seductive lure in convincing white men to violate unexplored (Black) land. Part of Marija's desire to be Sissie's friend is her realization of her subjugated existence in German colonial narrative; part of Sissie's hesitation is her realization of her subjugated existence in German colonial narrative and questions about who Marija can be to her.

15. See *Reconstructing Womanhood*, in which Carby notes marriage and motherhood as dually engaged in the social regulation of womanhood, especially for white women. While the same is true of Black women, it is arguable that in the United States, where marriages between Black women and Black men have not always been legal and then have not always carried a similar social relevance and purpose as marriage in other U.S. contexts (see, for example, Ann DuCille's *Coupling Convention*), motherhood is the greater site of regulation, even as legal decisions are made about Black women's lives in relation to their marriage status (see, for example, *The Moynihan Report*). Betty Friedan and Simone de Beauvoir have made foundational arguments about marriage as a state of women's subjection.

16. This idea is the crux of Adrienne Rich's *Of Woman Born*, in which she delineates between the experience of being a mother and the institutionalization of motherhood as a site of women's oppression, what she terms "motherhood as enforced identity and political institution" (*On Lies, Secrets, and Silence*, 196)

17. See Dorothy Roberts's essay "Racism and Patriarchy in the Meaning of Motherhood," which is the most cogent tracing of the history of the social meaning of motherhood for U.S. Black women that I have read. Also see her thorough critical analysis in *Killing the Black Body*.

18. I am thinking here of Black women in slavery but also of the particular ambivalence to marriage and motherhood that, according to Paula Giddings, was so common among women of the National Association of Colored Women. Ann DuCille notes, and my students have commonly also picked up on this, the particularity of Janie Crawford's being childless in Hurston's *Their Eyes Were Watching God*. The arc of these arguments have been made by Angela Davis, *Women, Race, Class*; Roberts, *Killing*; and Patricia Williams, *Alchemy* and "Spare Parts."

19. Quoted by Patricia Hill Collins in "Shifting the Center", originally from Gerda Lerner's *Black Women in White America*, 158.

20. Renee Larrier makes the astute observation that iconic motherhood is about having sons whose praises to sing ("Reconstructing Motherhood," 194). This particular translation I am using from Obioma Nnaemeka's introduction to *The Politics of (M)Othering* (1). Renee Larrier translates it slightly differently in her essay in the same text: "the nostalgic songs dedicated to the African Mother which express men's anxieties about Mother Africa are no longer sufficient" (202). Bâ's original statement, in French, is from the essay "La fonction politique des litteratures africaines ecrites," *Ecriture Française* 3.5 (1981): 4–7.

21. "In the Caribbean as in nearly every place in the world, any criticism of this most celebrated and procreative human role will more than likely be met with wild-eyed contempt by women and men, both of whom have so internalised the myths of motherhood as to ignore its harsh realities" (Liddell 321).

22. See Sara Ruddick, *Maternal Thinking*, one of the few works to consider the various epistemologies of a pregnant woman.

23. From a paper, "'A Drive from the Mother's Blood': Return Migrations in Audre Lorde's *Zami*," delivered at the MELUS conference in Nashville, TN, March 1999.

24. See "Shifting the Center: Race, Class, and Feminist Theorizing about Motherhood."

25. From *Bread out of Stone*.

26. From *Of Woman Born*.
27. From "The Laugh of the Medusa."
28. Bobby is aware of coalitions, as is evident in his recurring dreams about the Asian woman war prisoner whom he was forced to rape after she had been killed by his white military compatriots because they would not let him fuck her alive (149); his job as an organ harvester, gathering pieces of dead bodies; his time spent as a soldier who informed families that their enlisted sons were dead—all of which are acts that represent coalitions. Yet Bobby is too wounded to be Clare's an/other.
29. Raiskin further argues that the choices Harriet and (later) Clare make "challenge the boundaries of racial and sexual classification" (167). This issue of choice that Harriet relies on so explicitly and her connection of the choice available in identification to issues of nationalism posit a hybrid subjectivity in which identity is a politic writ large and small. See Ramchandran Sethuraman, "Evidence-cum-Witness: Subaltern History, Violence and the (De)Formation of Nation in Michelle Cliff's *No Telephone to Heaven*." Harriet's subjectivity and selffullness also situates sexuality and the erotic within the discourse of selfhood, which makes these issues also relevant to Clare's consideration of identity. Myriam Chancy's reading of *No Telephone* pays necessary attention to the erotic as a politic of identity (*Searching*, 136–165).
30. Earlier in the novel Clare wishes to have a child, which she believes would afford her a sense of completion. This idea of motherhood as an act of self-completion is the undercurrent of the question Eva asks Sula: "When you gone to get married? You need to have some babies. It'll settle you." Yet Sula's response reveals one of the tensions of motherhood for some Black women on their narrative journeys: "I don't want to make somebody else. I want to make myself" (92). And, still, Sula functions as a mother in a variety of contexts (to the Deweys; to Ajax, whose mother she is said to resemble; to the community).

What Sula is rejecting in her claim of wanting to make herself is the social construction of motherhood as a selfless process, which always and only means a woman's giving to and for her children (and, as a result, for their father), even to her own detriment. The agency that a woman might have in her life is refigured when she becomes a mother. Sula's rejection, or that found in other texts in which characters either choose to not have children or are unable to do so, is based on the limits the *construction* of motherhood seems to place on a woman's agency and is not based on motherhood itself. See Lucille P. Fultz's excellent reading "To Make Herself: Mother-Daughter Conflicts in Toni Morrison's *Sula* and *Tar Baby*," which argues against French feminist reclamation of the mother and toward a Black feminist selfhood that sometimes involves being a biological mother, sometimes not. See also Rita Dove, *Thomas and Beulah*, especially the poem "Daystar," which explores the difficulties and confinements that motherhood can place on a Black woman's desire to be an artist.

Chapter 3   *Liminality and Selfhood*

1. Again, I turn attention to Hortense Spillers's smart essay "All the Things You Could Be by Now."
2. Shange writes "i found god in myself / & i loved her / i loved her fiercely" (63).
3. Liminality is prevalent in many of the novels discussed in this section. In *Sula* Sula and Nel's moment of finding each other is described in ecstatic terms, a "delirium of . . . noon dreams" with galloping horses (51–52). And, in fact, Sula's meditation on Ajax's face ponders skin, flesh, bone, alabaster, gold, loam, and mud and moves toward (his) energy. At the end of the novel Sula herself is in the air, is a

part of the elements that facilitate the breaking of Nel's fear once again. Likewise, Shadrack undergoes a transformation whereby he emerges as a corporeal manifestation of a (stranger) spirit. This representation of spirit and energy is also evident in Cliff's *No Telephone to Heaven,* in which Christopher experiences a transformation into elemental self: "Christopher tightened his eyes. . . . He let go. A force passed through him. He had no past. He had no future. He was phosphorus. Light-bearing. He was light igniting the air around him. The source of all danger. He was the carrier of fire. He was the black light that rises from bone ash. The firelight passed through his feet and hands, and his blade quivered with his ignited fury" (47). Via this transformation, one that occurs because he has experienced extreme violence and otherness, Christopher becomes the island's stranger, the grotesque figure of fascination who is not human and not-me but is part of the community—like Sula, Shadrack, Juletane, and Harry/Harriet. These communal strangers are as much outsiders as they are viable and necessary members of the community, as the text's introduction of Harry/Harriet reveals: "Harry/Harriet, boy-girl . . . everyone tolerates him, as if measuring their normalness against his strangeness" (21). Yet it is Harry/Harriet who is committed to national health and who keeps a connection with Clare that initiates her return to the island and its struggle for self-determination.

4. For a discussion of the prevalence of self-divinity in African discourse, see, for example, Robert Farris Thompson, "Black Saints Go Marching In," in *Flash of the Spirit.* Also see Paul Carter Harrison, *The Drama of Nommo,* which describes the harmony between superhuman and human in Black expression. Sula is considered to be the fourth manifestation of God by the people in Medallion, for in a strange way she brings them closer to love: "They began to cherish their husbands and wives, protect their children, repair their homes" (117). Their loving each other in the face of Sula is motivated by their own fear, and, still, it reveals Sula's power for Godlike motivation. She is a spirit: "They would no more run Sula out of town than they would kill the robins that brought her back, for in their secret awareness of Him, He was not the God of three faces they sang about. They knew quite well that He had four, and the fourth explained Sula" (118). Sula is the fourth face of God. See Trudier Harris's description of Sula as "legendary" (*Fiction and Folklore,* 71–79); and Karen Stein's suggestion that Nel and Sula are epic heroes ("Toni Morrison's *Sula:* A Black Woman's Epic"). More directly, Michelle Pessoni suggests that Sula is a goddess. In "'She was Laughing at Their God': Discovering the Goddess Within in *Sula*" Pessoni argues against "the culturally ingrained 'patriarchal fear of the feminine'" in favor of Black women writers "like Gloria Naylor, Ntozake Shange, and Toni Morrison [who] . . . explore the possibility of discovering divinity and meaning from within, . . . which offers the promise of healing and life to an ailing world" (439).

   The relationship of the self to God is particular in Black women's religious traditions. Black theologians in general struggle to articulate a folk conceptualization of God, as asserted by the essays in James Cone's edited collection *Black Liberation Theology* (esp. the section titled "Black Theology and Pastoral Ministry" [79–177]). In Black womanist theological tradition the expression of a womanist God materializes in some cases in reading Jesus' relation to womanism or even reading Jesus as a Black woman (see 257–355, esp. essays by Jacquelyn Grant and Kelly Brown-Douglass; also see Brown-Douglass, "God Is as Christ Does: Toward a Womanist Theology"). But most scholars assert womanist theology directly through the principles and conceptualizations of God. In my own thinking about the matter, especially about the use of God (as opposed to Jesus) as a site of self-spirituality, it seems that the historicization of Jesus as a man is less pliable than the assignment of a masculine gender to God, who is supposed to be a spirit/force and therefore genderless. Hence, it is interesting that more of the Black women characters in these works reference God than Jesus (as it is with womanist theological scholars).

5. In further negotiating the relationship to God, Celie tells Shug that she (Celie) is not Christ (122), which highlights the differences between living like Christ and living like God (for one, Christ's well-referenced passivity, and the silence surrounding his anger, does not serve Celie's coming-to-selfhood; further, Christ's miracles manifest in a male body, differently than God, whose spirit is called male but is arguably genderless). Nettie makes a similar distinction in another letter to Celie, in which she narrates how the roofleaf became an object of worship by the Olinka people. In a ceremony of worship and celebration when the village presented Nettie with her roof, completing a five-year roofleaf restoration project, Olinka members proclaim, "We know a roofleaf is not Jesus Christ, but in its own humble way, is it not God?" (131). I read this comment to reflect the malleability of god(liness) as a concept, in contradistinction to Jesus as a human being; that is, God's eminent spirit form is highly conducive to the model of selfhood being argued for here.

6. The suggestion that godliness is about companionship—that even God has a girlfriend self—is echoed by Lucille Clifton's eight-poem sequence "Brothers" in *Book of Light*, which chronicles a conversation between Lucifer and God years after the Fall.

7. It is Celie's will—her engagement of her own power—that enables Nettie's transformation into some other thing. Hence, it is Celie's will that brings Nettie back to life. Similarly, once Nel claims her own resistance to missing and longing for Sula, her grey ball breaks, and she reconnects with her girlfriend—Sula returns and manifests in the air. This space beyond death, where connection between a woman and her other willfully supersedes the finality of death, also occurs in *Juletane* in the relationship between Juletane and Helene; in *No Telephone* between Clare and her mother; and in *The Salt Eaters* between Minnie, Old Wife, and Velma.

8. Julia Kristeva's work *Strangers to Ourselves* offers a meditation on foreignness that extends the consideration of the stranger into international relations and national histories. Kristeva argues that strangers disrupt time, place, and community and always gesture back to ourselves (7, 191). She also interestingly argues for the strangerhood as a feminine space (185), which correlates with Morrison's identification with this woman and my own suggestion that being a stranger is key to embracing the otherness of girlfriend selfhood. Although her arguments are sometimes cumbersome (especially her readings of Freud, Kant, Hegel, and others) and she also falls prey to racialized metaphors (shadow and Blackness) that are uneasy for me, Kristeva's theorization of the stranger is useful and evocative.

9. There are too many books to mention by title of meditation and reflection that have informed my thinking about the idea of "one," which is prominent in many non-Christian religious practices. Academically, a good reference is Hortense Spillers's "All the Things You Could Be."

10. *Kenosis* is a term used to describe a process of surrender, of yielding, most often in the biblical sense as Christ transforms from divine to human. I use it intentionally to suggest the fluency between liminality and materiality, to suggest the surrender that is willful and not.

11. This self(full)ness is similar to the ways that Trinh discusses identity (see *Woman, Native, Other*, esp. 36–44).

12. The reference to a tree in Shug's meditation is key to the negotiation of this moment. Trees manifest in other moments in the worlds of these novels: elsewhere

in *The Color Purple* Celie writes: "I say to myself, Celie, you a tree. That's how come I know trees fear man" (22). And, later, Albert is part redeemable because "every day [he] . . . git up, sit on the porch, look out at nothing. Sometime look at the trees out front the house" (27). The mango tree in *Juletane* sits right outside her window and is the first breathful thing she sees every morning, and her connection to herself and her life exists in part because of its presence. This aesthetic use of the tree as symbol references the idea of the collective-in-one but also of the fragility of the life at the collective's core. In *Salt Eaters* the tree is a gathering place for the spirits: "They passed the Old Tree where Minnie Ransom daily placed the pots of food and jugs of water for the loa that resided there. Old Tree the free coloreds of Claybourne planted in the spring of 1871. . . . The branches, reaching away from the winter destruction toward the spring renewal, the body letting go of its sap as the new halls and rooms were whitewashed, the branches stretching out and up over the first story as the collective mind grew " (145–146). This tree is a place where collectivity resides in a singular and vulnerable part of the earth.

13. These criticisms constitute Aidoo's revision of exile.

14. This merged voice reminds me of the alliance between the narrator and Janie in Hurston's *Their Eyes*, an alliance that manifests through Hurston's use of free indirect discourse. Kofi Owusu, in "Canons under Siege: Blackness, Femaleness and Ama Ata Aidoo's *Our Sister Killjoy*," keenly asserts that prior to the letter the novel has been polyvocal, an assertion he supports through the novel's mixed structure (351). I would maintain, however, that the position of the narrator, in the midst of the earlier polyvocality, is one of an outsider, a voice that is clearly omniscient and judgmental.

15. Chimalum Nwankwo suggests that the male partner is imaginary (158), an argument that is supported by Wilentz's pointed attention to the namelessness of the man who is subject of the letter. The namelessness, and potentially imaginary nature of the letter's subject, seems to suggest even further that the subject of the letter is not this man but, rather, Sissie/the narrator. See Nwankwo, "The Feminist Impulse and Social Realism in Ama Ata Aidoo's *No Sweetness Here* and *Our Sister Killjoy*."

16. I am borrowing this idea of "voice throwing" from Sija Jajne, a Senegalese concept known as "sani-baat." Against the idea of African women's invisibility and Western feminist construction of voicelessness, Jajne writes: "I would like to offer an alternate reading and locate myself within the concept of 'voice throwing.' I believe that by 'throwing' one's voice, a disruption of discourse can take place. The act of 'throwing' one's voice can create an epistemic violence to discourse that will create a space for hitherto unheard voices" (qtd. in Kolawole, *Womanism* 6). What I find most appealing about the idea of "throwing voice" is that it asserts that the voice was already present, already becoming, but not heard or received. Further, throwing voice seems to be different and less confined than mimicry, the latter which confounds and even limits agency.

17. Kristeva argues that universality is in one's particular foreignness (169–192). When Sula says to Nel, "I know what every Black woman in this world is doing," she speaks from the particularity of her own experience. This approach to universality is one that Alisha Coleman begins to assess in "One and One Make One: A Metacritical and Psychoanalytic Reading of Friendship in Toni Morrison's *Sula*," yet Coleman becomes entangled in other scholars' arguments and mostly expands Elizabeth Abel's psychoanalytic reading, thereby eluding the opportunity of her title.

18. The "singularity" of the self articulated here, and perhaps throughout these chapters, might resonate with some aspects of existential thought. In particular, I can

think of Hegel's expression of "being for others" or his delineation of a model of tension (what is termed *thesis, antithesis, synthesis*), which, when interpreted in relation to human populations, manifests as the master/slave dialectic; and how both of these ideas become foundational to the existential thinking of Sartre and de Beauvoir, for example, or even Fanon (who, especially in *White Skins*, is existential). It is Fanon who is most interesting to me here, for, while his attempt to express Black subjectivity is instructive, like other existential thinkers, he posits an identity that is *only* tension; his description of a subjectivity that attacks (in "The Fact of Blackness," for example) seems grounded in an anxiety that exists between subject and other; and an anxiety that also literally *is* the self's subjectivity. The prevalence of anxiety in Fanon is counter to the selfhood I am expressing here; this girlfriend selfhood is a model of tension but one that moves toward self-revelation. Furthermore, Fanon works from and stays enrapt in a concept of nothingness (what he calls a "zone of nonbeing" [8]), which is different than the achievement of an abundant "I am enough."

19. Mobility is not necessarily freedom; hence, I am arguing for a mobility with a center that remains politically aware, a mobility that is a kind of stillness. See Kimberle Crenshaw's argument against the overreliance on mobility. My fusing of integrity and mobility is inspired by Parker Palmer, who talks about identity as "an evolving nexus where all the forces that constitute my life converge in the mystery of self . . . identity is a moving intersection of the inner and outer forces that make me who I am, converging in the irreducible mystery of being human," and who later talks about integrity in a way that is compatible: "Whatever wholeness I am able to find within that nexus as its vectors form and re-form the pattern of my life . . . [this] wholeness . . . [is not] perfection" (13).

20. I am grateful to an anonymous student at a lecture I gave at the University of Maryland, College Park (November 2000), whose engagement with me propelled both of us to this conclusion.

21. Quoted from Valerie Gladstone's "The Long Shadow of Alvin Ailey's Great Cry," *New York Times*, 26 November 2000, 2:6.

22. I am revising Ralph Waldo Emerson's famous line: "Nothing is sacred but the integrity of the self."

Chapter 4   *An Indisputable Memory of Blackness*

1. This argument for a corporealized memory (and its implications for identity politics) exists within the historical consideration that has been given to the quality, character, and authenticity of bodies. Classical Western philosophies of human subjectivity often exhibit what Elizabeth Grosz calls "somatophobia" (*Volatile Bodies*, 5), an epistemological fear of the body as a source of knowledge. In these philosophies the body is summarily dismissed for two primary and contradictory reasons— either for being static and mute or for being unpredictable and mysterious. In both cases the body is discredited as inaccessible, unnecessary, and unreliable. More recent theoretical and philosophical considerations of corporeality have sought to embrace the body's conflicting character as exactly the reason for its relevance to scholarly study, and body composition has become central to understanding identity and selfhood (such is the case in Fanon, Spinoza, and Merleau-Ponty and in feminist revisions of psychoanalysis). The specificity of my argument for corporeal memory, then, generates from this moment in cultural studies that highlights the significance of the ideology of the body in the production of knowledge. But one of the risks of theorizing the body in Black female cultural contexts is that it may unwittingly give credibility to ideologies that overidentify Black women with

and through their bodies. Nonetheless, as Audre Lorde argues in her essay "The Erotic as Power," to acquiesce to the false ideas about Black women's bodies, which is also to surrender the body to an also-ran status in relation to the mind's discursive primacy, is detrimental to Black women's and in fact all people's lives (See *Sister Outsider*).

2. For example, Larry Neal cites memory as a key diasporic condition in "Some Reflections on the Black Aesthetic," and a similar appraisal can be gleaned from the arguments in James Baldwin's "Stranger in the Village" (from *Notes of a Native Son*). Frantz Fanon (*Black Skins, White Masks*) and Patricia Hill Collins's phrase "consciousness as a sphere of freedom" (*Black Feminist Thought* 103) also link memory, consciousness, and decolonization.

   What is more, *memory* has become an increasingly important scholarly term with the rise of cultural studies. One could cite, for example, George Lipsitz's *Time Passages*, Singh, Skerrett, and Hogan's *Memory and Cultural Politics*, and O'Meally and Fabre's *History and Memory* as key interventions in the area. See also Karla Holloway, "Cultural Narratives Passed On"; Houston Baker, "Critical Memory and the Black Public Sphere"; and Elizabeth Alexander's elegant essay "Can You Be BLACK and Look at This?" Certainly, my arguments about memory are indebted to Freudian psychoanalysis. Freud's investigation into the psyche asserts that memory is central to understanding human experience (and illness) and even seemingly corporealizes memory in suggesting that physical ailments originate in psychologically repressed encounters. Indirectly, he suggests that memory is both liberating (in that it can be engaged in understanding physical and psychic trauma) and unreliable (in that memory sometimes represses or disguises itself). Despite his predilection toward a sexual interpretation of memory, Freud articulated clearly the value of memory and of remembering (as an act) in the process of selfhood.

3. There are a couple ways that Grosz's arguments in the whole text are not useful. Particularly, I am called to ask questions about Grosz's theorized body, which is gendered but not raced, because I believe that her sweeping dismissal of memory (somewhat by default, although she argues against memory more directly in "Refiguring Lesbian Desire") is linked to a progressive disappearing of the Black body from her work. For example, central to Grosz's arguments is the specificity of bodies—that she wants to explore the textualities of literal, in-flesh bodies. She argues that "the specificity of bodies must be understood in its historical rather than simply its biological concreteness. Indeed, there is no body as such: there are only *bodies*—male or female, black brown, white, large or small—and gradations in between. Bodies can be represented or understood not as entities in themselves or simply on a linear continuum with its polar extremes occupied by male and female bodies . . . but as a field, a two-dimensional continuum in which race (and possibly even class, caste, or religion) form body specifications" (*Volatile* 19). This focus on specificity is a necessary move, for too often bodies are rendered silent under theoretical formulations that construct them. Still, this emphasis on specificity is dangerous, because it also suggests, or at least leaves open, the possibility that a particular body, or its known behaviors, becomes *the* body, the archetypal cast of what a whole set of bodies do. The danger here is that Grosz's feminine body becomes *the* feminine body, which Grosz is aware of but which nonetheless seems to occur in her work: as the rest of her argument develops, race slips from being articulated, to being parenthesized ("If the mind is necessarily linked to, perhaps even a part of, the body and if bodies themselves are always sexually [and racially] distinct"), to being unarticulated. This slippage is the result of race being unspecified and unarticulated and interferes with the lucidity and relevance of her

comment that "bodies are always irreducibly sexually specific, necessarily interlocked with racial, cultural, and class particularities" (19). It seems as if Grosz herself is aware of this slippage and the difficulty of negotiating the multiplicity that is the specificity of bodies in a paradigmatic formulation. In line with such awareness, she writes, "I do not want to suggest that there is a single homogeneous field on which all sorts of body types can, without any violence or transcription, be placed so that they can now be assessed fairly and equally" (23). To her further credit, at the end of *Volatile* she resists the notion that she has presented a "definitive model by which bodies and their sexual differences are to be understood" (209), to say nothing of other differences bodies might exhibit or inhabit. This becomes relevant, for example, when Grosz critiques the construction of the conscious/unconscious (and rightly notes the parallel between that binary and Descartes's body-mind as well as the larger binary of male/female in Western culture)—here, she fails to consider that (the) unconscious is also racialized, imagined as a "dark force," and literally conflated with Africa. Further, when she writes, "Insofar as women's body images are clearly different from men's and are modeled on lack and castration," it is apparent that she is talking about white women's bodies (and genitals), for Black women's bodies, in large and in part, are not fashioned as lack (73).

4. Generally, in the world of cultural discourse corporeality is feminine.
5. I was inspired here by Avery Gordon's amazing reading of *Beloved*.
6. I can't help but think of Shadrack's promise of "always" to Sula, a statement that figures prominently in my reading of subjectivity in that novel.
7. Earlier Sethe's brain is described as having a mind of its own, which she indicates as the source of the haunting memories: "[Sethe's] brain was not interested in the future. Loaded with the past and hungry for more, it left her no room to imagine, let alone plan for, the next day. Exactly like that afternoon in the wild onions—when one more step was the most she could see of the future. Other people went crazy, why couldn't she? Other people's brains stopped, turned around and went on to something new" (70). The narrator's commentary on Sethe's brain is important because the brain is, in vernacular, often used as a metaphor for memory; hence, the volatility of Sethe's brain, which seems to have a mind of its own, is also expressive of her memory's volatility.
8. Beloved herself refers to "a hot thing." I am grateful to Jadine Starmer for reminding me of the chaos that surrounds Beloved's arrival. This memory smell parallels the scene of rescue at the end of the novel and imbues memory with another corporeal characteristic: when the women came to see about Sethe, "it was three in the afternoon on a Friday so wet and hot Cincinnati's stench had traveled to the country: from the canal, from hanging meat and things rotting in jars; from small animals dead in the fields, town sewers, and factories. The stench, the heat, the moisture" (257–258).
9. I am borrowing the pairing of these terms from Sheila Smith McKoy's essay "Remnant Consciousness: Home, Desire, and Cultural Reclamation in Kofi Awoonor's *Comes the Voyager at Last*," delivered at the 1999 MELUS Conference in Nashville.
10. There are a number of solid critical essays that explore aspects of Beloved's multiplicity. See Deborah Horowitz, "Nameless Ghosts: Possession and Dispossession in *Beloved*"; Mae G. Henderson, "Toni Morrison's *Beloved*: Re-membering the Body as Historical Text"; and Linda Krumholz's essay "The Ghosts of Slavery: Historical Recovery in Toni Morrison's *Beloved*." Barbara H. Solomon's introduction to *Critical Essays on Toni Morrison's "Beloved"* has a useful and extensive summary of a wide range of scholarship on the novel.

11. Note Jane Olmsted's essay "The Pull to Memory and the Language of Place in Paule Marshall's *The Chosen Place, The Timeless People,* and *Praisesong for the Widow,*" which successfully argues for the connection between memory and Avey and Jay's bodies.

12. Having heard her mother's thoughts on memory, Denver becomes a child of memory, her body materializing via the told story of her birth, which are the scraps that she gives blood and a heartbeat to (78). Unlike other little girls in the nursery rhyme, Denver is made of remembered narratives, and memory is the literal constitution of her body.

13. It is memory who is the other-me that Alice Walker meets in her essay "Beauty: When the Other Dancer Is the Self." Memory, her own Beloved, this dancing other who is literally the memory of a young Alice, carefree and her father's most favorite child, smartly dressed; as well as the recovery of the Alice who loses the function and aesthetic of her eye to a vagrant BB gun pellet and who learns to adjust to this change that others refuse to remember.

14. See Paulette Brown-Hinds, "In the Spirit: Dance as Healing Ritual in Paule Marshall's *Praisesong for the Widow,*" which also asserts that the dance is a memory; and Barbara Frey Waxman, "Dancing Out of Form, Dancing into Self: Genre and Metaphor in Marshall, Shange and Walker," an excellent essay that addresses the dance as it relates to subjectivity.

15. Fanon asserts that memory is a necessary but not sufficient condition of decolonization (see *Wretched of the Earth*).

16. Beloved's self-colonization is the result of her disregard that is so rampant that her own body becomes its victim. I have come to this argument through Lenore Brady's suggestion that the novel itself is haunted.

17. There is an interesting voodoo term, *met-tet,* which refers to a head spirit that passes from person to person. See Karen McCarthy Brown, "The Moral Force Field of Haitian Vodou."

18. Houston Baker, in "Critical Memory and the Black Public Sphere," argues for a critical memory, though his proposal leans more toward a normative collectivity, while mine, imbedded in the notion of girlfriend subjectivity, is necessarily ambivalent about collectivity.

Chapter 5 *The Practice of a Memory Body*

1. The phrase is from the title story of John Edgar Wideman's collection.

2. George Lipsitz, in *Time Passages,* calls the relationship between memory and storytelling "counter-memory." *Counter-memory* acknowledges that "story-telling that combines subjectivity and objectivity, that employs the insights and passions of myth and folklore in the service of revising history, can be a powerful tool of contestation" (213), which he theorizes through the opening of Zora Neale Hurston's *Their Eyes Were Watching God* and Barbara Johnson's oft-cited essay "Metaphor, Metonomy and Voice." Lipsitz says that counter-memory is "sometimes dangerous terrain" because it involves revision, yet its value is that it is "a way of remembering and forgetting that starts with the local, the immediate, and the personal" (213). While I find Lipsitz's notion of counter-memory useful, I also want to argue for a memory process that is not only oppositional in relation to a master(ing) narrative; in fact, though memory as a body manifests through tensions, memory is also self-contained like the enough selfhood of the previous chapters. Furthermore, the case of *Beloved* as argued thus far seems to represent a memory body that is oppositional in relationship to itself as well as to other bodies. I was alerted to Lipsitz's formulation through Susan Comfort's essay "Counter-Memory,

Mourning, and History in Toni Morrison's *Beloved.*" Finally, it is worth citing Elizabeth Alexander's "Can You Be BLACK and Look at This?" in which she is "building a case for a collective memory that rests in the present moment . . . but which has been constructed as much by storytelling in multiple media as by personal, actual experience" (88).

3. See Lipsitz's *Time Passages* for a fine discussion of the simultaneously private and public aspects of memory.

4. Margaret Atwood, *The Handmaid's Tale*, 14.

5. Similarly, Paul D closes down his chest, pushing memory away in hopes of finding the peace that has eluded his last days at Sweet Home and all his days since: "It was some time before he could put Alfred, Georgia, Sixo, schoolteacher, Halle, his brothers, Sethe, Mister, the taste of iron, the sight of butter, the smell of hickory, notebook paper, one by one, into the tobacco tin lodge in his chest. By the time he got to 124 nothing in this world could pry it open" (113). Nothing could pry his locked memories open, except memory incarnate, a girl named Beloved.

6. In fact, Jones herself has cited voice as crucial to her narrative aesthetic: in a piece titled "About My Work" she writes: "I notice people more than landscape. I notice voices" (234). Jones's attention to voice is also notable in her first novel, *Corregidora*.

7. Of the myth Jones says that, because men perceive Eva as a whore, "she begins to feel she is, and eventually associates herself with the Queen Bee and the Medusa symbol. I put these images in the story to show how the myths or ways in which men perceive women actually define women's character" (Claudia Tate, "Gayl Jones," interview, 96).

8. Eva's cellmate Joanne coins the term *public hair* and articulates the absurdity of Black women's sexual awakening (156, 151). Interestingly, Shug Avery in *The Color Purple* is referred to as "Queen Honeybee" (24).

9. The text acknowledges her as the Queen Bee, with an image of Queen Eva in prison, sitting constipated on her throne / the toilet (151). This revision is an important difference between Eva and the "real" Queen Bee, because, as Carol Margaret Davison notes, the Queen Bee in some ways resigns herself to the oppressed condition (455).

10. Elvira is Eva's cellmate, who repeatedly solicits sex from Eva, almost mimicking the overtures that both she and Eva have endured from men. That Elvira's name mirrors Eva's, and is also another mythical defiant and unusual woman, might indicate the fragility of Eva's mythmaking, for, like Elvira, Eva is susceptible to internalizing and replicating male-gendered violence.

11. I engage Dixon's essay because it is the most famous of pieces on the controversies of this novel and is relevant to the issue of voice. Other evocative scholarly pieces of the novel's conundrum and use of myth include Biman Basu's essay "Public and Private Discourse and the Black Female Subject: Gayl Jones' *Eva's Man*"; Keith Byerman, "Intense Behaviors: The Use of the Grotesque in *The Bluest Eye* and *Eva's Man*" (on repetition); and Sally Robinson, *Gender and Self-Representation in Contemporary Women's Fiction* (166–188).

12. This assertion is similar to the familiar arguments that Alice Walker and others put forth in defense of the attack on Janie's silence in the courtroom scene near the end of Hurston's *Their Eyes* (see Mary Helen Washington's foreword to the Perennial edition).

13. I am referring to Davis's *Blues Legacies and Black Feminism*. See Sally Robinson's and Biman Basu's works here, which make powerful arguments that contest some of Dixon's claim (particularly about the quality of the orgasm at the end of the novel).

14. See Lipsitz's reading of Kristeva's essay "Woman's Time," through which he argues that "counter-memory understands the limits of historical time, but still tries to act within it" (229). Lipsitz identifies time as one of those elements that is relevant to (and sometimes impedes) memory and suggests that there is a need to rethink time in ways that might be more conducive for the process of counter-memory.

15. See Eugenia DeLamotte's argument for doubleness in *Places of Silence, Journeys of Freedom: The Fiction of Paule Marshall*, particularly her suggestion of double exposure as one of Marshall's narrative aesthetics (especially "Introduction: The Double Visions of Paule Marshall's Art," 1–9).

16. Interestingly, Marshall's use of this incident, which Cliff also uses in *No Telephone to Heaven*, is a manifestation of a Black collective unconscious. In fact, the Birmingham bombing might more accurately be called a *lieux de memoire*, a mythic and galvanized site of memory, because its presence is as much conscious as unconscious. Other similar incidents represented in Black literature are the MOVE bombing in Philadelphia in 1985, the March on Washington in 1968, and the U.S. invasion of Grenada.

17. I am using the term as inspired by the end of Octavia Butler's *Parable of the Sower*, which expresses a memory that is of the future.

18. The narrative voice of *A Small Place* has been largely considered arrogant and acerbic, but I have come to see it as more fluid and playful than that, moving between three narrative perspectives: it is critical and omniscient; it is a tourist (in telling readers what tourists will see); and it is one of the Antiguans whom it sometimes criticizes (for example, when it dreamily evokes love for Antigua's seas). In this respect the shifting between the three voices is a collective volatility that parallels corporeal memory as theorized here. In Kincaid's attempt to critique and articulate a (new) myth, she interfaces with a memory body that does not allow her solely to be a critic (those more strident and unrelenting moments). That the narrative voice is multiple—and, in fact, volatile and even somewhat unreliable—is missed by most reviewers. It was Moira Ferguson's suggestion that *A Small Place* is part of Kincaid's bildungsroman that challenged me to think differently about the work (78).

19. The latter phrase is from Alice Walker's "Foreword: Zora Neale Hurston—A Cautionary Tale and A Partisan View," in the biography of Hurston (xviii).

Chapter 6   *Toward a Language Aesthetic*

1. It is arguably in articulations of Negritude as well as in the Harlem Renaissance that Black subjectivity was first represented as being synonymous with aesthetics. See especially Aime Cesaire, Marita Bonner, Langston Hughes, Zora Neale Hurston and W. E. B. Du Bois, who in *The Gift of Black Folks* states that every Black person is essentially an artist. But for me Juliette Jarrett offers a citation that makes the point most clearly: "Every Black woman who survives art college fairy tales and repressive society to make images in her reality, deserves the name artist" (121).

2. This is the lovely argument made by the late Barbara Christian's essay "A Race for Theory" as well as "The Highs and Lows of Black Feminist Criticism"; see earlier references and discussion in the introduction. Additionally, see Gerry Smyth, "The Politics of Hybridity" (esp. 52–54), in which she discusses the gap between theory and history in a way relevant to my concerns about intellectual immunity; and Carole Boyce Davies, "Negotiating Theories," which covers a broad range of concerns about theory and Black women's cultural production (in *Migrations of Subject*).

3. See also salient comments on pages 20 and 53.
4. The larger issue here is a comment on the relationship between language and freedom. Aside from Nourbese Philips, I can also cite Henry Louis Gates Jr. (*The Signifying Monkey*), Ngugi Wa Thongo (*Homecoming*), and Edward Kamau Braithwaite (*The Development of Creole Society in Jamaica*) about the role of language in decolonization. Braithwaite summarily states: "It was in language that the slave was perhaps most successfully imprisoned by his master, and it was in his (mis) use of it that he perhaps most effectively rebelled" (237). Also see Oyekan Owomoyela's insightful and comprehensive "The Question of Language in African Literatures," which is a necessary read on this topic.

  In terms of the specificities of gender: Marlene Nourbese Philip cites the distrust and scorn a writing career generates in the Caribbean, in general as well as specifically related to women. See her opening essay "The Absence of Writing: Or How I Almost Became a Spy." Also see Alice Walker's crucial essay "In Search of Our Mother's Gardens"; Patricia Hill Collins, *Fighting Words* (esp. the chapter "Fighting Words with *Fighting Words*"); Ama Ata Aidoo's interview with Anuradha Dingwaney Needham; and Estella Conwill Majozo's *Come Out of the Wilderness*. Finally, I must also mention Susan Willis's successful discussion of the historical tension between the Black American woman writer and her community, in chapter 1 of *Specifying*.
5. There are many successful scholarly considerations on exile as part of Black literary production. See George Lamming, *The Pleasures of Exile*; Myriam Chancy, *Caribbean Women Writers in Exile*; Carole Boyce Davies, "Other Tongues," in *Migrations of Subject*; and Ngugi Wa Thongo, *Homecoming*.
6. This is what Chantal Zabus calls "relexification"; also see Nourbese Philip (17).
7. For a capable theorization of exile, see Chancy, *Caribbean Women Writers in Exile* (esp. xi–xix and 1–7, 22–30). My own discussion of language here is informed by Chancy's reading of Brand and Nourbese Philips (esp. 99–117).
8. The narrator in Aidoo's *Our Sister Killjoy* notes a similar situation in which language (and education, for both are often paired in colonized situations) seductively confers special status and poses a barrier between the educated Black artist and her people:
  Post-graduate awards.
  Graduate awards.
  It doesn't matter
  What you call it.
  . . . .
  What
  Dainty name to describe
  This
  Most merciless
  Most formalised
  Open,
  Thorough,
  Spy system of all time:
  For a few pennies now and a
  Doctoral degree later,
  Tell us about
  Your people
  Your history
  Your mind. (86)
9. My thoughts on "modernity" here are influenced by Anthony Giddens, *The*

Consequences of Modernity; and especially Walter Benjamin, "The Work of Art in the Age of Mechanical Reproduction" (in *Illuminations*), especially his suggestion that one impact of modernity is that more people (can) consume art and less people (are afforded to) produce it. Also see A. O. Balcomb, "Modernity and the African Experience."

10. I must make some comment on my aversion to hybridity and my affinity for difference: as a central postcolonial, postmodern, and cultural studies metaphor, hybridity has been useful in rethinking dangerous notions of racial purity and cultural exclusivity. Ideologically, hybridity implies border crossing and mobility and represents the radical and trangressive quality of movement in and out of established boundaries. As such, hybridity disrupts common binaries, for example, the opposition of black and white or colonized and colonizer. In fact, hybridity in deconstructionist and poststructuralist thought has become a vaunted cultural ideology especially in the case of language. But the engagement of hybridity is not without unease, particularly because the concept has become an overinvested episteme. Much interpretation of work by people of color can be labeled "hybrid," without requisite attention to power differences among artist, text, and aesthetic tradition. Further, as Robert Young notes in *Colonial Desire: Hybridity in Theory, Culture, and Race*, the notion of hybridity has a complicated historical foundation that in many ways validates racist essentialism, leaving intact the poles of purity that make the hybrid possible. Or the reverse, as Gerry Smyth makes clear in arguing about the inattention to textual coherence left in the wake of hybridity's in-vogueness: "Hybridity is also hegemonically recuperable, easily absorbed by those with an interest in denying the validity of a coherent discourse of resistance" (43). In the case Smyth imagines the so-called hybrid text is privileged over and above that which seems less marked by a merging of aesthetic principles, an appraisal that ultimately affirms the dominant traditions for whatever improvement the hybrid text is deemed to have over a more marginal one. The very discourse of hybridity itself becomes insular, accessible only to a small group of people, further disallowing marginal and often colored bodies from an imagined field intended to speak about and of them, reifying that which is already powerful and endowed. I can say it no more clearly than these words from bell hooks:

> Working with students and families from diverse class backgrounds, I am constantly amazed at how difficult it is to cross boundaries in this white supremacist, capitalist patriarchal society. And it is obviously most difficult for individuals who lack material privilege or higher levels of education to make the elaborate shifts in location, thought, and life experience cultural critics talk and write about as though it is only a matter of individual will. To claim border crossing, the mixing of high and low, cultural hybridity, as the deepest expression of a desired cultural practice within multicultural democracy means that we must dare to envision ways such freedom of movement can be experienced by everyone. (*Outlaw Culture*, 5)

This is the poison of hybridity, its depoliticized and ahistoricized reinforcement of intellectual immunity and real-world relevance, what makes it less useful for my consideration of the conundrum of language. I am not arguing here that hybridity is not useful; see, for example, Gates, *The Signifying Monkey*; Houston A. Baker Jr., *Modernism and the Harlem Renaissance*; Paul Gilroy, *Black Atlantic*; and especially Homi Bhabha's explication of mimicry in "Signs Taken for Wonders," which argues that hybridity can and does interrupt the perception of unilateralism—that knowledge and impact travels only from colonizer to colonized. Trinh, Anzaldúa, and even Smyth, as well as Young and hooks also value hybridity as a necessary concept in cultural discourse. But there is the need for caution, which is what my comment here highlights—a commitment to an appreciation of hybridity that does not reject wholeness, oversimplify complicated literary and cultural traditions, or re-privilege/recenter the dominant aesthetic.

There are many successful discussions of the concerns of hybridity, including Donna Haraway, *Simian, Cyborgs, and Women* (which attempts to infuse hybridity with a keen sense of radical, transformative politics); Anthony Appiah, *In My Father's House* (which grapples with both the imperialism of hybridity and the fallacy of nativism); Tariq Modood, "'Difference,' Cultural Racism and Anti-Racism" (also note Pnina Werbner's introduction in the same collection); Anne McClintock, *Imperial Leather* (especially her comment on progress and postcoloniality); and Benita Parry, essay "Resistance Theory / Theorizing Resistance," in *Colonial Discourse, Postcolonial Theory* (it was Gerry Smyth's work that alerted me to Parry and this useful collection).

In terms of difference Trinh's suggestion is from *Woman, Native, Other*. Audre Lorde also uses this term *difference* in *Sister Outsider*, and much of bell hooks's argument about choosing the margin is predicated on maintaining the critical posture of difference (in *Yearning*). *Difference* is also the key term of Derrida's definition of *deconstruction*, though academic deconstructive practice too often disintegrates into depoliticized high-play. Although *difference* itself is not without criticism (see, for example, Appiah and Modood), it does seem to suggest a more critical disposition than hybridity.

11. It might be hard to imagine someone of Morrison's poise as capable of anxiety, but for sure the lecture is an anxious textuality. Michael Nowlin, in a lovely essay, argues convincingly that Morrison's *Jazz* is a treatise of being an American writer, that the novel is nearly autobiographical (154). Nowlin's conviction is guidance and inspires me to think that all of Morrison's canon, but especially her interviews and nonfiction, are about her place and fit as a writer.

12. In "The Storyteller" Walter Benjamin has argued that the story is counsel, in contradistinction to the novel, a modern form, which is solitary and without counsel; see *Illuminations*. Also see Barbara Smith's essay "The Race for Theory," in which she argues for story as Black culture's theory.

13. The title of Alice Walker's early collection of essays.

14. This idea of "epic" speech is indebted to Susan Willis's discussion of condensation in Black women's narrative aesthetic (see esp. 20–22 in *Specifying*).

Chapter 7   **My Own, Language**

1. Before knowing who Roland Flint was, I had only a fragment of the poem that was my version of my friend's memoried one. I took the license to imagine that Ethan was a young Black boy, which he may still have been though his father is white, and adored the possibility that he had encountered language in a way that is so similar to Black women. It is no less profound, now, that Ethan was likely white and that his father is too, for the model I am suggesting is not essentialist, and Flint's poem serves as a useful epigraph. My overall argument for this chapter, that writing is an act of (un)becoming, is influenced by Trinh T. Minh-ha's breathtaking exploration of a similar premise in chapter 1 of *Woman, Native, Other*.

2. I am indebted to Wayne Booth, *The Rhetoric of Fiction*, for the notion of a compact between author and reader; and to Seymour Chatman, *Story and Discourse*, for the diagrammatic model that introduces the notion of realness (151).

3. See David Lodge, *The Art of Fiction*.

4. Again, I am talking about distinctions between the novels and stories, as explicated more fully in the textual notes of the previous chapter.

5. I am especially indebted to Shlomith Rimmon-Kenan, *Narrative Fiction: Contemporary Poetics*, in forming this insight (esp. 1–5 and 106–116).

6. Chatman and Rimmon-Kenan's works are especially good on free-indirect discourse; Rimmon-Kenan on unreliable narration; and Booth and Chatman on the fictions of narration.

7. See Donald Pease's useful and readable definition "Author," in *Critical Terms for Literary Study;* my use of the term *demotion* should be credited to him.

8. The question of the narrator's gender is the site of much conversation about Morrison's novel. Early on, in his *New York Times* review, Henry Louis Gates Jr. names the narrator as "indeterminate: it is neither male nor female; neither young nor old; neither rich nor poor. It is both and neither" ("Review of Jazz" 54). From there many have either agreed with Gates's notion of indeterminacy (often as an ambiguity juxtaposed against the city's authority; see, for example, Jocelyn Chadwick Joshua, Patricia McKee, Janis Stout, and Michael Wood) or have insisted on the narrator's femininity (see, for example, Denise Heinze or, more subtly, Caroline Rody's essay on "first-person omniscient anonymous" that calls the narrator "she" [622]). Michael Nowlin identifies the narrator as female in consideration of the goddess voice announced by the novel's epigraph from the Nag Hammadi text "The Thunder: Perfect Mind" and points my attention to Eusebio Rodrigues's essay that does the same. But Nowlin also encouraged me to acknowledge that, though the gender of the narrator is under heavy discussion, the narrator is largely assumed to be African-American. Surely, Morrison's last of her love trilogy, *Paradise* (as well as her short story "Recitatif"), would unsettle this racial determinacy (as would jazz as an art form). In any case, I here choose to think of the narrator as Black and female, especially because of the overall argument I am making. Such identification is at once determinate, even singular, and wildly indeterminate—a vagaried and unfamiliar Black and female body.

9. Nowlin's is easily one of the best essays on Morrison's *Jazz* that I have ever encountered. For the sake of my summary here, see especially 151–160.

10. This is a dangerous premise, but it seems that if not all then maybe most Black art is self-reflexive, especially if the impulse of Du Bois's double consciousness is true. For an effective discussion of metafiction, see Madelyn Jablon, *Black Metafiction*, especially its discussion of Morrison.

11. In an endnote from her book *Blues Legacies and Black Feminism* Angela Y. Davis makes a useful comment on the relationship between performer and audience in Black cultural practice that I think is evocative here. She argues: "Popular musical culture in the African-American tradition continues to actively involve the audience in the performance of music. The distinction, therefore, is not between the relatively active and relatively passive stances of the audience. Rather, it is between a mode of musical presentation in which everyone involved is considered a 'performer'—or perhaps in which no one, the song leader included, is considered a 'performer'—and one in which the producer of the music plays a privileged role in calling forth the responses of the audience" (362). This is in the context of Davis talking about the blues as a modern expression in which "the borders of performer and audience [become] increasingly differentiated" (5).

12. My consideration of the role of photography is influenced largely from reading the essays in Liz Wells's edited work, *Photography: A Critical Introduction;* John Berger, *Ways of Seeing;* and Anne McClintock, *Imperial Leather.* I am also influenced here

by Sander Gilman's essay "Black Bodies, White Bodies"; Anthony Appiah's essay "Race"; and John Tagg's smart study *The Burden of Representation: Essays on Photographies and Histories,* the latter which Wells's collection introduced me to.

13. One of the foundational debates of photography is actually whether the form is art or mere technology. See especially Derrick Price and Liz Wells, "Thinking about Photography: Debates, Historically and Now." This debate turns upon the potential nuance of photography's art. Another consideration here is the argument Roland Barthes raises about the sign system invoked in every photograph (see *Camera Lucida*); Price and Wells suggest that, as such, looking at and engaging a photograph is phenomenological (30).

14. See Ida Lewis, "Conversation: Ida Lewis and James Baldwin" 92.

15. Interestingly, Brand, in an interview from 1991, refers to Mammy Prater's patience and talks of it with a respect and self-referentiality that echoes my larger argument in the chapter:

> Q: I see in militancy in *No Language Is Neutral,* for instance, in "Blues Spiritual for Mammy Prater" where you celebrate the memory of an ex-slave woman whose patience pays off. There is a definite spirit of resistance and defiance in the poem. But it is a sober militancy.
> A: Maybe it's more steadfast. Some of the other poems may be forgotten, but I have faith that this one will survive, because this woman sits and survives for one hundred and fifteen years waiting for a photograph.
> Q: I think you've come through, both technically and ideologically, to a position of great maturity and poise. You've found a voice that lets you interpret your experience smoothly and openly, without special pleading, anxiousness or self-doubt.
> A: I think for me the voice is now unshakable: it can say anything it wants, with certainty. (Birbalsingh 135–136)

The discussion easily moves from Mammy Prater's patience to Brand's authorial voice, a slip that reflects that tension and energy between subject and author. Also see Diana Brydon's brief "Reading Dionne Brand's 'Blues Spiritual for Mammy Prater,'" which does well to talk about the use of repetition and the realization of the subject in the poem.

16. As Trinh notes, though story is joy, there are parts of it that can be distressing (119).

17. I am signifying here on the title of Barbara Smith, Patricia Bell Scott, and Gloria Hull's *All the Women Are White, All the Blacks Are Men, but Some of Us Are Brave.*

18. Berlant also cites descriptions of subjectivity that resonate with and inform her notion of Diva Citizenship, many of which implicitly resonate with my own discussion here: Donna Harraway, bell hooks, and Wayne Koestenbaum (223).

19. Thich Nhat Hanh, *Teachings,* 51.

20. I am also reminded here of Cornel West's argument for a balance between individual agency and the recognition of profound social odds of Black life; see his chapter on nihilism in *Race Matters.*

21. "Rough Road Ahead" is the title of a section of Brand's poems.

22. This latter argument is the thesis of Bhabha's edited *Nation and Narration.* For explorations of migration and movement in Black subjectivity, see Carole Boyce Davies (*Black Women, Writing, and Identity,* and *Moving beyond Boundaries,* vols. 1–2), Farah Jasmine Griffin (*"Who Set You Flowin'?"*), and Melvin Dixon (*Ride Out the Wilderness*).

23. From *A Small Place* 77.

24. I am indebted to David Chariandry's discussion of "territorial belonging," which propelled my own thinking about *Land to Light On.*

25. Brand is playing with Joseph Conrad's classic modernist text, *Heart of Darkness* (here and esp. 77).
26. For an effective discussion of home and art, see especially the introduction and "Writing Home" in Davies, *Black Women, Writing, and Identity*; also see Barbara Smith's edited anthology, *Homegirls*.

Conclusion   . . . What Is Undone

1. The phrase *center without walls* is from the Black Radical Congress's Statement of Unity.
2. There are other versions of this story that claim Truth revealed her arm, which seems like a contemporary euphemism for breast (see esp. Nell Painter).
3. See William Andrews on slave narratives' use of "I am" as a centering of subjectivity.
4. I am borrowing the phrase "life relevantly lived" from Aidoo's *Killjoy* (129).
5. I am signifying on Luce Irigaray's title *This Sex Which Is Not One*. I intend here to imply at least ways of reading the phrase: a wholeness that is not singular or uncomplicated; a wholeness that is, in the spiritual sense of the word, one; and a wholeness that is and is not a subject's essence.

Works Cited

Abel, Elizabeth. "(E)Merging Identities: The Dynamics of Female Friendship in Contemporary Fiction by Women." *Signs* 6 (1981): 413–435.

Aidoo, Ama Ata. "Literature, Feminism and the African Woman Today." In *Reconstructing Womanhood, Reconstructing Feminism: Writings on Black Women*. Ed. D. Jarrett-Macauley. New York: Routledge, 1996.

———. *Our Sister Killjoy: Or Reflections from a Black-Eyed Squint*. London: Longman, 1992.

Alexander, Elizabeth. "Can You Be BLACK and Look at This? Reading the Rodney King Video(s)." In *The Black Public Sphere*. Ed. Black Public Sphere Collective. Chicago: U of Chicago P, 1995. 81–98.

Anatol, Giselle Liza. "'A Drive from the Mother's Blood': Return Migrations in Audre Lorde's *Zami*." Paper delivered at the Thirteenth Annual Meeting of the Society for the Study of Multi-Ethnic Literature of the United States, Nashville, TN, 20 March 1999.

Anderson, Benedict. *Imagined Communities: Reflections on the Origin and Spread of Nationalism*. 1983. Reprint. New York: Verso, 1991.

Andrews, William L. *To Tell a Free Story: The First Century of Afro-American Autobiography, 1760–1865*. Urbana: University of Illinois Press, 1986.

Anzaldúa, Gloria. *Borderlands: The New Mestiza = La Frontera*. San Francisco: Spinsters / Aunt Lute, 1987.

Anzaldúa, Gloria, and Cherríe Moraga, eds. Introduction to *This Bridge Called My Back: Writings by Radical Women of Color*. Watertown, MA: Persephone, 1981.

Appiah, Kwame Anthony. *In My Father's House: Africa in the Philosophy of Culture*. New York: Oxford UP, 1992.

———. "Race." In *Critical Terms for Literary Study*. Ed. Frank Lentricchia and Thomas McLaughlin. Chicago: U of Chicago P, 1995. 274–287.

Atwood, Margaret. *The Handmaid's Tale*. Boston: Houghton, 1986.

Awkward, Michael. "A Black Man's Place in Black Feminist Criticism." *Negotiating Difference: Race, Gender, and the Politics of Positionality*. Chicago: U of Chicago P, 1995. 43–58.

Babb, Valerie. "Women and Words: Articulating the Self in *Their Eyes Were Watching God* and *The Color Purple*." In *Alice Walker and Zora Neale Hurston: The Common Bond*. Ed. L. P. Howard. Westport, CN: Greenwood P, 1993. 83–93.

Badders, Anne-Lancaster. "Les plis dans les puits: Identity and Narrative in Myriam Warner-Vieyra's *Juletane*." *Paroles Gelees: UCLA French Studies* 8 (1995): 75–90.

Baker, Houston A., Jr. "Critical Memory and the Black Public Sphere." In *The Black*

Public Sphere. Ed. Black Public Sphere Collective. Chicago: U of Chicago P, 1995. 5–38.

———. *Modernism and the Harlem Renaissance*. Chicago: U of Chicago P, 1987.

Balcomb, A. O. "Modernity and the African Experience." *Bulletin for Contextual Theology in Southern Africa and Africa* 3.2 (June 1996): 12–20.

Baldwin, James. *Notes of a Native Son*. 1955. Reprint. New York: Dial, 1963.

Bambara, Toni Cade. *The Salt Eaters*. 1980. Reprint. New York: Vintage, 1981.

Baraka, Imanu Amiri. "Black Art." In *The Black Poets*. Ed. D. Randall. New York: Bantam. 223–224.

Barthes, Roland. *Camera Lucida*. 1981. Reprint. New York: Hill and Wang, 1984.

Basu, Biman. "Public and Private Discourse and the Black Female Subject: Gayl Jones' *Eva's Man*." *Callaloo* 19 (1996): 193–208.

Bell, Derrick. Foreword to *Critical Race Feminism, A Reader*, ed. A. Katherine Wing. New York: New York UP, 1997. xiii–xvi.

Belton, Don. "Where We Live: A Conversation with Essex Hemphill and Issac Julien." In *Speak My Name: Black Men on Masculinity and the American Dream*. Ed. Belton. Boston: Beacon, 1995. 209–219.

Benjamin, Walter. *Illuminations*. Trans. Harry Zohn. New York: Schocken, 1969.

Bergenholtz, Rita A. "Toni Morrison's Sula: A Satire on Binary Thinking." *African American Review* 30 (1996): 89–98.

Berger, John. *Ways of Seeing*. Harmondsworth, UK: Penguin, 1972.

Berlant, Lauren. *The Queen of America Goes to Washington City: Essays on Sex and Citizenship*. Durham: Duke UP, 1997.

Bhabha, Homi K. "Cultural Diversity and Cultural Differences" in *The Post-Colonial Studies Reader*. Ed. B. Ashcroft, G. Griffiths, and H. Tiffin. New York: Routledge, 1995. 206–209.

———. "Signs Taken for Wonder: Questions of Ambivalence and Authority under a Tree outside Dehli, May 1817." In *"Race," Writing, and Difference*. Ed. Henry Louis Gates Jr. Chicago: U of Chicago P, 1995. 163–184.

Birbalsingh, Frank, ed. *Frontiers of Caribbean Literature in English*. New York: St. Martin's, 1996.

Black Radical Congress. "Statement of Unity." In *Let Nobody Turn Us Around: Voices of Resistance, Reform, and Renewal: An African American Anthology*. Ed. M. Marable and L. Mullings. Lanham, MD: Rowman and Littlefield, 2000. 625–626.

Blanck, Rubin, and Gertrude Blanck. *Beyond Ego Psychology: Developmental Object-Relations Theory*. New York: Columbia UP, 1986.

Bonner, Marita. "On Being Young—A Woman—And Colored." In *Frye Street and Other Environs: The Collected Works of Marita Bonner*. Ed. Joyce Flynn and Joyce Occomy Sticklin. Boston: Beacon, 1987. 3–8.

Booth, Wayne. *The Rhetoric of Fiction*. 2 ed. Chicago: University of Chicago Press, 1983.

Brady, Lenore L. "Haunting the Slave Narrative: The Sacred Apprehension of Time in Toni Morrison's *Beloved*." MS.

Braithwaite, Edward. *The Development of Creole Society in Jamaica, 1770–1820*. New York: Oxford UP, 1971.

Brand, Dionne. *Primitive Offense*. Toronto: Williams-Wallace International,1982.

———. *No Language Is Neutral*. 1990. Reprint. Toronto: McClelland and Stewart, 1998.

———. *Bread Out of Stone*. Toronto: Coach House, 1994.

———. *Land to Light On*. Toronto: McClelland and Stewart,1997.

Brown, Karen McCarthy. "The Moral Force Field of Haitian Vodou." In *Face the Facts: Moral Inquiry in American Scholarship*. Ed. R. Fox and R. Westbrook. Cambridge: Cambridge UP, 2002. 181–200.

Brown-Douglass, Kelly. "God Is as Christ Does: Toward Womanist Theology." *Journal of Religious Thought* 46.1 (Summer–Fall 1989): 7–16.

Brown-Hinds, Paulette. "In the Spirit: Dance as Healing Ritual in Paule Marshall's *Praisesong for the Widow.*" *Religion and Literature* 21 (1995): 107–117.

Brydon, Diana. "Reading Dionne Brand's 'Blues Spiritual for Mammy Prater.'" In *Inside the Poem: Essays and Poems in Honour of Donald Stephens.* Ed. W. H. New. Toronto: Oxford UP, 1992. 81–87.

Butler-Evans, Elliott. *Race, Gender and Desire: Narrative Strategies in the Fiction of Toni Cade Bambara, Toni Morrison and Alice Walker.* Philadelphia: Temple UP, 1989.

Butler, Octavia. *Parable of the Sower.* New York: Warner, 1993.

Byerman, Keith. "Intense Behaviors: The Use of the Grotesque in *The Bluest Eye* and *Eva's Man.*" *CLA* 25 (1982): 447–457.

Canaan, Andrea. "Girlfriends." In *Making Face, Making Soul. Haciendo Caras: Creative and Critical Perspectives by Feminists of Color.* Ed. by Gloria Anzaldúa. San Francisco: Aunt Lute, 1990. 302–303.

Carby, Hazel. *Reconstructing Womanhood: The Emergence of the Afro-American Woman Novelist.* New York: Oxford UP, 1987.

Chadwick-Joshua, Jocelyn. "Metonymy and Synecdoche: The Rhetoric of the City in Toni Morrison's *Jazz.*" In *The City in African American Literature.* Ed. Yoshinobu Hakutani and Robert Butler. Madison: Fairleigh Dickinson UP, 1995. 168–180.

Chancy, Myriam J. A. *Searching for Safe Spaces: Afro-Caribbean Women Writers in Exile.* Philadelphia: Temple UP, 1997.

Chariandry, David. "Landing Lightly: Dionne Brand and the Question of Territorial Belonging." Paper delivered at the Thirteenth Annual Meeting of the Society for the Study of Multi-Ethnic Literature of the United States, Nashville, TN, 20 March 1999.

Chatman, Seymour. *Story and Discourse: Narrative Structure in Fiction and Film.* Ithaca, NY: Cornell UP, 1978.

Chetin, Sara. "Reading from a Distance: Ama Ata Aidoo's *Our Sister Killjoy.*" In *Black Women's Writing.* Ed. G. Wisker. New York: St. Martin's, 1993.

Chickering, Arthur. *Education and Identity.* San Francisco: Jossey-Bass, 1975.

Chodorow, Nancy J. *Feminism and Psychoanalytic Theory.* New Haven: Yale UP, 1989.

Christian, Barbara. "The Highs and Lows of Black Feminist Criticism." In *Reading Black, Reading Feminist: A Critical Anthology.* Ed. Henry Louis Gates Jr. New York: Penguin-Meridian, 1990. 44–51.

———. "The Race for Theory." In *Making Face, Making Soul. Haciendo Caras: Creative and Critical Perspectives by Feminists of Color.* Ed. G. Anzaldúa. San Francisco: Aunt Lute, 1990. 335–345.

Cixous, Hélène. *The Newly Born Woman.* Trans. Betsy Wing. Minneapolis: U of Minnesota P, 1986.

Clarke, Cheryl. "Living the Texts Out: Lesbians and the Uses of Black Women's Traditions." In *Theorizing Black Feminisms: The Visionary Pragmatism of Black Women.* Ed. A. Busia and S. James. New York: Routledge, 1993. 214–227.

Clasby, Nancy Tenfelde. "Sula the Trickster." *Literature, Interpretation and Theory* 6 (1995): 21–34.

Clement, Catherine. *The Weary Sons of Freud.* Trans. Nicole Ball. London: Verso, 1987.

Cliff, Michelle. *Abeng.* 1990. New York: Penguin, 1991.

———. *No Telephone to Heaven.* 1987. New York: Vintage, 1989.

Clifton, Lucille. *The Book of Light.* Port Townsend, WA: Copper Canyon, 1993.

Coleman, Alisha. "One and One Make One: A Metacritical and Psychoanalytic Reading of Friendship in Toni Morrison's *Sula.*" *CLA Journal* 37.2 (December 1993): 145–155.

Collins, Patricia Hill. *Black Feminist Thought: Knowledge, Consciousness, and the Politics of Empowerment*. New York: Routledge, 1991.

———. "Shifting the Center: Race, Class, and Feminist Theorizing about Motherhood." In *Representations of Motherhood*. Ed. D. Basin, M. Honey and M. M. Kaplan. New Haven: Yale UP, 1994. 56–74.

———. "What's Going On? Black Feminist Thought and the Politics of Postmodernism." *Fighting Words: Black Women and the Search for Justice*. Minneapolis: U of Minnesota P, 1998. 124–154.

Combahee River Collective. "A Black Feminist Statement." In *All the Women Are White, All the Blacks Are Men, but Some of Us Are Brave: Black Women's Studies*, ed. G. T. Hull, P. B. Scott, and B. Smith. New York: The Feminist P, 1982. 13–22.

Comfort, Susan. "Counter-Memory, Mourning, and History in Toni Morrison's *Beloved*." *Literature, Interpretation, and Theory* 6.1–2 (1995 April): 121–132.

Cone, James H., and Gayraud S. Wilmore, eds. *Black Theology: A Documentary History*. Vol. 2: *1980–1992*. New York: Orbis, 1993.

Cooper, Anna Julia. "Woman versus the Indian." *A Voice from the South*. 1892. Reprint. New York: Oxford UP, 1988. 80–126.

Couser, G. Thomas. "Oppression and Repression: Personal and Collective Memory in Paule Marshall's *Praisesong for the Widow* and Leslie Marmon Silko's *Ceremony*." In *Memory and Cultural Politics: New Approaches to American Ethnic Literatures*. Ed. A. Singh, J. T. Skerret Jr., and R. E. Hogan. Boston: Northeastern UP, 1996. 106–120.

Crenshaw, Kimberle. "Mapping the Margins: Intersectionality, Identity, Politics, and Violence against Women of Color." *Stanford Law Review* 43.6 (1991): 1241–1299.

Cudjoe, Selwyn. Introduction to *Caribbean Women Writers*. Ed. Cudjoe. Wellesley, MA: Callaloux, 1990. 1–48.

Davidson, Carol Margaret. "'Love 'Em and Lynch 'Em': The Castration Motif in Gayl Jones' *Eva's Man*." *African American Review* 29.3 (1995): 393–410.

Davies, Carole Boyce. *Black Women, Writing, and Identity: Migrations of the Subject*. London: Routledge, 1994.

———. "Mothering and Healing in Recent Black Women's Fiction." *Sage* 2.1 (Spring 1995): 41–43.

———. *Moving beyond Boundaries: Black Women's Diasporas*. New York: New York UP, 1995.

Davies, Carole Boyce, and Elaine Savory Fido. "African Women Writers: Toward a Literary History." In *A History of Twentieth Century African Literatures*. Ed. Oyekan Owomoyela. Lincoln: U of Nebraska P, 1993. 311–346.

Davies, Carole Boyce, and Molara Ogundipe Leslie, eds. *Moving beyond Boundaries: International Dimensions of Black Women's Writing*. New York: New York UP, 1995.

Davis, Angela Y. *Blues Legacies and Black Feminism: Gertrude "Ma" Rainey, Bessie Smith, and Billie Holiday*. 1998. Reprint. New York: Vintage, 1999.

———. *Women, Culture and Politics*. New York: Random, 1989.

Dawson, Emma J. Waters. "Redemption through Redemption of the Self in *Their Eyes Were Watching God* and *The Color Purple*." In *Alice Walker and Zora Neale Hurston: The Common Bond*. Ed. Lillie P. Howard. Westport, CN: Greenwood P, 1993. 69–82.

DeAbruna, Laura Niesen. "Twentieth-Century Women Writers from the English-Speaking Caribbean." In *Caribbean Women Writers: Essays from the First International Conference*. Ed. S. R. Cudjoe. Wellesley, MA: Callaloux, 1990. 86–97.

DeLamotte, Eugenia C. *Places of Silence, Journeys of Freedom: The Fiction of Paule Marshall*. Philadelphia: U of Pennsylvania P, 1998.

DeLauretis, Teresa. *The Practice of Love: Lesbian Sexuality and Perverse Desire.* Bloomington: Indiana UP, 1994.

———. "Upping the Anti (sic) in Feminist Theory." In *The Cultural Studies Reader.* 2d ed. Ed. Simon During. New York: Routledge, 1999. 307–319.

Dixon, Melvin. *Ride Out the Wilderness: Geography and Identity in Afro-American Literature.* Urbana: U of Illinois P, 1987.

———. "Singing a Deep Song: Language as Evidence in the Novels of Gayl Jones." In *Black Women Writers (1950–1980): A Critical Evaluation.* Ed. M. Evans. New York: Anchor/Doubleday, 1984. 236–248.

Dove, Rita. *Thomas and Beulah.* Pittsburgh: Carnegie-Mellon UP, 1986.

DuCille, Ann. *The Coupling Convention: Sex, Text, and Tradition in Black Women's Fiction.* New York: Oxford UP, 1993.

———. *Skin Trade.* Cambridge, MA: Harvard UP, 1996.

Du Bois, W. E. B. *The Autobiography of W. E. B. Du Bois: A Soliloquy on Viewing My Life from the Last Decade of Its First Century.* New York: International, 1968.

———. *The Souls of Black Folk.* 1903. Ed. D. Blight and R. Gooding-Williams. Boston: Bedford Books, 1997.

Eagleton, Terry. *Literary Theory: An Introduction.* Minneapolis: U of Minnesota P, 1983.

Fanon, Frantz. *Black Skins, White Masks.* Trans. Charles Lam Markmann. New York: Grove, 1967.

———. *Wretched of the Earth.* Trans. Constance Farrington. 1963. Reprint. New York: Grove, 1968.

Felman, Shoshana. *Writing and Madness.* Trans. Martha Noel Evans, S. Felman, and Brian Massumi. Ithaca, NY: Cornel UP, 1995.

Ferguson, Moira. *Jamaica Kincaid: Where the Land Meets the Body.* Charlottesville: UP of Virginia, 1994.

FitzGerald, Jennifer. "Selfhood and Community: Psychoanalysis and Discourse in *Beloved.*" *Modern Fiction Studies* 39 (1993): 669–687.

Flint, Roland. "A Poem Called George, Sometimes." *Resuming Green.* New York: Dial, 1983. 55.

Fromm, Erich. "Politics and Psychoanalysis." In *Critical Theory and Society: A Reader.* Ed. Stephen Eric Bonner and Douglas Kellner. New York: Routledge, 1989. 213–218.

Fultz, Lucille P. "To Make Herself: Mother-Daughter Conflicts in Toni Morrison's *Sula* and *Tar Baby.*" In *Women of Color: Mother-Daughter Relationships in 20th-Century Literature.* Ed. E. Brown-Guillory. Austin: U of Texas P, 1996. 228–243.

Fusco, Coco. "Uncanny Dissonance: The Work of Lorna Simpson." *Third Text* 22 (Spring 1993): 27–32.

Gates, Henry Louis, Jr. "Review of *Jazz.*" In *Toni Morrison: Critical Perspectives Past and Present.* Ed. Gates and K. A. Appiah. New York: Amistad, 1993

———. *The Signifying Monkey: A Theory of African-American Literary Criticism.* New York: Oxford UP, 1988.

Giddens, Anthony. *The Consequences of Modernity.* Stanford: Stanford UP, 1990.

Giddings, Paula. *When and Where I Enter: The Impact of Black Women on Race and Sex in America.* New York: William Morrow, 1984.

Gillespie, Diane, and Missy Dehn Kubitschek. "Who Cares? Woman-Centered Psychology in *Sula.*" *Black American Literature Forum* 24 (1990): 21–48.

Gilman, Sander. "Black Bodies, White Bodies: Toward an Iconography of Female Sexuality in Late Nineteenth Century Art, Medicine and Literature." *Critical Inquiry* 12 (Fall 1985): 204–239.

Gilroy, Beryl. "Writing, Ancestry, Childhood and Self." In *Moving beyond Boundaries.*

Vol. 1: *International Dimensions of Black Women's Writing*. Ed. C. B. Davies and M. Ogundipe-Leslie. New York: New York UP, 1995. 53–60.

Gilroy, Paul. *The Black Atlantic: Modernity and Double Consciousness*. Cambridge, MA: Harvard UP, 1993.

Gladstone, Valerie. "The Long Shadow of Ailey's Great Cry." *New York Times*, 26 November 2000, 2:6.

Goldsby, Jackie. "Queen for 307 Days: Looking B[l]ack at Vanessa Williams and the Sex Wars." In *Afrekete: An Anthology of Black Lesbian Writing*. Ed. Catherine E. McKinley and L. Joyce DeLaney. New York: Anchor/Doubleday, 1995. 165–188.

Gordon, Avery F. *Ghostly Matters: Haunting and the Sociological Imagination*. Minneapolis: U of Minnesota P, 1997.

Griffin, Farah Jasmine. *"Who Set You Flowin'?" The African-American Migration Narrative*. New York: Oxford UP, 1995.

Grosz, Elizabeth. *Jacques Lacan: A Feminist Introduction*. London: Routledge, 1990.

———. *Space, Time, and Perversion: Essays on the Politics of Bodies*. New York: Routledge, 1995.

———. *Volatile Bodies: Toward a Corporeal Feminism*. Bloomington: Indiana UP, 1994.

Guth, Deborah. "A Blessing and a Burden: The Relation to the Past in *Sula, Song of Solomon*, and *Beloved*." *Modern Fiction Studies* 39 (1993): 575–596.

Hammonds, Evelyn. "Black (W)holes and the Geometry of Black Female Sexuality." In *African American Literary Theory: A Reader*. Ed. Winston Napier. New York: New York UP, 2000. 482–497.

Haraway, Donna. "Cyborgs at Large: An Interview with Donna Haraway." In *Technoculture*. Ed. C. Penley and A. Ross. Minneapolis: U of Minnesota P, 1991. 1–20.

———. *Simians, Cyborgs, and Women: The Reinvention of Nature*. New York: Routledge, 1991.

Harris, Angela P. "Race and Essentialism in Feminist Legal Theory." In *Critical Race Feminism, A Reader*. Ed. A. K. Wing. New York: New York UP, 1997. 11–18.

Harris, Trudier. *Fiction and Folklore: The Novels of Toni Morrison*. Knoxville: U of Tennessee P, 1991.

Harrison, Paul Carter. *The Drama of Nommo*. New York: Grove, 1972.

Heinze, Denise. *The Dilemma of the "Double Consciousness": Toni Morrison's Novels*. Athens: U of Georgia P, 1993.

Henderson, Mae G. "Speaking in Tongues: Dialogics, Dialectics, and the Black Women's Writers Literary Tradition." In *Changing Our Own Words: Essays on Criticism, Theory, and Writing by Black Women*. Ed. C. A. Wall. New Brunswick, NJ: Rutgers UP, 1989. 16–37.

———. "Toni Morrison's *Beloved*: Re-Membering the Body as Historical Text." In *Toni Morrison's "Beloved": A Casebook*. Ed. W. L. Andrews and N. Y. McKay. New York: Oxford UP, 1999. 79–106.

Hernton, Calvin C. *The Sexual Mountain and Black Women Writers: Adventures in Sex, Literature, and Real Life*. New York: Anchor/Doubleday, 1987.

Holloway, Karla F. C. "Cultural Narratives Passed On: African American Mourning Stories." In *African American Literary Theory: A Reader*. Ed. Winston Napier. New York: New York UP, 2000. 653–659.

———. *Moorings and Metaphors: Figures of Culture and Gender in Black Women's Literature*. New Brunswick, NJ: Rutgers UP, 1992.

hooks, bell. "Eating the Other." In *Black Looks: Race and Representation*. Boston: South End, 1992. 21–39.

———. *Feminist Theory: From Margin to Center*. Boston: South End, 1984.

———. *Sisters of the Yam: Black Women and Self-Recovery*. Boston: South End, 1993.

————. *Yearning: Race, Gender and Cultural Politics*. Boston: South End, 1990.

Horowitz, Deborah. "Nameless Ghosts: Possession and Dispossession in *Beloved*." *Studies in American Fiction* 17.2 (Fall 1989): 157–167.

Hull, Gloria T. "'What It Is I Think She's Doing Anyhow': A Reading of Toni Cade Bambara's *The Salt Eaters*." In *Conjuring: Black Women, Fiction, and Literary Tradition*. Ed. M. Pryse and H. J. Spillers. Bloomington: Indiana UP, 1985. 216–232.

Hurston, Zora Neale. *Their Eyes Were Watching God*. 1937. New York: Harper, 1990.

Irigaray, Luce. *This Sex Which Is Not One*. Trans. Catherine Porter with Carolyn Burke. Ithaca, NY: Cornell UP, 1985.

Jablon, Madelyn. "Rememory, Dream Memory, and Revision in Toni Morrison's *Beloved* and Alice Walker's *The Temple of My Familiar*." *CLA* 37.2 (1993 December): 136–144.

Jarrett, Juliette. "Creative Space? The Experience of Black Women in British Art Schools." In *Reconstructing Womanhood, Reconstructing Feminism: Writings on Black Women*. Ed. D. Jarrett-Macauley. New York: Routledge, 1996. 121–135.

Jones, Gayl. "About My Work." In *Black Women Writers (1950–1980): A Critical Evaluation*. Ed. M. Evans. New York: Anchor/Doubleday, 1984. 233–235.

————. *Corregidora*. 1975. Reprint. Boston: Beacon, 1986.

————. *Eva's Man*. 1976. Reprint. Boston: Beacon, 1987.

Kelley, Margot Anne. "'Damballah Is the First Law of Thermodynamics': Modes of Access to Toni Cade Bambara's *The Salt Eaters*." *African American Review* 27.3 (Fall 1993): 479–493.

Kelley, Robin D. G. *Yo Mama's Disfunktional! Fighting the Culture Wars in Urban America*. Boston: Beacon, 1997.

Kincaid, Jamaica. *Lucy*. 1990. Reprint. New York: Plume, 1991.

————. *A Small Place*. 1988. Reprint. New York: Plume, 1989.

Kolawole, Mary E. Modupe. *Womanism and African Consciousness*. Trenton, NJ: Africa World Press, 1997.

Kristeva, Julia. *Strangers to Ourselves*. Trans. Leon S. Roudiez. New York: Columbia UP, 1991.

Krumholz, Linda. "The Ghosts of Slavery: Historical Recovery in Toni Morrison's *Beloved*." *African American Review* 26 (Fall 1992): 395–408.

Lacan, Jacques. "The Mirror Stage as Formative of the Function of the I as Revealed in Psychoanalytic Experience." *Ecrits*. Trans. Alan Sheridan. New York: W. W. Norton, 1977. 1–7.

Lamming, George. *The Pleasures of Exile*. 1960. Reprint. London: Alison and Busby, 1984.

Larrier, Renee. *Francophone Women Writers of Africa and the Caribbean*. Gainesville: U of Florida P, 2000.

————. "Reconstructing Motherhood: Francophone African Women Autobiographers." In *The Politics of (M)Othering: Womanhood, Identity, and Resistance in African Literature*. Ed. Obioma Nnaemeka. London: Routledge, 1997. 192–204.

Lee, Rachel. "Notes from the (non)Field: Teaching and Theorizing Women of Color." *Meridians* 1 (2002): 85–109.

Lewis, Ida. "Conversation: Ida Lewis and James Baldwin." In *Conversations with James Baldwin*. Ed. Fred L. Standley and Louis H. Pratt. Jackson: U of Mississippi P, 1989. 83–92.

Lewis, Vashti Crutcher. "African Tradition in Toni Morrison's *Sula*." *Phylon* 48 (1987): 91–97.

Liddell, Janice Lee. "The Narrow Enclosure of Motherdom/Martyrdom: A Study of Gatha Randall Barton in Sylvia Wynter's *The Hills of Heborn*." In *Out of the Kumbla: Caribbean Women and Literature*. Ed. C. B. Davies and E. S. Fido. Trenton, NJ: Africa World Press, 1990. 321–330.

Lipsitz, George. *Time Passages: Collective Memory and American Popular Culture*. Minneapolis: U of Minnesota P, 1990.

Lodge, David. *The Art of Fiction: Illustrated from Classical and Modern Texts*. New York: Penguin, 1994.

Lorde, Audre. *The Black Unicorn: Poems*. New York: Norton, 1978.

———. *Sister Outsider: Speeches and Essays*. New York: Crossing P, 1984.

———. "School Note." *The Black Unicorn*. New York: Norton, 1978. 55.

———. *Sister Outsider: Essays and Speeches*. Tramansburg, NY: Crossing P, 1984.

MacKinnon, Catherine. *Toward a Feminist Theory of the State*. Cambridge, MA: Harvard UP, 1989.

Majozo, Estella Conwill. *Come Out of the Wilderness: Memoir of a Black Woman Artist*. New York: The Feminist P, 1999.

Marshall, Paule. *Praisesong for the Widow*. 1983. Reprint. New York: Dutton, 1984.

Martin, Joan. "The Notion of Difference for Emerging Womanist Ethics: The Writings of Audre Lorde and bell hooks." *Journal of Feminist Studies in Religion* 9 (1993): 39–52.

McClintock, Anne. *Imperial Leather: Race, Gender, and Sexuality in the Colonial Contest*. New York: Routledge, 1995.

McDowell, Deborah E. *"The Changing Same": Black Women's Literature, Criticism, and Theory*. Bloomington: Indiana UP, 1995.

———. "'The Self and the Other': Reading Toni Morrison's *Sula* and the Black Female Text." In *Critical Essays on Toni Morrison*. Ed. N. Y. McKay. Boston: G. K. Hall, 1988. 77–90.

McKee, Patricia. *Producing American Races: Henry James, William Faulkner, Toni Morrison*. Durham: Duke UP, 1999.

McKoy, Shelia Smith. "Remnant Consciousness: Home, Desire, and Cultural Reclamation in Kofi Awoonor's *Comes the Voyager at Last*." Paper delivered at the Thirteenth Annual Meeting of the Society for the Study of Multi-Ethnic Literature of the United States, Nashville, TN, 19 March 1999.

Mitchell, Stephen A., and Margaret J. Black. *Freud and Beyond: A History of Modern Psychoanalytic Thought*. New York: Basic Books, 1995.

Mirza, Helen Safia, ed. *Black British Feminism: A Reader*. London: Routledge, 1997.

Modood, Tariq. "'Difference,' Cultural Racism, and Anti-Racism." In *Debating Cultural Hybridity: Multi-Cultural Identities and the Politics of Anti-Racism*. Ed. Pnina Werbner and Modood. Atlantic Highlands, NJ: Zed, 1997. 154–172.

Mohanty, Chandra Talpade. "Introduction: Cartographies of Freedom—Third World Women and the Politics of Feminism." In *Third World Women and the Politics of Feminism*. Ed. A. R. Mohanty and L. Torres. Bloomington: Indiana UP, 1991. 1–47.

Morrison, Toni. *Beloved*. 1987. Reprint. New York: Plume Penguin. 1988.

———. *The Bluest Eye*. 1969. Reprint. New York: Plume. 1996.

———. *Jazz*. New York: Knopf, 1992.

———. *Lecture and Speech of Acceptance upon Award for the Nobel Prize in Literature*. New York: Knopf, 1994.

———. "Strangers." *New Yorker* 74.31, 12 October 1998, 68–71.

———. *Sula*. 1973. Reprint. New York: Plume Penguin. 1982.

Mudimbe-Boyi, Elisabeth. "Narrative 'je(ux)' in *Kamaouraska* by Anne Herbert and *Juletane* by Myriam Warner-Vieyra." In *Postcolonial Subjects: Francophone Women Writers*. Ed. Mary Jean Green et al. Minneapolis: U of Minnesota P, 1996. 124–139.

Mullen, Harryette. "Runaway Tongue: Resistant Orality in *Uncle Tom's Cabin, Our Nig, Incidents in the Life of a Slave Girl*, and *Beloved*." In *The Culture of Sentiment:*

Race, Gender, and Sentimentality in Nineteenth Century America. Ed. S. Samuels. New York: Oxford UP, 1992. 244–264.

Munoz, Jose Esteban. *Disidentifications: Queers of Color and the Performance of Politics.* Minneapolis: U of Minnesota P, 1999.

Neal, Larry. "Some Reflections on the Black Aesthetic." In *The Black Aesthetic.* Ed. Addison Gayle. New York: Doubleday, 1972. 12–16.

Needham, Anuradha D. "An Interview with Ama Ata Aidoo." *Massachusetts Review* 36.1 (Spring 1995): 23–32.

Ngate, Jonathan. "Reading *Juletane.*" *Callaloo* 9.4 (Fall 1986): 553–564.

Ngugi, Wa Thiongo. *Homecoming: Essays on African and Caribbean Literature, Culture, and Politics.* New York: Lawrence Hill, 1973.

Nhat Hanh, Thich. *Teachings on Love.* Berkeley: Parallax, 1997.

Nichols, Grace. *I Is a Long-Memoried Woman.* London: Karnak House, 1983.

Nnaemeka, Obioma. "Introduction: Imag(in)ing Knowledge, Power, and Subversion in the Margins." In *The Politics of (M)Othering: Womanhood, Identity, and Resistance in African Literature.* Ed. Nnaemeka. London: Routledge, 1997. 1–25.

Nourbese Philip, Marlene. 1989. Reprint. *She Tries Her Tongue, Her Silence Softly Breaks.* Charlottetown, PEI, CN: Ragweed P, 1999.

Nowlin, Michael. "Toni Morrison's *Jazz* and the Racial Dreams of the American Writer." *American Literature* 71.1 (March 1999): 151–174.

Nwankwo, Chimalum. "The Feminist Impulse and Social Realism in Ama Ata Aidoo's *No Sweetness Here* and *Our Sister Killjoy.*" In *Ngambika: Studies of Women in African Literature.* Ed. C. B. Davies and A. A. Graves. Trenton, NJ: Africa World Press, 1996. 151–159.

O'Callahan, Evelyn. "Interior Schisms Dramatised: The Treatment of the 'Mad' Woman in the Work of Some Female Caribbean Novelists." In Davies and Fido, *Out of the Kumbla.* 89–109.

Olmstead, Jane. "The Pull to Memory and the Language of Place in Paule Marshall's *The Chosen Place, The Timeless People* and *Praisesong for the Widow.*" *African American Review* 31 (1997): 249–267.

O'Meally, Robert, and Genevieve Fabre. *Introduction to History and Memory in African-American Culture.* Ed. O'Meally and Fabre. New York: Oxford UP, 1994. 3–17.

Owomoyela, Oyekan. "The Question of Language in African Literatures." In *A History of Twentieth Century African Literatures.* Ed. Owomoyela. Lincoln: U of Nebraska P, 1993. 347–368.

Owusu, Kofi. "Canons under Siege: Blackness, Femaleness, and Ama Ata Aidoo's *Our Sister Killjoy.*" *Callaloo* 13 (1990): 331–363.

Page, Philip. "Traces of Derrida in Toni Morrison's *Jazz.*" *African American Review* 29.1 (Spring 1995): 66.

Painter, Nell Irvin. *Sojourner Truth: A Life, A Symbol.* New York: Norton, 1996.

Palmer, Parker J. *The Courage to Teach: Exploring the Inner Landscape of a Teacher's Life.* San Francisco: Jossey-Bass, 1998.

Parker, Pat. "For the White Person Who Wants to Know How to Be My Friend." *Movement in Black: The Collected Poetry of Pat Parker, 1961–1978.* 1978. Reprint. Ithaca, NY: Firebrand, 1989. 99.

Parry, Benita. "Resistance Theory / Theorizing Resistance; or Two Cheers for Nativism." In *Colonial Discourse, Postcolonial Theory.* Ed. Frances Barker, Peter Hulme, and Margaret Iversen. New York: Manchester UP, 1994. 172–196.

Pease, Donald. "Author." In *Critical Terms for Literary Study.* Ed. Frank Lentricchia and Thomas McLaughlin. Chicago: U of Chicago P, 1995. 105–116.

Perez-Torres, Rafael. "Between Presence and Absence: *Beloved,* Postcolonialism and

Blackness." In *Toni Morrison's "Beloved": A Casebook*. Ed. W. L. Andrews and N. Y. McKay. New York: Oxford UP, 1999. 179–202.

Pessoni, Michelle. "'She Was Laughing at Their God': Discovering the Goddess Within in *Sula*." *African American Review* 29 (1995): 439–451.

Price, Derrick, and Liz Wells. "Thinking about Photography: Debates Historically and Now." In *Photography: A Critical Introduction*. 2d ed. Ed. Wells. New York: Routledge, 2000. 9–64.

Proudfit, Charles L. "Celie's Search for Identity: A Psychoanalytic Developmental Reading of Alice Walker's *The Color Purple*." *Contemporary Literature* 32 (1991): 12–37.

Quindlen, Anna. "Mother's Choice." *Ms.* (February 1988): 55+.

Rabasa, Jose. "Allegories of Atlas." In *The Post-Colonial Studies Reader*. Ed. B. Ashcroft, G. Griffiths, and H. Tiffin. London: Routledge, 1995. 358–564.

Raiskin, Judith. "Inverts and Hybrids: Lesbian Rewritings of Sexual and Racial Identities." In *The Lesbian Postmodern*. Ed. L. Doan. New York: Columbia UP, 1994. 156–172.

Renan, Ernest. "What Is a Nation?" In *Nation and Narration*. Ed. H. K. Bhabha. London: Routledge, 1990. 8–22.

Rich, Adrienne. "For Memory." *A Wild Patience Has Taken Me This Far: Poems 1978–1981*. New York: Norton, 1981. 21–22.

———. *Of Woman Born: Motherhood as Experience and Institution*. 1976. Reprint. New York: Bantam, 1977.

———. *On Lies, Secrets, and Silence: Selected Prose, 1966–1978*. New York: Norton, 1979.

Rigney, Barbara Hill. "'A Story to Pass On': Ghosts and the Significance of History in Toni Morrison's *Beloved*." In *Haunting the House of Fiction: Feminist Perspectives on Ghost Stories by American Women*. Ed. L. Carpenter and W. K. Kolmar. Knoxville: U of Tennessee P, 1991. 229–235.

Riley, Denise. *The Words of Selves: Identification, Solidarity, Irony*. Stanford: Stanford UP, 2000.

Rimmon-Kenan, Shlomith. *Narrative Fiction: Contemporary Poetics*. London: Methuen, 1983.

Roberts, Dorothy. *Killing the Black Body: Race, Reproduction, and the Meaning of Liberty*. New York: Pantheon, 1997.

———. "Racism and Patriarchy in the Meaning of Motherhood." In *Mothers in Law: Feminist Theory and the Legal Regulation of Motherhood*. Ed. M. A. Fineman and I. Karpin. New York: Columbia UP, 1995. 224–249.

Robinson, Sally. *Engendering the Subject: Gender and Self-Representation in Contemporary Women's Fiction*. Albany, NY: SUNY P, 1991.

Rodrigues, Eusebio L. "Experiencing *Jazz*." *Modern Fiction Studies* 39.3–4 (Fall-Winter 1993): 733–754.

Rody, Caroline. "Impossible Voices: Ethnic Postmodern Narration in Toni Morrison's *Jazz* and Karen Tei Yamashita's *Through the Arc of the Rain Forest*." *Contemporary Literature* 41.4 (Winter 2000): 618–641.

Ruddick, Sara. *Maternal Thinking: Towards a Politics of Peace*. Boston: Beacon, 1989.

Rushdy, Ashraf H.A. "Daughters Signifyin(g) History: The Example of Toni Morrison's *Beloved*." In *Toni Morrison's "Beloved": A Casebook*. Ed. W. L. Andrews and N. Y. McKay. New York: Oxford UP, 1999. 37–66.

Savage, Monique J. Personal communications, n.d. (1996–2000).

Sethuraman, Ramchandran. "Evidence-cum-Witness: Subaltern History, Violence, and the (De)Formation of Nation in Michelle Cliff's *No Telephone to Heaven*." *Modern Fiction Studies* 43 (1997): 249–287.

Shange, Ntozake. *For colored girls who have considered suicide, when the rainbow is enuf.* 1975. Reprint. New York: Scribner, 1997.

Silverman, Kaja. *Threshold of the Visible World.* New York: Routledge, 1996.

Singh, Amritjit, Joseph T. Skerrett Jr., and Robert E. Hogan. Introduction to *Memory and Cultural Politics: New Approaches to American Ethnic Literatures.* Boston: Northeastern UP, 1996. 3–18.

Smith, Anna Deveare. *Fires in the Mirror: Crown Heights, Brooklyn, and Other Identities.* New York: Anchor/Doubleday, 1993.

Smith, Barbara. "Towards a Black Feminist Criticism." In *All the Women Are White, All the Blacks Are Men, but Some of Us Are Brave: Black Women's Studies.* Ed. G. T. Hull, P. B. Scott, and B. Smith. New York: The Feminist P, 1982. 157–175.

———. *Homegirls: A Black Feminist Anthology.* New York: Kitchen Table, 1983.

Smith, Valerie. "Black Feminist Theory and the Representation of the 'Other.'" In *Changing Our Own Words: Essays on Criticism, Theory, and Writing by Black Women.* Ed. C. A. Wall. New Brunswick, NJ: Rutgers UP, 1989. 38–57.

———. *Self-Discovery and Authority in Afro-American Narrative.* Cambridge, MA: Harvard UP, 1987.

Smyth, Gerry. "The Politics of Hybridity." In *Comparing Postcolonial Literatures: Dislocations.* Ed. Ashok Bery and Patricia Murray. New York: St. Martin's, 2000. 43–55.

Solomon, Barbara H. Introduction to *Critical Essays on Toni Morrison's "Beloved."* Ed. Solomon. New York: G. K. Hall, 1998. 1–35.

Spelman, Elizabeth V. *Inessential Woman: Problems of Exclusion in Feminist Thought.* Boston: Beacon, 1988.

Spillers, Hortense. "'All the Things You Could Be by Now if Sigmund Freud's Wife Was Your Mother.'" *Critical Inquiry* 22 (Summer 1996): 710–734.

———. "Mama's Baby, Papa's Maybe: An American Grammar Book." *Diacritics* 17 (1987): 65–81.

Stanley Love Group. "About *Calico*." Cited in Work and Show Festival, Tribeca Performing Arts Center, Artists in Residence 2001–2002, New York.

Steele, Claude M. "Thin Ice: 'Stereotype Threat' and Black College Students." *Atlantic Monthly* 284.2 (August 1999): 44–54.

Stein, Karen. "Toni Morrison's *Sula*: A Black Woman's Epic." *Black American Literature Forum* 18.4 (1984 Winter): 146–150.

Stout, Janis. *Through the Window, Out the Door: Women's Narrative of Departure from Austen and Cather to Tyler, Morrison and Didion.* Tuscaloosa: U of Alabama P, 1998.

Sweet Honey in the Rock. "No Mirrors in My Nana's House." On *Still on the Journey: The Twentieth Anniversary Album.* Redway, CA: Earthbeat, 1993.

Tagg, John. *The Burden of Representation: Essays of Photographies and Histories.* London: Macmillan, 1988.

Tate, Claudia. "Gayl Jones." Interview. In *Black Women Writers at Work.* Ed. Tate. New York: Continuum, 1990. 89–99.

Taylor-Guthrie, Danielle, ed. *Conversations with Toni Morrison.* Jackson: U of Mississippi P, 1994.

Thompson, Robert Farris. *Flash of the Spirit: African and Afro-American Art and Philosophy.* New York: Vintage, 1984.

Thomson, Rosemarie Garland. *Extraordinary Bodies: Figuring Disability in American Culture and Literature.* New York: Columbia UP, 1997.

Toomer, Jean. *Cane.* 1923. Reprint. New York: Liveright, 1975.

Trinh T. Minh-ha. "Not You / Like You: Post-Colonial Women and the Interlocking Questions of Identity and Difference." In *Dangerous Liaisons: Gender, Nation, and*

Postcolonial Perspectives. Ed. A. McClintock, E. Shohat, and A. Mufti. Minneapolis: U of Minnesota P, 1997. 415–419.

———. *Woman, Native, Other: Writing Postcoloniality and Feminism*. Bloomington: Indiana UP, 1989.

Walker, Alice. *Anything We Love Can Be Saved: A Writer's Activism*. New York: Random, 1997.

———. *The Color Purple*. New York: Harcourt, 1982.

———. "Foreword: Zora Neale Hurston—A Cautionary Tale and a Partisan View." In *Zora Neale Hurston: A Literary Biography*, by Robert E. Hemenway. Urbana: U of Illinois P, 1977.

———. *In Love and Trouble: Stories of Black Women*. New York: Harcourt, 1974.

———. "Womanist," "In Search of Our Mothers' Gardens," and "Beauty: When the Other Dancer Is the Self." In *In Search of Our Mothers' Gardens: Womanist Prose*. New York: Harcourt, 1983. xi–xii, 231–243, 361–370.

Wall, Wendy. "Lettered Bodies and Corporeal Texts in *The Color Purple*." *Studies in American Fiction* 16 (1988): 83–97.

Wallace, Michele. "A Black Feminist's Search for Sisterhood." In *All the Women Are White, All the Blacks Are Men, but Some of Us Are Brave: Black Women's Studies*. Ed. G. T. Hull, P. B. Scott, and B. Smith. New York: The Feminist P, 1982. 5–12.

Warner, Michael. "Homo-Narcissism; or Heterosexuality." In *Engendering Men: The Question of Male Feminist Criticism*. Ed. Joseph A. Boone and Michael Cadden. New York: Routledge, 1990. 190–206.

Warner-Vieyra, Myriam. *Juletane*. 1982. Trans. Betty Wilson. Portsmouth, NH: Heinemann, 1987.

Washington, Mary Helen. "Disturbing the Peace: What Happens to American Studies if You Put African American at the Center?" *American Quarterly* 50 (1998): 1–23.

———. Foreword to *Their Eyes Were Watching God*, by Zora Neale Hurston. New York: Harper, 1990. vii–xiv.

———. "Teaching Black-Eyed Susans: An Approach to the Study of Black Women Writers." In *All The Women Are White, All the Blacks Are Men, but Some of Us Are Brave: Black Women's Studies*. Ed. G. T. Hull, P. B. Scott, and B. Smith. New York: The Feminist P, 1982. 208–220.

Waxman, Barbara Frey. "Dancing Out of Form, Dancing into Self: Genre and Metaphor in Marshall, Shange, and Walker." *MELUS* 19.3 (1994 Fall): 91–106.

Weems, Carrie Mae. *Not Manet's Type*. Exhibit. In *Reflections in Black: A History of Black Photographers, 1840 to the Present*. Ed. Deborah Willis. New York: Norton, 2000. 312.

Wells, Liz, ed. *Photography: A Critical Introduction*. 2d ed. New York: Routledge, 2000.

Werbner, Pnina. "The Dialectics of Cultural Hybridity." In *Debating Cultural Hybridity: Multi-Cultural Identities and the Politics of Anti-Racism*. Ed. Werbner and Tariq Modood. London: Zed, 1997. 1–26.

West, Cornel. *Race Matters*. Boston: Beacon, 1993.

Wideman, John Edgar. *All Stories Are True*. New York: Vintage, 1993.

———. *Brothers and Keepers*. 1985. Reprint. New York: Vintage, 1994.

Wiegman, Robyn. "What Ails Feminist Criticism? A Second Opinion." *Critical Inquiry* 25 (Winter 1999): 362–380.

Wilentz, Gay. "The Politics of Exile: Ama Ata Aidoo's *Our Sister Killjoy*." In *Arms Akimbo: Africana Women in Contemporary Literature*. Ed. J. L. Liddell and Y. B. Kemp. Gainesville: UP of Florida, 1999. 162–175.

Williams, Patricia J. *The Alchemy of Race and Rights: Diary of A Law Professor.* Cambridge, MA: Harvard UP, 1991.

———. "Spare Parts, Family Values, Old Children, Cheap." In *Critical Race Feminism: A Reader.* Ed. A. K. Wing. New York: New York UP, 1997. 151–158.

Willis, Susan. *Specifying: Black Women Writing the American Experience.* Madison: U of Wisconsin P, 1987.

Wilson, Elizabeth. "'Le voyage et espace close': Island and Journey as Metaphor." In Davies and Fido, *Out of the Kumbla.* 45–57.

Wilson, Mary Ann. "'That Which the Soul Lives By': Spirituality in the Works of Zora Neale Hurston and Alice Walker." In *Alice Walker and Zora Neale Hurston: The Common Bond.* Ed. L. P. Howard. Westport, CT: Greenwood, 1993. 57–68.

Wing, Adrien Katherine. "Brief Reflections toward a Multiplicative Theory and Praxis of Being." In *Critical Race Feminism: A Reader.* Ed. Wing. New York: New York UP, 1997. 27–34.

Wood, Michael. *Children of Silence: On Contemporary Fiction.* New York: Columbia UP, 1998.

Wyatt, Jean. "Giving Body to the Word: The Maternal Symbolic in Toni Morrison's *Beloved.*" In *Critical Essays on Toni Morrison's "Beloved."* Ed. B. H. Solomon. New York: G. K. Hall, 1998. 211–232.

Yearwood, Gladstone. "Expressive Traditions in Afro-American Visual Arts." In *Expressively Black: The Cultural Basis of Ethnic Identity.* Ed. Geneva Gay and Willie L. Baber. New York: Praeger, 1987. 137–163.

Zabus, Chantal. "Relexification." In *The Post-Colonial Studies Reader.* Ed. Bill Ashcroft, Gareth Griffiths, and Helen Tiffin. London: Routledge, 1995. 314–318.

Index

Abel, Elizabeth, 194n17
abjection, 9, 10
absence, 8–9
"Absence of Writing or How I Almost Became
    a Spy" (Nourbese Philip), 130–131
activism, community and, 54
"acts of Diva Citizenship" (Berlant), 161
aesthetics, 133, 176. See also language,
    aesthetics of
African folk tale, 98–99, 142
agency, 142, 147, 153, 173, 177
Aidoo, Ama Ata, 60–61, 90, 92, 108–109,
    141, 171, 189n13, 201n4, 201n8, 206n4
Ailey, Alvin, 95
"Ain't I a Woman" (Truth), 176
Akron, Ohio, 176
Albert (The Color Purple), 37–38, 39, 59–60,
    161
Alexander, Elizabeth, 180n12, 196n2, 198–
    199n2
Allen, Brenda, 182n5
Anatol, Giselle, Liza, 67
Andrews, William, 206n3
an/other, 31–32; body, 149; coalition with, 97;
    in Juletane, 44, 50; Mammy Prater as,
    155; in No Telephone to Heaven, 70, 76;
    in Our Sister Killjoy, 92; self and, 39, 90,
    140, 153; in Sula, 58; as third woman, 80;
    Walker's, 33; woman, 25, 26, 30. See also
    other and self
anti-essentialism, 10. See also essentialism
Antigua, 115, 127
anti-identity, 1, 7, 14. See also identity
Anzaldua, Gloria, 185n26, 202n10
Appiah, Anthony, 203n10, 205n12
art, 148. See also aesthetics

artist, 2, 142, 145, 150, 164, 172; freedom of,
    160–61; subject as, 130; as witness, 160
Atwood, Margaret, 199n4
Aunt Cuney (Praisesong), 105, 106, 122, 123
Autobiography (Du Bois), 100
Avatara/Avey (Praisesong), 105–8
aversions, 161–62
Avery, Shug (The Color Purple), 22, 28, 37,
    43, 60, 85, 87, 89, 93, 199n8
Avey (Praisesong), 122, 123, 125, 128
Awa (Juletane), 44, 46, 48, 49
Awkward, Michael, 182n17

Bâ, Mariama, 66, 190n20
Baby Suggs (Beloved), 103, 127, 147, 162
Badders, Anne Lancaster, 188n5
Baker, Houston A. Jr, 196n2, 198n18, 202n10
Balcomb, A.O., 202n9
Baldwin, James, 9, 160, 180n9, 196n2
Bambara, Toni Cade, 51, 53, 80, 81, 88, 97
Barthes, Roland, 150, 205n13
Basu, Biman, 199n11, 199n13
Beam, Joseph, 184n18
"Beauty: When the Other Dance is the Self"
    (Walker), 18–19
becoming, 55. See also (un)becoming
be-ing, 1, 7. See also self; subjectivity
Beloved (Beloved), 102–105, 113–114, 116,
    122, 128
Beloved (Morrison), 15, 102–105, 112, 115,
    125, 147
Benjamin, Walter, 143, 202n9, 203n12
Berger, John, 204n12
Berlant, Lauren, 161, 205n18
Bhabha, Homi K., 30, 124, 185n23, 185n26,
    202n10, 205n22

Bible, 112

binary system, 13, 140, 180n10

Black female subject, 5, 9, 10, 17, 25

Black feminists, 12, 16. *See also* feminists

"Black Feminist Statement, A" (Combahee River Collective), 4

Black men, 32, 38, 58

Blackness, 8–9, 11, 98–110. *See also* memory of Blackness

Black Radical Congress, 206n1

"Blues Spiritual for Mammy Prater" (Brand), 155–160

Bobby *(No Telephone to Heaven)*, 73

body, 12, 66, 117, 142, 146, 177; communal, 128; ghost, 103–104; home and, 170; language of, 162; limits of, 9; memory as a, 13, 99, 105; race or gender and, 78; re-materializing, 147; in *Salt Eaters*, 80; of Shadrack, 32; surfaces as, 101; as symbolic text, 105; (un) becoming, 8; volatile, 101. *See also* corporeality; memory body

bombing, Birmingham church, 70

Bonner, Marita, 3, 200n1

Booth, Wayne, 203n2, 204n6

Boy Savage *(No Telephone to Heaven)*, 69, 71

Brady, Lenore, 198n16

Braithwaite, Edward Kamau, 201n4

Brand, Dionne, 68, 130, 132–135, 141, 155, 161–162, 164–167, 170, 171, 205n15, 205n21

Brown, Karen McCarthy, 198n17

Brown-Douglass, Kelly, 192n4

Brown-Hinds, Paulette, 198n14

Brydon, Diana, 205n15

Butler, Octavia, 200n17

Canaan, Andrea R., 17–18

"Canto II" (Brand), 130

"Can You be BLACK and Look at This?" (Alexander), 180n12

Carby, Hazel, 190n15

Carter, Davis *(Eva's Man)*, 116, 117, 119, 121, 122

Cartesian dichotomy, 47, 147, 101, 180n10, 182n6, 197n3. *See also* binary system

Celie *(The Color Purple)*, 22, 31, 42–43, 94, 129; girlfriendship with Shug, 28, 37, 39, 43, 60, 85, 87, 93; Nettie, God and, 84–86; relationship with Albert, 37–38, 39, 59–60; sin against Sofia of, 187–188

Chancy, Myriam J.A., 189n13, 191n29, 201n5, 201n7

"Changing Same, The" (McDowell), 5

Chariandry, David, 205n24

Chatman, Seymour, 203n2, 204n6

Chickering, Arthur, 186n30

Christian, Barbara, 12, 180n11, 181n16, 200n2

Christianity, 84

Civil Rights Movement, 51, 52

Cixous, Helene, 183n15, 185n20, 185n23

Clarke, Cheryl, 36

Claybourne *(Salt Eaters)*, 52, 55, 80, 88

Clement, Catherine, 184–185n20, 185n24

Cliff, Michelle, 39–40, 57, 68, 69, 187n38, 191n29, 192n3, 200n16

Clifton, Lucille, 97, 193n6

coalition: with an/other, 97; mother-daughter, 72, 74, 76; of selves, 79, 81, 86

Coard, Phyllis, 133

Coleman, Alisha, 194n17

Collins, Patricia Hill, 67, 180n12, 183n11, 183n12, 186n28, 190n19, 196n2, 201n4

colonialism, 60–61, 66, 78, 90, 91, 92, 108, 131, 140

colonization, 74, 78, 108, 116, 124, 130, 136; sexuality and, 60–65

Color Purple, The (Walker), 22, 28, 37–38, 39, 42–43, 112, 161, 187–188n39, 193–194n12; God concept in, 84–87. *See also* Celie *(The Color Purple)*

Combahee River Collective, 4, 12, 174

Comfort, Susan, 198n2

community, 88, 121–122, 128, 139, 143; in *Our Sister Killjoy*, 90; in West African story, 98–99; writing and, 137. *See also* self(full)ness and community

Cone, James, 192n4

Conrad, Joseph, 206n25

Cooper, Anna Julia, 3–4, 9, 12, 179n4

corporeality, 82, 102, 127, 149, 154, 155, 176, 187n37. *See also* body; memory body

Corregidora (Jones), 120

coupling, 39, 41, 62

Crenshaw, Kimberle, 195n19

Cry (Ailey), 95

Cudjoe, Selwyn, 181n13

cultural ideology, 10, 11

cultural production, 11, 17, 175–176

culture, 33, 78–79, 101

dance, 95, 96

Davies, Carole Boyce, 181n13, 185n26, 188n4, 200n2, 201n5, 205n22, 206n26

Davis, Angela, 34, 104, 120, 186n31, 190n18, 204n11

Davison, Carol Margaret, 199n9

"Death of the Author" (Barthes), 150

DeBeauvoir, Simone, 190n15, 195n18

deconstructionalist, 131, 141

DeLamotte, Eugenia, 200n15

de Lauretis, Teresa, 6, 9, 10, 180n10, 184–185n20

Denver *(Beloved)*, 103, 105, 106, 109

"Dialectics," 139

diaspora, 66, 83, 128

difference, 4, 5, 140, 141, 202n10

disidentification, 16, 17, 78, 182n2. *See also* identity

diva subjectivity, 160–163

Dividing Lines (Simpson), 25

Dixon, Melvin, 120–121, 199n11, 205n22

Dove, Rita, 191n30

Du Bois, W.E.B., 2–3, 9, 12, 100, 200n1, 204n10

DuCille, Ann, 9, 180n10, 180n9, 180n10, 190n15, 190n18

Eagleton, Terry, 17

Easy for Who to Say (Simpson), 25, 29–30

Elvira *(Eva's Man)*, 119, 120, 199n10

English language, 13, 132, 133; in Caribbean, 131; mastering, 136–140

enoughness, 79, 90, 93–97

epic speech, 146–147, 162

essentialism, 2, 3–4, 6, 7, 9, 16, 99–100, 173, 174, 176, 180n10

ethics, 130, 133

Eurocentricity, 173. *See also* colonialism

Eva's Man (Jones), 116–121, 122

"Every Chapter of the World" (Brand), 135

Fabre, Genevieve, 100

Fanon, Frantz, 9, 124, 180n9, 182n6, 182n7, 193n8, 195n18, 195n1, 196n2, 198n15

fearlessness, 94

Felman, Shoshana, 188n5

feminism, 8, 9, 11–12, 16, 40, 74, 174, 180n10

Ferguson, Moira, 200n18

Flint, Ethan, 148, 155

Flint, Roland, 148, 203n1

"For the White Person Who Wants to Know How to Be My Friend" (Parker), 10

Foucault, Michel, 150

freedom, 160–161

Freud, Sigmund, 17, 66–67, 182n6, 182n9, 184n19

Friedan, Betty, 190n15

friendship, 65. *See also* girlfriend

Fromm, Erich, 17, 29

Fultz, Lucille P., 191n30

Fusco, Coco, 25, 184n16

Gates, Henry Louis Jr., 201n4, 202n10, 204n8

Germany, 62, 64

Ghana, 62, 92

ghost body, 103–104. *See also* memory body

Giddings, Paula, 190n18

Gilman, Sander, 185n21, 205n12

Gilroy, Beryl, 175

Gilroy, Paul, 202n10

girlfriend, 1, 13, 113, 155; God as, 83, 84; intimacy and, 155; memory and, 108, 110; memory as, 99

girlfriend selfhood/subjectivity, 15–41, 18, 21, 30; aesthetic of, 17; an/other and, 31–32, 33, 34, 38, 40–41; beholding of, 33; black feminist idiom of, 15–17, 20; as coalitional subject, 42; community and, 39, 50, 55; as dance, 95–96; healing of, 87; home and, 170; identity and, 7–8, 20; imagination, 81; in *Juletane*, 47, 50; Lacan and, 28–29; language and, 130, 135, 147; liminality of, 78, 79; Lorna Simpson on, 22–27, 29–30; mobility and, 33–35, 41, 82, 126; mothers and daughters and, 67; as narrative construct, 17; narrator and, 151; nationalism and, 76; oscillations of, 43; process of, 16, 31; productive and nonbinary character of, 22; as relationship, 16; in *Salt Eaters*, 51; self-discovery and, 95; selflessness and, 87; self-serving, 26; sexuality and, 36, 57; specificity of, 34; story and, 112, 143; subject to subject relation in, 33; in *Sula*, 19–20; unbelonging and, 169; unsettling nature of, 40; as ur-principle, 79; violence and, 89

Gladstone, Valerie, 195n21

God, 192–193n4, 193n5; in *The Color Purple*, 84–87; "girlfriend self" and, 83–84

Goldsby, Jackie, 181n12

Gordon, Avery, 197n5
Grant, Jacquelyn, 192n4
Great Expectations (Dickens), 75
Griffin, Farah Jasmine, 205n22
Grosz, Elizabeth, 40, 100–101, 184–185n20, 187n37, 195n1, 196n3, 196–197n3
Gubar, Susan, 180n10

Halle *(Beloved)*, 162
Hammonds, Evelyn, 17, 179n5, 183n10, 186n32
Haraway, Donna, 187n34, 203n10
Harris, Trudier, 192n4
Harrison, Paul Carter, 192n4
Harry/Harriet *(No Telephone to Heaven)*, 73–75
Helene Parpin *(Juletane)*, 45–48, 93
Henderson, Mae G., 31, 197n10
Herbert, Anne, 188n5
Henry, Velma *(Salt Eaters)*, 51–55, 56, 79–80, 81, 88
Hernton, Calvin, 184n18
heterosexuality, 56, 57, 61, 63, 91
Heywood, Sophie, *(Salt Eaters)*, 52
History and African-American Culture (Fabre and O'Meally), 100
Holloway, Karla F.C., 179n6, 196n2
home, 13, 64, 124, 149, 163–70, 171, 172; as collective voice, 111; land and, 166–168, 170; language and, 165; truth and, 173
hooks, bell, 145, 146, 180n12, 181n14, 182n4, 185n23, 185n26, 186n27, 187n35, 189n9
Horowitz, Deborah, 197n10
Hurston, Zora Neale, 15, 175, 183n13, 190n18, 194n14, 200n19, 200n1
hybridity, 141, 202–3n10

identification, 18, 28–29, 40, 68; *(as and with)*, 16, 17, 26, 41
identity, 1, 4, 5, 9, 30; collective, 100; in *Juletane*, 44, 46, 47; lesbian, 5; liminality and, 78; margins of, 20; national, 68–69; otherness as locus of, 13; policing fictions of social, 95; politics of, 6, 17, 56; and subjectivity compared, 7–8. *See also* self
"I is a long memoried woman" (Nichols), 99
image, 30, 131
imagination, 81, 95, 155
individuality, 2, 33, 111
interiority, politics of, 6

intersectionality, 4–5, 9, 11–12
intimacy, 148, 149, 154, 155
Irigaray, Luce, 185n23, 206n5

Jajne, Sija, 194n16
Jamaica, 68, 69, 72, 74
James *(Eva's Man)*, 117
Jamison, Judith *(Cry)*, 95
Jane Eyre (Brönte), 73
Jarrett, Juliette, 200n1
Jay *(Praisesong)*, 106, 122
Jazz (Morrison), 151–55, 171–172
Joe *(Jazz)*, 151–153
Jones, Gayl, 116, 120, 199n6, 199n7
Joshua, Jocelyn Chadwick, 204n8
Jude *(Sula)*, 21, 26, 28, 54, 59
Juletane *(Juletane)*, 81, 83; friendship with Helene, 45–48, 93 *Juletane* (Warner-Vieyra), 43–51, 55, 82–83, 112
Julien, Issac, 184n18

Kelley, Robin, 182n7
Kennedy, John F., 71
Kincaid, Jamaica, 115–16, 117, 124–125, 127, 166, 200n18
Kitty *(No Telephone to Heaven)*, 69, 70, 71, 75–76
Klein, Melanie, 182n9
Kristeva, Julia, 185n23, 193n8, 194n17
Krumholz, Linda, 197n10

Lacan, Jacques, 28–29, 30, 32, 33, 39, 182n6, 182n9, 184n19, 184–185n20, 185n24, 188n5
Lamming, George, 201n5
land, 167, 168, 170
Land to Light On (Brand), 134–135, 138–140, 160, 161–162, 164–165, 166–169
language, aesthetic of, 2, 5, 129–147, 130, 135, 148, 149; African languages, 132; contention with, 134; corporeality of, 147; diva subjectivity and, 160–165; English, 13, 131, 132, 133, 136–140; home and, 163–70; in Lacan, 28–29; mastery and, 149, 162, 171; narrator and, 149–155; politics of black, 130–135, 146; self, love and, 170; as soul mate, 170–172; story and, 140–146; unreliability of, 141; witness and, 155–160. *See also* narrator
Larrier, Renee, 181n13, 190n20

Lauretis, Teresa de, 6, 9–10, 180n10
Lee, Rachel, 180n10
Lerner, Gerda, 190n19
lesbians, 5, 36, 59. *See also* sexuality
Lewin, S. S., 136
Lewis, Ida, 205n14
Lewis, Vashti Crutcher, 187n33
liminality, 48, 174, 178, 191–192n3; space and, 79
liminality and selfhood, 78–97; being enough and, 93–97; in *The Color Purple*, 84–87; divinity and, 79–87; selffullness and, 87–92
Lipsitz, George, 196n2, 198n2, 199n3, 200n14
Literary Theory: An Introduction (Eagleton), 17
Lodge, David, 149, 204n3
"Look, a Negro" (Fanon), 9
Lorde, Audre, 148–149, 149, 162–163, 186n28, 188n1, 195–196n1
love, 41, 55, 95, 175; language, self and, 170, 171–172. *See also* self-love
"Love Letter, The" (Aidoo), 90
Love, Stanley, 186n29

MacKinnon, Catherine, 189n10
Majozo, Estella Conwill, 201n4
Mamadou (*Juletane*), 44–45, 46, 50
Marshall, Paule, 105, 123, 200n15, 200n16
matrophobia, 68. *See also* motherhood
McDowell, Deborah, 5
McClintock, Anne, 183n10, 203n10
McKee, Patricia, 204n8
McKoy, Sheila Smith, 197n9
Medallion (*Sula*), 54, 55 Medina, Eva (*Eva's Man*), 116–121, 122; selfhood of, 118
memory, 2, 13, 115; ancestors and, 108; as body, 13, 99, 105; community and, 98–99
memory body, 108, 110, 111–128, 112; in *Beloved*, 102, 104, 112–116; collectives of, 121–126; colonization and, 116; community and, 98–99; diasporic, 128; essentialism and, 99–100; in *Eva's Man*, 116–121; as girlfriend an/other, 106; Grosz and, 100–101; history and, 101; home and, 124; magical, 122; Middle Passage, 112, 122; nationalism and, 124–25, 127–28; ontology of, 111, 126; in *Our Sister Killjoy*, 108–110; placelessness of, 125; possession and, 104; in *Praisesong*, 107,

122–124; product and process, 100; repetition and, 114; revised, 121; story and, 112, 116; time as, 123
migration, 165, 166
mirror, 31, 33, 89
Mirror, Mirror (Weems), 30
"Mirror Stage" (Lacan), 28–29
mobility (movement), 33–35, 41, 82, 126; 167; ritual of, 126–128
modernity, 8, 141, 149
Modood, Tariq, 203n10
Mohanty, Chandra, 6–7
Morrison, Toni, 12, 146, 186n32, 187n36, 189n12, 191n30, 193n8, 203n11, 204n8; *Beloved* and, 15, 102–105, 114; *Jazz* and, 151–155, 171–172; "Nobel lecture" of, 135, 137–138, 141, 142–145, 147, 170–171; "Strangers" essay of, 81–82; *Sula* and, 19, 32, 89. *See also Beloved*; *Jazz*; "Nobel Lecture"; *Sula*
mother-daughter relationship, 65–77; Clare and Kitty (*No Telephone*) and, 68–73, 76–77; as coalition, 72, 74, 76; colonialism and, 66, 68, 74; girlfriend subjectivity, 67, 68, 69, 76; Harry/Harriet (*No Telephone*), 73–75; matrophobia and, 68
motherhood, 65–67, 76, 77, 191n 30
Mudimbe-Boyi, Elisabeth, 188n5
multiplicity, 1, 29, 34, 88
Munoz, Jose, 182n2
mutuality, 20, 38, 82, 95–96

narcissism, 40, 50
narrator, 141, 149, 160; agency of, 168; authority of, 149; in "Blues Spiritual of Mammy Prater," 156; body of, 149–55; objectivity and, 149; tenderness and, 150–151; unfunctioning of, 172
narrator (*Jazz*), 152–154
nation, 13, 92, 174; house as, 129
nationalism, 2, 9, 72–73, 111, 125, 127, 129; black, 124; memory as, 128; mother-daughter relations and, 73, 74, 76, 77; terms of, 164
nationality, 55, 62
Naylor, Gloria, 187n36
Ndeye (*Juletane*), 45
Neal, Larry, 196n2
Nel (*Sula*), 21–22, 54
Nettie (*The Color Purple*), 22
New Criticism, 150

Ngate, Jonathan, 188n5
Ngugi, Wa Thiongo, 201n4, 201n5
Nichols, Grace, 99
Nnaemeka, Obioma, 190n20
"Nobel Lecture" (Morrison), 10–171, 135, 137–138, 141, 143–145, 147, 153
No Language is Neutral (Brand), 132–134, 138–139, 155–160, 165, 166
Nora, Pierre, 100
No Telephone to Heaven (Cliff), 39–40, 57, 68–77, 88, 147; mother/daughter relations in, 68–73, 76–77
Notes of a Native Son (Baldwin), 163
Not Manet's Type (Weems), 160
Nourbese Philip, Marlene, 130–132, 201n4, 201n6, 201n7
novel, 143, 154
Nowlin, Michael, 154–155, 203n11, 204n9
Nwankwo, Chimalum, 194n15

Obie *(Salt Eaters)*, 53, 56
O'Callaghan, Evelyn, 188n5
"Occult of True Black Womahood" (DuCille), 180n10
Old Wife (Salt Eaters), 79–80
Olmstead, Jane, 198n11
O'Meally, Robert, 100
other as self, 13, 16, 21, 25, 30–31, 44, 82, 153. *See also* an/other
otherness, 40–41, 72, 78
Our Sister Killjoy: Or Reflections of a Black-Eyed Squint (Aidoo), 60–65, 90–92, 108–110, 141, 171; colonialism and, 60, 61–62, 64; Europe in, 62, 63
outsiderness, 43–55; in *Juletane*, 43–50; overidentification and, 50, 53–54
Owomoyela, Oyekan, 201n4
Owusu, Kofi, 194n14

Page, Philip, 154
Painter, Nell, 206n2
Palmer, Parker, 195n19
Parker, Pat, 10
Parry, Benita, 203n10
patriarchy, 6, 17, 164; heterosexuality and, 91
Paul D *(Beloved)*, 15, 104, 126, 147
Peace, Eva *(Sula)*, 38–39
Pease, Donald, 204n7
Pemberton, Esther, 174
Pessoni, Michelle, 192n4
photography, 158, 159. *See also* Simpson, Lorna; Weems, Carrie Mae

Pip *(Great Expectations)*, 75
plural body, 2. *See also* community; nation
"Poem Called George, Sometimes, A" (Flint), 148
politics, 17, 73, 91, 92; of black language, 130–135, 146; of identity, 6, 17, 56; of race, 73; sexual, 56; of writing, 154
"Politics and Psychoanalysis" (Fromm), 17
possession, 104, 118
postcolonial discourse, 141. *See also* colonialism
postmodern blackness, 11, poststructuralism, 1, 4, 8, 9, 10, 11, 12, 131, 174
Praisesong for the Widow (Marshall), 105, 122–124, 125, 127
Prater, Mammy, 133, 155–160, 161, 163, 170; 205n 15; as an/other, 155; patience and, 157
Price, Derrick, 205n13
Primitive Offense (Brand), 130
psychoanalysis, 17, 28, 29, 66–67, 182–183n9, 188n8

Quashie, Kevin Everod, 185n26
Queen Bee *(Eva's Man)*, 118–120, 199n9
Quindlen, Anna, 40

Rabasa, Jose, 189n14
race, 2, 9, 62–63, 70; gender and, 3, 20, 30, 78; politics of, 73; racism and sexism, 121, 176
Raiskin, Judith, 191n29
Ransom, Minnie *(Salt Eaters)*, 51, 54, 79–80, 81
"Refiguring Lesbian Desire" (Grosz), 40
relationality, 5, 38. *See also* girlfriend; mother and daughter relationship
Renan, Ernest, 124
repetition, 114, 126
Rich, Adrienne, 68, 186n28, 190n16
Riley, Denise, 14, 179n1
Rimmon-Kenan, Shlomith, 204n5, 204n6
Roberts, Dorothy, 190n17, 190n18
Robinson, Sally, 199n11, 199n13
Romans, Book of, 112–113
Ruddick, Sara, 190n22

Salt Eaters (Bambara), 79–80, 81, 88; self(full)ness and community in, 51–57
Sartre, Jean Paul, 195n18
Savage, Clare *(No Telephone to Heaven)*, 30,

57, 68–77, 88, 147; relationship with mother of, 68–73, 71–72

Savage, Monique, 129, 179n6

"School Note" (Lorde), 148–49

self, 1, 2, 4, 6, 41, 127, 194–195n18; an/other and, 33, 39, 140, 153; authenticity of, 92; belonging and, 163; boundaries of, 56; colonization of, 62; decolonization of, 109; discourses of, 7–11; divinity of, 83, 192n4; God and, 86; loss of, 34; love, language and, 170; other as, 13, 16, 21, 25, 30–31, 44, 82; revelation of, 107; of Shadrack (*Sula*), 32; specificity of, 80; truth and, 173; untenable aspects of, 9

self(full)ness and community, 42–77; of Clare and Kitty (*No Telephone*) and, 68–73, 76–77; colonialism and, 60–65; girlfriend subjectivity and, 50, 51, 55; of Harry/Harriet (*No Telephone*) and, 73–75; heteropathic anxiety of, 55; individual and, 65; in *Juletane*, 43–50; motherhood and, 65–68; overidentification and, 50, 53; paradox of, 42; in *The Salt Eaters*, 51–57; sexuality and, 57–60; subjectivity and, 16, 55. *See also* community

selffullness (selfishness, self-centeredness), 40, 87–92, 88, 89, 96, 130, 161, 162, 174; female, 77; in *Juletane*, 47; language of, 172; in *No Telephone to Heaven*, 57

selfhood, 13, 17, 101, 111; coalitioned, 51; community and, 51; in *Juletane*, 46; model of, 43; or narrator, 154; selfish, 68. *See also* girlfriend selfhood/subjectivity; liminality and selfhood

selflessness, 26, 29, 40, 42, 50, 51, 171, 174

self-love, 25, 26, 34, 79

Sethe (*Beloved*), 15, 103, 126, 129, 147; Beloved as body memory of, 102, 104, 113, 114, 116; on the power of memory, 102–103, 114–115

Sethuraman, Ramchandran, 191n29

sexuality, 55–60, 118; heterosexual, 56, 57, 61, 63, 91; lesbian, 5, 36, 59

sexual violence, 74, 116, 118, 119

Shadrack (*Sula*), 12, 32, 38, 43

Shange, Ntozake, 79, 84, 191n2

She Tries Her Tongue, Her Silence Softly Breaks (Nourbese Philip), 130–132

"Signs Taken for Wonder" (Bhabha), 30–31

Silverman, Kaja, 183n10, 184–185n20, 188n8

Simpson, Lorna, 22–25, 26, 27, 29–30

"Singing a Deep Song" (Dixon), 120

Sissie (*Our Sister Killjoy*), 61–65, 90–92, 94, 141, 171

sisterhood, 18, 36

Sister Outsider (Lorde), 163

Sisters of Yam (hooks), 145–146 *Small Place, A* (Kincaid), 115–116, 124–125, 200n18

Smith, Anna Deveare, 185n25

Smith, Barbara, 5, 9, 20, 179n5, 183n12, 186n28, 203n12, 205n17, 206n26

Smith, Valerie, 185n23, 188n2

Smyth, Gerry, 200n2, 202n10

solidarity, 25, 73

Solomon, Barbara, 197n10

Sommer, Marija (*Our Sister Killjoy*), 61–65, 90

Souls of Black Folk (Du Bois), 2–3

South African Freedom Charter, 100

Space, Time and Perversion (Grosz), 100–101

"Speaking in Tongues" (Henderson), 31

Spelman, Elizabeth V., 180n10

Spillers, Hortense, 17, 183n10, 185n24, 191n1, 193n9

spirituality, 79, 95

Staples, Robert, 184n18

Starmer, Jadine, 197n8

Steele, Claude, 182n2

Stein, Karen, 192n4

story: African folk tale, 98–99, 142; body of, 140–146; language of, 147; memory and, 111; power of, 113; restorative, 120; telling of, 112, 141, 150. *See also* narrator

Stout, Janice, 204n8

stranger, 89. *See also* other

"Strangers" (Morrison, Toni), 81–82

subject, 1–5, 12, 15, 31, 155; artist as, 130; being of, 7; Black female, 5, 9, 10, 17, 25; coalitional, 42, 87; impulses informing, 79; in *Our Sister Killjoy*, 91; traceable, and notable, 8; (un)becoming and, 97; will of, 126

subjecthood/subjectivity, 9, 120, 128, 129–130, 154, 158, 172, 174, 177; artist's, 142, 149, 165; black feminist idiom of, 1; change and, 176–177; community and, 16, 55; contested claims to, 99; as dance, 96; diva, 160–163; in *Eva's Man*, 116; healing of, 87; in *Juletane*, 44, 47, 48, 49; language and, 129, 140; liminal, 78, 83; "me" and "us," 89–90, 93; mother-daughter, 68; movement of, 95; and nation, 92, 129; objectivity and, 149; as past, 105; potentiality and, 79; selffull

subjecthood/subjectivity, (*continued*)
    enterprise of, 110; sex as communal, 55–
    56; truth and, 176; unreliable, 141; of
    Velma and Sula, 55; writer and, 137;
    writing and, 131. *See also* girlfriend
    selfhood/subjectivity
Sula (Morrison), 13–14, 19–20, 21–22, 26, 32,
    38–39, 54–55, 89; sexuality in, 57–59
Sula (*Sula*), 54, 55, 147, 155, 161, 184n17;
    coupling with Ajax of, 58–59; girlfriend
    selfhood between Nel and, 19–22, 28, 31,
    36, 80, 81, 83, 89, 147, 189n12; ridicule
    of Jude by, 26, 28, 59
surrender, 14, 20, 49, 50, 54–60, 62–63, 65,
    78, 87, 90, 93–96, 115, 118, 127, 149,
    151–155
Sweet Honey in the Rock (singing group), 33

Tagg, John, 205n12
Tate, Claudia, 17, 183n10
Tatem (*Praisesong*), 124
tenderness, 150–151, 155, 172
theory, 2, 5, 8, 11, 29
"There Were No Mirrors in My Nanas House"
    (Sweet Honey in the Rock), 33
Thich Nhat Hanh, 205n19
third body, 33
third space, 87
*Third World Women and the Politics of
    Feminism"* (Mohanty, intro), 6–7
Thompson, Robert Farris, 192n4
Time Piece (Simpson), 25
Toni Morrison's *Jazz"* (Nowlin), 154–155
"Toward Black Feminist Criticism"
    (Smith), 5
Trinh T. Minh-ha, 40, 140, 141, 142–143,
    182n3, 185n23, 193n11, 202n10, 203n1,
    205n16
truth, 141, 173; subjectivity and, 176
Truth, Sojourner, 3, 9, 12, 176, 186n31, 206n2
Tyrone (*Eva's Man*), 119

(un)becoming, 8, 14, 22, 28, 33, 93–97;
    authorship and, 47; in *Juletane*, 50;
    language and, 133, 146, 147; liminality
    and, 79; "Mammy Prater" and, 155, 159;
    in *Our Sister Killjoy*, 92; process of, 36; in
    relation to non-black women, 16;
    selffullness of, 40; subjecthood and, 31,
    32 (un)belonging, 169. *See also* belonging
"Upping the Anti [*sic*] in Feminist Theory"
    (de Lauretis), 6

violence, 33, 89. *See also* sexual violence
Violet (*Jazz*), 151–153
visual culture, 29, 33. *See also* culture
voice, 113, 114, 120
Volatile Bodies: Toward a Corporeal Feminism
    (Grosz), 100
volatility, 101, 126, 176

Walker, Alice, 18, 28, 31, 33, 42, 79, 81,
    84, 112, 186n28; definition of
    womanist, 35–36, 186n32, 198n13,
    200n19, 201n4, 203n13; motherhood
    and, 67. *See also Color Purple, The*
Wall, Wendy, 188n6
Warner-Vieyra, Myriam, 43, 46, 47, 112,
    188n5, 188n7
Washington, Mary Helen, 12, 179n4, 181n15,
    199n12
Weems, Carrie Mae, 20, 22, 160, 185n21,
    185n22
Weigman, Robyn, 180n10
Wells, Liz, 204n12, 205n13
West, Cornel, 205n20
West African folk story, 98–99
"What Ails Feminist Criticism?" (Gubar),
    180n10
"What Is an Author" (Foucault), 150
wholeness, 13, 130, 177
Wideman, John Edgar, 198n1
Wilentz, Gay, 189n13
Williams, Patricia, 127–128, 190n18
Willis, Susan, 201n4, 203n14
Wilson, Elizabeth, 188n3
witness, 155–164
Woman, Native, Other (Trinh), 143
womanist, 35–37
"Woman Versus the Indian" (Cooper), 4
Women's Rights Convention (Akron, 1851),
    176
Wonder, Stevie, 19
Wood, Michael, 143, 204n8
Words of Selves, The (Riley), 14
writing, 131, 137, 160; politics of, 154

Yearning (hooks), 180
Yearwood, Gladstone, 136
Yoruba peoples, 95
Young, Robert, 202n10

Zabus, Chantal, 201n6

About the Author

Kevin Everod Quashie is an Assistant Professor in Afro-American Studies at Smith College, where he teaches cultural studies and theory. He is coeditor of *New Bones: Contemporary Black Writers in America* (2001).